THE ROLES OF
CHRIST'S HUMANITY
IN SALVATION

Frederick G. McLeod, S.J.

THE ROLES
OF CHRIST'S
HUMANITY IN
SALVATION

Insights from
Theodore of Mopsuestia

The Catholic University of America Press
Washington, D.C.

Copyright © 2005

The Catholic University of America Press

All rights reserved

Library of Congress Cataloging-in-Publication Data

McLeod, Frederick G.

    The roles of Christ's humanity in salvation: insights from
Theodore of Mopsuestia / Frederick G. McLeod.

       p. cm.

    Includes bibliographical references and index.

    ISBN-13: 978-0-8132-1396-5 (cloth : alk. paper)

    ISBN-10: 0-8132-1396-7 (cloth : alk. paper)

    1. Theodore, Bishop of Mopsuestia, ca. 350–428 or 9.

  2. Jesus Christ—Person and offices.   3. Salvation.

  I. Title.

BR1720.T35M35 2005

232′.8′092—dc22

                                     2004004193

To my Sisters, Marjorie and Carol,

Now Deceased,

Whose Generous Willingness to Support My Family

after My Father's Death in 1954

Enabled Me to Continue as a Jesuit

CONTENTS

PREFACE

The present work has a lengthy history. It began with my dissertation on the soteriology of Narsai, a fifth-century Syrian theologian. He gained fame as the outstanding Syriac proponent of Theodore of Mopsuestia's thought by successfully passing on Theodore's teaching through the use of metric homilies. One feature of Narsai's soteriology that intrigued me was his view of how Adam as God's "image" serves as a type of Christ's human archetypal role as the visible, perfect "image" of God. This led to the publication of a monograph and then an article on the image of God in Narsai.[1] Since Narsai closely adhered to Theodore's soteriological outlook, I decided to determine whether he was dependent on Theodore and, if so, to what extent. I was not surprised to discover in my research that Narsai reproduced Theodore's idea of the "image of God." But I was not prepared to learn that Theodore and Narsai's viewpoint on "image" differed notably from that of Diodore, John Chrysostom, and Theodoret, the other leading theologians of the School of Antioch. This is significant in that Theodore and Narsai were

1. Frederick G. McLeod, *The Soteriology of Narsai* (Rome: Pontificium Institutum Orientalium Studiorum, 1973); and "Man as the Image of God: Its Meaning and Theological Significance in Narsai," *Theological Studies* 42 (Sept. 1981): 458–68.

both fully committed to the School's emphasis upon a literal, historical, and rational method of interpretation and on its defense of Christ's integral human nature within his personal union with the Word of God. This showed me how the Antiochenes could employ their method of biblical exegesis and arrive at different interpretations. It also made me aware of Theodore's independent, speculative mind. I then published a book on this topic entitled *The "Image of God" in the Antiochene Tradition*.[2]

In my inquiry into Theodore's understanding of "image," I was particularly struck by his inclusion of various other "roles" within that of Adam and Christ's humanity as the "image of God." The one that stood out was Adam's role as the "bond" of the universe. I could understand how Adam and Christ's humanity functioned as visible images who reveal God's existence and will. Nor did it seem strange that Adam could receive honor from other creatures because of his unique role within creation, or for that matter that God would require other creatures to offer their glory and worship for God by caring for the physical and spiritual needs of humans as his "image" within the cosmos. I began to discern more clearly a connection between all these when I published a long article for the *Journal of Early Christian Studies* on "The Christological Ramifications of Theodore of Mopsuestia's Understanding of Baptism and the Eucharist."[3] This study was invaluable in enabling me to comprehend in general what Theodore intended by a true type and more particularly how he considered the sacraments of baptism and the Eucharist to be true types. They not only "image" a future immortal existence in heaven but also have a spiritual effect in the present life, for they unite and nourish a person's union with the body of Christ. If one is so joined in a true corporate way with Christ's body, one is assured of sharing in a potential way in the immortal bodily existence that Christ's humanity now possesses. Such an understanding of Theodore's outlook unlocked for me a number of his key concepts regard-

2. Frederick G. McLeod, *The Image of God in the Antiochene Tradition* (Washington, D.C.: The Catholic University of America Press, 1999).
3. Frederick G. McLeod, "The Theological Ramifications of Theodore of Mopsuestia's Understanding of Baptism and the Eucharist," *Journal of Early Christian Studies* 10 (spring 2002): 41–50.

ing the meaning of a "true type" and "salvation" and the correlation that he made between how Adam and Christ's humanity constitutes the "bonds" of universe and at the same time "images of God." By relating all these to Theodore's idea of what is a "person," I had confirmation for a long-held conviction that Theodore and Nestorius were really advocating a functional kind of Christology and were being judged by an essentialistic one. This means that one ought to pursue Theodore's Christology in light of and within his soteriology.

Two years ago I began to connect these pieces into a coherent whole. I was fortunate to have a year's sabbatical during which I read all of Theodore's extant works. I then attempted to spell out how Theodore used typology to explain Adam's and Christ's roles in the history of salvation and to relate this to Theodore's understanding of "person." For him, a "person" is not one defined in a metaphysical sense as a complete self-subsisting subject but as one whose inner self is known from his activity and speech. While it is true that one's external way of acting may not always be revelatory of the real inner person, nevertheless it can still reveal this inner person when there exists a true correspondence between the inner and outer person, such as in the case of Christ. This is best exemplified in the way the Synoptics portray Jesus as the Christ who acts as one being in human and divine ways. Such double activity indicates that he is both God and man in a unity where both his divine and human natures are complete and function as one without either nature being compromised, much as the soul and body function as one, and how Christ's human nature recapitulates all of creation in one body. The present work intends to give flesh to these views, arguing from Christ's humanity's roles to an understanding of how Theodore conceives of Christ as a "person" whose humanity is related to the Word and all other creatures in a unique relationship that transcends all other relationships. As such he serves as the mediator between God and the cosmos. All these conclusions will then be used to review the charges of heresy that the fathers at the Council of Constantinople II in 553 leveled against Theodore's works and his very person and to reassess them in light of the present study.

Since few of Theodore's extant works have been translated into modern languages—the exceptions are his *Catechetical Homilies*,[4] his *Commentary on the Psalms*[5] (in part), his *Commentary on the Twelve Minor Prophets*,[6] as well as those fragments that have been translated in studies about Theodore—I have decided to weave into my work English translations of those passages from Theodore that I believe substantiate my interpretations. Since his extant works are not generally available and are, for the most part, available only in Syriac and Latin versions, I believe that my frequent use of citations in the text itself will enable the reader to form his or her own opinion of whether mine is really justified. The translations are, generally speaking, my own and are based on the Greek and Syriac texts rather than the Latin and French translations derived from them. This is meant to allow Theodore to speak for himself in a text that is closer to his original text. Also, when I refer to the Syriac versions given in Raymond Tonneau, E. Sachau, J.-M. Vosté, and Lucas van Rompay, I cite in the first entry the Syriac text and then, after a slash, the page or folio where it has been translated. In Tonneau's references, I also mention the homily and section number for those who may be using an English or German translation of Theodore's *Catechetical Homilies*. When there is a string of references to the same work, I include the page reference in the text itself.

As for my dependence on other scholarly studies of Theodore, I will not repeat what these have uncovered other than to accept what I consider to be positive in their research. Since little has been written about my own approach, I will discuss only those points and arguments I believe are rele-

---

4. I have used Raymond Tonneau's edition in this volume: *Les Homélies Catéchétiques de Théodore de Mopsueste*, trans. Raymond Tonneau, with Robert Devreese (Vatican City: Biblioteca Vaticana, 1949), hereafter abbreviated *THC*. When page numbers are cited, the numbers on the left side of the slash are to the Syriac text, and on the right to the French translation on the opposite page. Unless otherwise indicated, all English translations from this work are my own based on the Syriac text.

5. Theodore of Mopsuestia, *Commentaire sur les Psaumes I–LXXX*, ed. Robert Devreese, Studi e Testi 93 (Vatican City: Biblioteca Vaticana, 1939). This work needs to be supplemented by *Théodore de Mopsueste: Fragments Syriaque du Commentaire des Psalmes* (Ps. 118 and Pss. 138–48), ed. and trans. Lucas van Rompay, CSCO 189–90 (Louvain: Peeters, 1982).

6. Theodore of Mopsuestia, *Commentary on the Twelve Prophets*, trans. Robert Hill, Fathers of the Church 108 (Washington, D.C.: The Catholic University of America Press, 2003).

vant, either in positive or negative ways, to my own position. For instance, I do not want to be caught up in disputes about what has influenced Theodore's exegesis. I want simply to present what I have found to be Theodore's invariable method of interpreting Scripture in a literal, historical, and rational way and his understanding of a "true type." My concern is to point out how the salvific roles that Christ's humanity plays as the head of the body of the Church, the recapitulating bond of the universe, and the "image of God," can help to enlighten us as to what Theodore means by "person" and the unity of Christ's natures as an "indwelling of good pleasure as in God's true Son." This is not to overlook the debt that I owe to earlier and present-day scholars who have studied Theodore and shared their insights publicly. I have benefited in no small measure from their careful, thorough, and nuanced research. For they have enabled me to build upon their achievements and forced me to defend my own interpretations of what I believe to be the theological synthesis that Theodore has developed regarding the roles of Christ's humanity in salvation.

I am very grateful to those who have assisted me in this venture. I want especially to thank those at Saint Louis University who approved my request for a year-long sabbatical, my Jesuit community in Saint Louis who supported me during these past two years, and my brother, Bill, who allowed me the use of his house on Cape Cod to write this book during my sabbatical. I am also indebted to Dr. Rowan A. Greer for his insightful corrections, comments, and suggestions on how to improve this work and grasp what Theodore actually intended to say, Dr. Charles Kannengiesser for his emendations and empathetic support, and William Crawford, my graduate assistant, for his onerous efforts in checking my notes and index for accuracy, as well as Dr. Gregory LaNave and Ms. Susan Needham, my guiding editors at The Catholic University of America Press, and especially Ms. Suzanne Wolk and Grindstone Editorial Services. They have all in their own ways enabled me to bring this present venture to a successful completion.

ABBREVIATIONS

CH   *Catechetical Homilies.* I have used Tonneau's edition of the catechetical homilies, as it has the Syriac and French translations on opposite pages. I have translated from the Syriac rather than from the French translation, except in a few places where the Syriac is illegible, in which case I have followed the French. Homily and section numbers are provided for those using the English and German translations.

CUS   *Concilium Universale Constantinopolitanum Sub Justiniano Habitum.* Ed. Johannes Straub. Acta Conciliorum Oecumenicorum. Tome 4, vol. 1. Berlin: De Gruyter, 1971.

EEC   *Encyclopedia of the Early Church.* 2 vols. Ed. Angelo Di Berardino, trans. A. Wolford. New York: Oxford University Press, 1992.

NEM   *Cyril of Jerusalem and Nemesius of Emesa,* by Nemesius of Emesa. Ed. and trans. William Telfer. Library of Christian Classics 4. Philadelphia: Westminster, 1955.

NPNF   *The Nicene and Post-Nicene Fathers,* 2d ser., ed. Philip Schaff and Henry Wace. 1896. Reprint, Peabody, Mass.: Hendrickson, 1994.

PG   Patrologia Graeca.

PL   Patrologia Latina.

TEP   *Theodori Episcopi Mopsuesteni in Epistolas B. Pauli Commentarii,* ed. H. B. Swete. 2 vols. Cambridge: Cambridge University Press, 1880, 1882.

TFS   *Theodori Mopsuesteni Fragmenta Syriaca,* ed. and trans. Edward Sachau. Leipzig: G. Engelmann, 1869.

THC   *Les Homélies Catéchétiques de Théodore de Mopsueste,* trans. Raymond Tonneau, with Robert Devreese. Vatican City: Vaticana, 1949.

TJA   *Theodori Mopsuesteni Commentarius in Evangelium Johannis Apostoli,* ed. and trans. J.-M. Vosté. Corpus Scriptorum Christianorum Orientalium, 115–16/Syr. 62–63. Louvain: Officina Orientali, 1940.

THE ROLES OF
CHRIST'S HUMANITY
IN SALVATION

1. INTRODUCTION

T HE MOST ENIGMATIC and controversial Christian theologian in the fifth-century Byzantine Empire was Theodore of Mopsuestia (ca. 350–ca. 428). At his death he was eulogized as one of the most respected church-men of his day.[1] He was hailed as the foremost exponent of the Antiochene literal, historical interpretation of the Bible and as the most sophisticated analytical opponent of Origen's alle-gorical method. He was also widely admired for the original, insightful ways in which he systematized authentic church tra-ditions and defended the humanity of Christ. Yet, within a few years of his death, he became the target of unrelenting criti-cism for the next century and a quarter. His adversaries

---

1. For a recent well-documented summary of Theodore's life and works, see Theodore of Mopsuestia, *Teodoro di Mopsuestia: Replica a Guil-iano Imperatore*, trans. Augusto Guida (Firenza: Nardini, 1994), 9–30; and for a fuller theological background of this period, see Alois Grillmeier, *Christ in Christian Tradition from the Apostolic Age to Chalcedon (451)*, trans. J. Cawte and P. Allen, 2 vols. 2d rev. ed. (Atlanta: John Knox, 1975), 2:411–62.

claimed that even though he had not been condemned at the Council of Ephesus in 431, he was the source of Nestorius's (ca. 380–451) "impious" teaching. Cyril of Alexandria (ca. 370–444), while he agreed with this assessment, was initially very hesitant to mention Theodore by name, for Theodore was already dead and was still widely admired.[2] He was concerned, too, not to disturb his Pact of Reunion (433)[3] with John of Antioch (bishop 428–ca. 441), the leader of the Syrian bishops. For this pact had reunited the Syrian bishops with Cyril and the Alexandrians as well as with those from the East who had condemned Nestorius at Ephesus.

The attacks against Theodore became more pronounced around the mid-430s, when Rabboula, the bishop of Edessa, and Basil, a deacon at Constantinople, attacked Theodore and his teacher, Diodore of Tarsus (ca. 330–ca. 394). They tried to goad Cyril into doing the same, claiming that Nestorius's followers were now rallying around the thought of Diodore and Theodore. Cyril openly attacked both around 438 in his now lost work *Against Diodore and Theodore.*[4] After Cyril died in 444, the fierce attacks against Theodore subsided, as attention was focused on the rise of Eutychianism. The issue of Theodore's orthodoxy, in fact, seemed to have been definitively settled when the fathers at the Council of Chalcedon in 451 made no explicit reference to him, although they once again condemned Nestorius.

Theodore was mentioned, however, at the council in a letter written by Ibas of Edessa (d. 457). When the council fathers reinstated Ibas as the bishop of Edessa, he insisted as a sign of his orthodoxy that his letter, condemned at the "Robbers Council" in 449, be read at one of the council sessions. The fathers listened without any adverse reaction, so it appears, to

2. In his "Epistle 72 ad Proclum," PG 77:344–45, Cyril affirmed that he wanted to avoid having to condemn a person like Theodore, who had died as a respected member of the Church. Later, the fathers at Constantinople II declared that a person could be anathematized after his death. See *Concilium Universale Constantinopolitanum Sub Justiniano Habitum,* ed. Johannes Straub, Acta Conciliorum Oecumenicorum, tome 4, vol. 1 (Berlin: De Gruyter, 1971), 209–10; and Grillmeier, *Christ in Christian Tradition,* 2:445.
3. An English translation of the pact can be found in Cyril's letter to John of Antioch, in *The Seven Ecumenical Councils,* ed. H. R. Percival, *NPNF,* 251–53.
4. See Grillmeier, *Christ in Christian Tradition,* 2:414–15.

the praise Ibas lavished upon Theodore in this letter. Those hostile to Chalcedon reacted negatively, assuming that Ibas's eulogy for Theodore indicated that the fathers favored Theodore's Christology and were therefore Nestorians. Throughout the rest of the fifth century and the first half of the sixth, the person of Theodore became a bête noire for the anti-Chalcedonians. They increasingly regarded him as a symbol of what was wrong with Chalcedon. This is ironic, for the number of Theodore's adherents within the empire had diminished from the late fifth century through the first half of the sixth. His views were known principally from the collections of supposedly heretical statements that his enemies had selectively culled from his writings. For the most part, only the East Syrians in the Persian Empire were familiar with his complete works and still esteemed his memory.

After the death of Theodoret of Cyr (ca. 393–ca. 458), Theodore's influence, as well as that of the famed School of Antioch, simply vanished within the Byzantine Empire.[5] He was, of course, still regarded as a common enemy by the Apollinarians, the Origenists, the Orthodox and, above all, the Monophysites. His name, in fact, was despised by all who regarded the Council of Chalcedon as seriously infected by Nestorianism. For all the Monophysites, or non-Chalcedonians, were convinced that Theodore's customary manner of speaking about Christ had been incorporated into Chalcedon's assertion that "we confess one and the same our Lord Jesus Christ [who is] the same perfect in godhead, the same perfect in humanity, truly God and truly human, the same of a reasonable soul and body; *homoousios* with the Father in godhead, and the same *homoousios* with us in humanity, like us in all things except sin . . . one and the same Christ, Son, Lord, unique acknowledged in two natures without confusion, without change, without division, without separation."[6]

As the Monophysites of all persuasions grew both in number and in

5. Grillmeier observes: "The attack on Theodore of Mopsuestia was all the more striking as he had already been forgotten within the borders of the Imperial Church." Ibid., 2:420.

6. For an English translation of the whole passage, see Percival, *Seven Ecumenical Councils, NPNF,* 264.

power, especially in Egypt and Syria, their fierce religious antagonism toward the Orthodox was also dangerously undermining the political unity of the empire. Finally, in a desperate effort to reunite the feuding parties, the emperor Justinian (483–565, reigned 527–565) first attempted in about 532 to "bring about the union of post-Chalcedonian parties which were denouncing each other."[7] In 545 he issued an imperial edict condemning Theodore, the anti-Cyrillian writings of Theodoret, and the letter he claimed was falsely attributed to Ibas of Edessa (2:421–25). These then became known as the "Three Chapters." Later Justinian wrote a letter, probably to those members of an Illyrian synod who had refused to subscribe to his earlier edict. He replied that his intent was to allay any fears that his previous condemnations were designed to undermine the Council of Chalcedon and insisted that he wanted to condemn only the heresy of those cited in his edict (2:419–23, 426–27). He also seems to have recognized that this approach offered him a way to reconcile the Orthodox and the Monophysites in a declaration of faith against a common Nestorian enemy.

To further his aims, Justinian summoned Pope Vigilius (537–555) to Constantinople in 547. Before the pope arrived, the Roman clergy, and later the Sardinian and African bishops, admonished him not to condemn Theodore, Theodoret, and the letter of Ibas. They were afraid that this would undermine, if not repudiate, the Council of Chalcedon. After his arrival, however, Vigilius secretly accepted Justinian's edict on the "Three Chapters" in two letters sent to the emperor and his wife, the empress Theodora (2:426). In 548 the pope published an official *Judicatum* in which he condemned the "Three Chapters." The West, especially Africa, reacted in such a hostile way to this *Judicatum* that the pope sought to annul it. Under intense pressure, however, Vigilius again wavered and swore an oath to Justinian that he would indeed accede to the condemnations.

In 551 Justinian issued a decree noteworthy not only for its condemnation, once again, of the "Three Chapters" but also for the distinction he made between the words *hypostasis* and *physis,* as well as for his rejection

---

7. Grillmeier, *Christ in Christian Tradition,* 2:418. Hereafter cited parenthetically in the text.

of the soul-body analogy, which he argued implied that Christ's two natures had been synthesized into a new nature rather than what the Christian faith required: a union of a divine Subject with a created nature (2:248). Justinian recognized that such a distinction was critical, for the non-Chalcedonians regarded the three Greek terms *physis, ousia,* and *hypostasis* as equivalent. Indeed, they interpreted the Chalcedonian passage declaring the presence of two natures in Christ to mean that the Chalcedonians held for two "persons" (2:430). Justinian's distinction meant that Chalcedon's declaration could also be interpreted as affirming one *hypostasis,* as the non-Chalcedonians wanted, while at the same time allowing for the existence of two natures subsisting in or "inexisting" in one *hypostasis* or "person" (2:437).

To resolve the continuing reluctance to his edicts, Justinian sought a new ecumenical council, to which Pope Vigilius agreed on January 7, 553. It convened at Constantinople on May 5 and is now popularly dubbed the "Council of the Three Chapters." Since the pope adamantly refused to attend any of the sessions, the patriarch Eutychius served as president, with the largest number of bishops coming from the East. Justinian ordered that a declaration be read to the full assembly at the outset, in which he insisted that the true faith of Chalcedon could be protected only by the condemnation of the "impious Three Chapters" (2:438). The council fathers acceded to his wish. When pressed to sign the decrees, Vigilius issued a *Constitutum* in which he agreed to declare that sixty of Theodore's excerpts were heretical. But he did not want Theodore to be mentioned by name, as he was already dead.[8] Justinian refused to accept Vigilius's stipulations and threatened the pope with excommunication by distinguishing between the pope's person and his office. Justinian maintained that if Theodore were not condemned by name, his enemies would not be fully mollified, believing that the refusal of the fathers at Chalcedon to protest Ibas's letter praising Theodore expressed approval of his heretical views. The pope finally relented, and in a letter of December 8, 553, agreed to the decrees about the

---

8. For a summary treatment of how Pope Vigilius wavered before finally condemning Theodore as a person, see Grillmeier, *Christ in Christian Tradition,* 2:440–42.

"Three Chapters"—a capitulation which deeply appalled and angered many in the West, especially in Africa and Aquileia, for they understood this to be, in fact, a rejection of Chalcedon.[9] While Justinian succeeded in obtaining his condemnations, he failed in his overall objective of reuniting the Orthodox and the non-Chalcedonians. The split became permanent when the Muslim armies overran the Middle East in the following century.

Contemporary Assessments

From the time of Theodore's condemnation at the Second Council of Constantinople in 553 until around the beginning of the twentieth century, he was generally proclaimed the real "Father of Nestorianism." His rejection has been echoed by such famous Christian personages as Cyril of Alexandria, the emperor Justinian, the fathers of the Second Council of Constantinople, and many modern-day theologians. They have each examined Theodore's Christological writings and have concluded that Theodore has indeed been rightly condemned for so overemphasizing Christ's humanity that he depicted him as an individual human being with a separate existence from God the Word. In fact, the fathers at Constantinople II were so alarmed by the threat they perceived in Theodore's teaching that they also anathematized "all those who accept or even defend him or who say that he has expounded in an orthodox way or who have written on his behalf and his impious writings or who think or have ever thought the same and persist in such a heresy as his until the end."[10] This blanket suppression of any effort to understand Theodore's thought shows how utterly persuaded the council fathers were that Theodore's way of speaking about Christ was not only heretical but dangerous. Their refusal to allow any reexamination of Theodore's teaching contributed in no small way to his enduring reputation as one of the foremost heretics in the history of Christianity. Several other factors have reinforced this view, among them the

9. Manlio Simonetti, "Three Chapters," *EEC* 2:838.

10. *Conciliorum Oecumenicorum Decreta,* 3d ed., ed. Josepho Alberigo et al. (Bologna: Scienze Religiose, 1973), 120. I have translated the passage from the original Greek text. All subsequent translations from non-English texts are my own, unless otherwise indicated.

fact that relatively few of Theodore's biblical commentaries and theological treatises have survived. We have only six in number, together with a number of fragments that have been preserved as examples of his heterodoxy and a number of his scriptural interpretations.[11] In addition, only his *Catechetical Homilies,* his *Commentary on the Twelve Prophets,* and part of his *Commentary on the Psalms* have been translated into modern Western languages. Most of the others are available only in the original Greek text or in their Syriac and Latin versions, apart from occasional passages that modern authors have cited.

Until the beginning of the twentieth century, only the Syrian Church of the East contested Theodore's longstanding reputation as a heretic.[12] Then, when the Syriac texts of his *Commentary on John's Gospel* and *Catechetical Homilies*[13] were published and scrutinized, a troubling question arose over whether the fragments used at Constantinople II to condemn Theodore accurately portray his Christological views, or whether these can now be reinterpreted in an orthodox way in light of the newly recovered documents. Two scholars, R. Devreese and Marcel Richard,[14] challenged the reliability of the council excerpts on the grounds that they had been altered.

11. Considering the effort to destroy Theodore's writings in the fifth and sixth centuries, we are fortunate today to possess six of his complete or almost complete works: his commentaries on the Psalms, the twelve minor prophets, the Gospel of John, and the minor Pauline epistles, and a work on his controversy with the Macedonians, as well as his *Catechetical Homilies* (which include his treatises on the Nicene Creed, the Our Father, and the sacraments of baptism and the Eucharist). In addition, a significant portion of his commentaries on Matthew's Gospel and Paul's Epistle to the Romans have survived in the catenae.

12. The Church of the East is the official title today of those East Syrians who still maintain the orthodoxy of Diodore, Theodore, and Nestorius.

13. J.-M. Vosté, ed., *Theodori Mopsuesteni Commentarius in Evagelium Johannis Apostoli,* Corpus Scriptorum Christianorum Orientalium 115–16/Syr. 62–63 (Louvain: Officina Orientali, 1940), hereafter abbreviated *TJA,* with page numbers of the Syriac text found to the left of the slash, Vosté's translation to the right (I have translated the text here and subsequently directly from the Syriac); *THC.* I have relied on Tonneau's French translation and Syriac text for the present work. For a rather free English translation, see A. Mingana, ed. and trans., *Commentary of Theodore of Mopsuestia on the Nicene Creed,* Woodbrooke Studies 5 (Cambridge: Heffer, 1932); and A. Mingana, *Commentary of Theodore of Mopsuestia on the Lord's Prayer and on the Sacraments of Baptism and the Eucharist,* Woodbrooke Studies 6 (Cambridge: Heffer, 1933).

14. Robert Devreese, *Essai sur Théodore de Mopsueste,* Studi e Testi 141 (Vatican City:

If this were true, then one could no longer cite these excerpts as grounds for condemning both the works and the person of Theodore. Francis Sullivan ended this controversy over the authenticity of the excerpts with a brilliant textual analysis and established that, except for the three that belong to Diodore, all the other fragments are definitively Theodore's.[15]

Even while granting this, Robert Devreese, Émile Amann, and Paul Galtier[16] continued to argue that Theodore can be reinterpreted in an acceptable orthodox way. Other theologians, such as Rowan A. Greer, Richard A. Norris Jr., José Maria Lera, J.N.D. Kelly, and Simon Gerber argue that Theodore came to his Christology from a different approach and framework from that of Cyril and Constantinople II and ought not be judged solely by the latter.[17] Others, among them Martin Jugie, Wilhelm de Vries, Kevin McNamara, F. Sullivan, John Romanides, Arthur Vööbus, and, to some extent, Alois Grillmeier, strongly disagree.[18] These theologians praise Theodore for his sincere efforts to safeguard the full humanity of Christ but con-

Biblioteca Vaticana, 1948); Marcel Richard, "La tradition des fragments du Traité Περί ἐνανϑπωπήδεως Théodore de Mopsueste," Le Muséon 46 (1943): 55–75.

15. Francis A. Sullivan, The Christology of Theodore of Mopsuestia, Analecta Gregoriana 82 (Rome: University Gregorian, 1956). Sullivan has carefully shown that, with the possible exception of a few minor places, the excerpts cited by the fathers at the Second Council of Constantinople are authentic (158).

16. Émile Amann, "Théodore de Mopsueste," in Dictionnaire de Théologie Catholique, vol. 15, part 1 (Paris: Letouzey, 1946), 235–79; Paul Galtier, "Théodore de Mopsueste: Sa vraie pensée sur l'incarnation," Recherches de science religieuse 45 (1957): 161–86, 338–60.

17. Rowan A. Greer, Theodore of Mopsuestia: Exegete and Theologian (Westminster: Faith, 1961); Richard A. Norris Jr., Manhood and Christ: A Study in the Christology of Theodore of Mopsuestia (Oxford: Clarendon Press, 1963); José Maria Lera, "Théodore de Mopsueste," in Dictionnaire de Spiritualité Ascétique et Mystique: Doctrine et Histoire, ed. M. Viller et al., 15:385–400 (Paris: Beauchsne, 1991); J.N.D. Kelly, Early Christian Doctrines, rev. ed. (San Francisco: Harper, 1978); Theodore of Mopsuestia Theodor von Mopsuestia und das Nicänum: Studien zu den katechetischen Homilien, trans. Simon Gerber (Leiden: Brill, 2000). For a detailed summary of this work, see the review by Charles Kannengiesser in Revue des Études Augustiniennes 49 (2003): 194–96.

18. Martin Jugie, "Le Liber ad baptizandos de Théodore de Mopsueste," Echoes d'Orient 34 (1935): 257–71; Wilhelm de Vries, "Der 'Nestorianismus' Theodors von Mopsuestia in seiner Sakramentenlehre," Orientalia Christiana Periodica 7 (1941): 91–148; Kevin McNamara, "Theodore of Mopsuestia and the Nestorian Heresy," Irish Theological Quarterly (July 1952): 254–78, and (April 1953): 172–91; John Romanides, "Highlight in the Debate over Theodore of Mopsuestia's Christology and Some Suggestions for a Fresh

clude that he ultimately failed to anchor the true unity of Christ's natures in the Person of the Word. Such a judgment has prevailed up to the present.

A New Approach

This work will not repeat what previous scholars have set forth at length, especially as regards the possible influence of rhetorical and philosophical thought upon Theodore. Rather it will enter into topics that have yet to be explored: the three principal roles that Theodore assigns to Christ in salvation as the head of the "body" that is his church; the head who recapitulates the "body" of the universe; and the perfect visible image whose "bodily" nature reveals the invisible God. My intent here is to bring into sharper focus what Theodore affirms to be Christ's humanity's indispensable roles in implementing God's plan for salvation for creation. I contend that this awareness provides useful insights into how Theodore conceived of the union, in general, between a spiritual and bodily component and, in particular, between the divine and human natures of Christ. This knowledge will clarify what Theodore means by a union of Christ's natures occurring within a "common *prosôpon*" and being "an indwelling of good pleasure as in His Son [a translation that I shall defend]." It will reveal not only how Theodore's understanding of the term "person" differs from the one that Cyril and others employ to justify a logical and linguistic basis for uttering such statements as "the Word suffered" and "Mary is truly the mother of God." All these points will, I hope, provide a new and wider context for reassessing the excerpts cited at the Second Council of Constantinople as certain proof that Theodore actually held, despite his impassioned denials, for a voluntary, moral kind of union of Christ's natures that is operational and, therefore, heretical.

Underlying my approach is the belief that we can uncover the theological framework that governs Theodore's thought about universal salvation

---

Approach," *Greek Orthodox Theological Review* 5 (winter 1959–60): 140–85 (Romanides provides an excellent summary of the literature up to the date of his article's publication); Arthur Vööbus, "Regarding the Theological Anthropology of Theodore of Mopsuestia," *Church History* (June 1964): 115–24; Grillmeier, *Christ in Christian Tradition*, 2:421–39.

through an understanding of the roles that Christ plays in this venture. While granting that a sizeable portion of Theodore's writings have been lost, I have found that there is more than enough material to deal with this subject of salvation, particularly in Theodore's commentaries on Paul's minor epistles and John's Gospel, and in his *Catechetical Homilies.* There is admittedly a problem in that Theodore wrote at a time when Christological terminology was still evolving. Yet there does appear to be present in his writings a truly consistent outlook that shaped his thought. This will be evident in the steadfast positions that he takes in opposition to Origen's defense of allegory as an acceptable way of interpreting God's revelation in Scripture and even more so in his rejection of Apollinaris's endorsement of a "Word-flesh" rather than a "Word-man" Christology. Since Theodore was a student and young theologian during a troubled time, when the Church was convulsed by the Arian crisis and the Antiochene dispute with Apollinaris, Theodore's synthetic theological outlook regarding God's plan for salvation probably belongs to his later life as a bishop at Mopsuestia. This is also suggested by the likelihood that most of the material with which we will be dealing dates from this period of his life.

Outline

Theodore lived during an era in which paradigmatic shifts were occurring in Christianity—not only regarding the correct ways to exegete a scriptural text and to speak of both the Word and Jesus as the Christ in accordance with creedal, liturgical, and pious traditions, but also regarding the best way to explain the meaning and effects of the sacraments of baptism and the Eucharist. Affected significantly by the Christological dispute over how the Word and Jesus are "one and the same," as well as by the patristic understanding and use of typology, the sacraments began to be described no longer as types, signs, and symbols (the way Theodore described them), but in realistic terms as divinely revealed sacramental ways to participate in God's divine life such that those who received the sacraments were "divinized." For, as Cyril reasoned, to receive the body of Christ is to share in the life of the Word.

My approach, therefore, to the question of Theodore's views of the roles that Christ's humanity plays within the history of salvation will be to move forward in ever-descending and reinforcing spirals. Since none of the salvific roles that will be discussed in the following chapters is fully explained as such in Theodore's extant works, I intend to show how the same pattern is repeated in each one of the roles in which Christ's humanity serves as the head of his body that is the church and the head of the "body" of the universe, as well as the perfect "visible image of God." All of this bolsters my conviction that an underlying theological viewpoint guides Theodore's thought on salvation. In other words, we can infer from his treatment of the roles of Christ's humanity in God's salvific plan for all creation that Theodore had evolved a comprehensive outlook that he adapted to each of these roles. This will not only highlight the mediating role that Christ's human "body" plays in salvation but will also prepare us to realize what Theodore means by "person" and the union of Christ's natures as a "common *prosôpon*" and an "indwelling of good pleasure as in His Son." This outlook makes sense only if there is a link between Theodore's soteriology and his Christology.

The chapters proceed through logical and ever-narrowing stages. I begin in Chapter 2 with a consideration of Theodore's own method of exegesis. I do not belabor what others have already done or enter into disputed questions other than to highlight what will help us to understand how and why Theodore interprets Scripture as he does. For, besides being conscious of how he was influenced by his rhetorical training, we want to be more sensitive to what appears to have been the intellectual impact upon him of such diverse sources as his teacher Diodore, the early Antiochene tradition that he inherited, possible Jewish, Stoic, and Aristotelian elements, his own temperament, and the evolution of his own thought. I am most interested in answering two questions: first, why is Theodore so committed to a literal, historical, rational kind of interpretation and so antagonistic to Origen's allegorical exegesis? And, second, what are his criteria for a true typology? The second question is critical, because Theodore developed his understanding of the roles of Christ's humanity in salvation on the basis of his archetypal relationship to Adam as the head of a mortal human existence, the bond of the universe, and the favored "image of God."

The next three chapters—3, 4, and 5—explore Theodore's literal and rational method of exegesis and his drawing out the typological meaning he discerns in Adam and Christ's roles as the heads of human and cosmic existence and as the "images of God." I begin in Chapter 3 with a brief elaboration of Theodore's understanding of salvation and the roles Adam and Christ's humanity in salvation as the heads of two kinds of "bodily" existence. Adam is the head of an earthly mortal existence. When he sins, he keeps all creation in a mortal state that then disposes other humans to sin. Christ's humanity, by contrast, is the head of an immortal existence. His sinless life enables all those who are united to him by nature to participate also in the immortal life that his humanity now enjoys in heaven. To share in this new life in a heavenly union with God, a human being must be united vitally to Christ as the living members of a body are to their head. This continuing "bodily" union means that those who are united directly to his humanity are also indirectly in a true union with God because of his humanity's true "exact" union with the Word. So, just as Adam affected the union of creation with God in a negative way, so Christ's humanity enables humans also to participate in his victory over sin and death.

I then consider in the same chapter the two sacramental ways Theodore believes that humans can now share in the immortal life of Christ's humanity as members of his "body." To clarify how Theodore conceived of the spiritual effects that baptism and the Eucharist have upon their recipients, I examine the principal arguments raised by Wilhelm de Vries, on one side, and by Ignatio Oñatibia and Luise Abramowski, on the other, concerning Theodore's conclusions about the real efficacy of these sacraments. De Vries believed that Theodore looked at baptism and the Eucharist as types, symbols, and signs that are effective in three ways: they provide forgiveness of sins, they provide actual grace for living a present virtuous life, and they provide a sense of hope that one can attain immortality in the next life, but without any real participation in the divine life of the risen Christ. I next summarize the major arguments advanced by Oñatibia and Abramowski against de Vries and elaborate on their chief arguments by showing how Theodore's understanding of a type also provides a clearer insight into the present spiritual effects he attributes to the sacraments. For

Theodore, baptism constitutes one as a living member of Christ's body and the Eucharist nourishes this life. Both of these sacraments typify for Theodore the future immortal life that awaits a person in heaven in a way similar to how an embryo grows into an adult human being, provided no obstacle intervenes to block his or her development. This dynamic element within a type indicates why Theodore was convinced that the sacraments provide not merely some sort of hope but a hope that God has guaranteed will be fulfilled because one is participating even here and now in Christ's humanity's immortal life and union with God.

Chapter 4 assesses Theodore's understanding of Christ's role in the salvation of the rest of creation. As Paul affirms, the spiritual powers and the material world are groaning, too, to share in the salvation God has promised to the members of Christ's body. To explain this role, Theodore turns once again to the typology he found in the New Testament. He regards both Adam's and Christ's humanity as the bonds uniting the spiritual and material worlds to form one "body," with themselves as their heads, for the angelic and spiritual powers are akin to the human soul, and the material world to the human body. When Adam sinned, allowing death to become an actuality, this meant that the human soul not only departed from its body but also broke the bond uniting the spiritual and material worlds with humans and thus severed their harmonious union with one another and with God. Adam's initial role in salvation history, however, is both a prefiguring and a type of the role Christ will play in recapitulating creation within his own human nature and bringing all to fulfillment by his death and resurrection. This integrating and peaceful union of all creation with its Creator through Christ's humanity is the archetypal fulfillment God has intended from the beginning. In the next life in heaven, this existence will be become permanent because of the immortality and immutability that Christ has achieved for all creation.

Theodore's two references to humans as the bond uniting all creation and to the universe as a "body" raise two questions: what is his source for the view that humans are the bonds of the universe? And is the idea of the universe constituting "one" body to be taken literally, or as a metaphor? Ulrich Wickert believes that Theodore depends upon a Stoic understanding of humans as the bond of the universe and has adapted this to cohere with his view of salvation. Wickert is also convinced that Theodore's notions of the universe as a "body" and of those united to Christ as the "body" of Christ are metaphorical. To amplify this view we must inquire into how Theodore interprets the passages in Colossians and Ephesians where Christ is said to be the one who "recapitulates" the universe and serves as the divine *"plerôma."* As the root meaning of "recapitulation" illustrates, Christ's humanity as the visible "image of the invisible God" is also the one who "re-heads" the "body" of the universe. For Theodore, since the cosmos forms the "body" of Christ, it can share in the immortality of Christ's humanity. As for the term *"plerôma,"* Theodore interprets this in a unique way among the fathers. He is convinced that Paul is asserting that Christ is fully not only in the "body" that is his church but also in the "body" that the universe forms. Christ's humanity permeates all those existing within the cosmos in such a way that all form one "body," with him as their head. This view raises further questions as to whether the source of Theodore's understanding of humans as the "bond" of the universe is from Paul rather than from Stoicism, and whether Theodore understands the universe as constituting one "body" in some sort of an organic way.

Chapter 5 provides us with clues as to how Theodore used typology to illuminate the roles of both Adam's and Christ's humanity in salvation. He compares and contrasts how Adam and Christ serve as God's true images. In a way that is unique among the fathers (including his three fellow Antiochenes, Diodore, John Chrysostom [ca. 350–407], and Theodoret), Theodore explains the phrase "image of God" as the functional way that Adam reveals God's existence and will, acts as the master of the material world, serves as the bond of the universe, and provides the means whereby creatures can give glory to God by their caring for the needs of other human beings. If one takes all these roles, especially that of Adam as the bond of the universe, as typical, in inferior ways, of those roles that the early chapters of Colossians assign to Christ's humanity as the perfect "image of God," then we have grounds to bolster our arguments that Theodore has drawn these functional roles of how Christ's humanity images God from a

Pauline source. It also further strengthens what I have argued for in the previous chapter: that Theodore has derived them from what he saw as Paul's view of the universe forming one "body."

To gain further insight into the relational bond that Theodore saw existing between Christ's humanity as the visible "image of God" and the Word as the "invisible image," I apply Theodore's criterion that a true type must not only image its reality but be related to it in a dynamic way whereby the fulfillment is guaranteed. Because God has decreed the bond, one is assured that Christ's humanity is truly, visibly imaging in a most perfect way the Word, and therefore that those who see the visible Christ are also seeing the Father and the Word because of the Word's unity in one nature with his Father. As we shall see, Theodore explains this in terms of John 14:9: "the one who sees me sees the Father." Thus, because Christ's humanity functions in this union as God's true visible "image," his visible humanity can receive the worship due God not because he is human but because his humanity perfectly images God. For Christ's human exterior reveals the presence of the Word dwelling within his humanity, just as in Jewish thought the body cannot be conceived apart from its soul. Theodore does not have a dualistic outlook but a unitary one.

By connecting the role of Christ's humanity as the "image of God" with his mediating roles as the one who binds and recapitulates all humanity, the spiritual powers, and the corporeal world within himself, Theodore reveals how these roles overlap with one another and convey a synthetic view of salvation. The term "Christ," signifying the union and unity of his human with his divine nature, truly symbolizes and effects the harmonious union of the whole universe with God. Because all human beings and the angelic and material worlds are bound in a "corporeal" way to Christ's humanity, they all can be rightly said to be "one" in Christ's human nature and therefore able to share in his immortal union with God. So too do humans, provided they remain living members of his "body" by freely pursuing a life of virtue. By being the one "head" to whom all other creatures are "bodily" united, Christ's humanity serves as their binding mediator with God. Because Christ is also God, the union of his two natures as "one" means that he is the perfect mediator who effects as well as images the peaceful harmony God has willed to exist in heaven between all created beings and himself.

Chapters 3 through 5 prepare us for a deeper reflection on what Theodore means by his term *prosôpon* and his two phrases for the union, the "common *prosôpon*" and an "indwelling of good pleasure as in His Son." Because of confusion as to what Theodore intends by these terms, I examine the words the fathers used to express who Christ is and the kind of union that has to exist between the Word and Christ's humanity, first in general and then in Theodore's own usage. I then look at what he meant by the first of his two phrases for the unity of Christ's natures: his "common *prosôpon*." We shall learn that he uses this phrase not in a metaphysical sense but to portray how the Synoptics depict who Christ is by the visible ways that he acts as "one" in human and divine ways. I then examine the three analogies Theodore uses to exemplify why one can rightly affirm the possibility of the existence of two natures in one common *prosôpon*. Theodore likens the union of Christ's natures to those between God and his temple, a husband and his wife in one flesh, and the soul and its body forming one person. I elaborate at length on the implications of the last analogy for grasping what Theodore means by a common *prosôpon*, for this analogy is the clearest example of why he says Christ's two natures can be "two yet one." But more tellingly, it suggests why and how Theodore insists that it is possible for Christ's two natures to operate as one. Chapter 6 concludes with an examination of how Christ's salvific roles as the heads of the church and the universe and as the "image of God" not only relate to but also clarify what Theodore intends by his phrase "one *prosôpon*."

Chapter 7 continues the explanation of what Theodore intends by the union of Christ's divinity and humanity in "one *prosôpon*." When pressed to state what kind of union the common *prosôpon* is, Theodore excludes both a substantial and an operational union. Resorting to scriptural terms, he describes it as being an "indwelling of good pleasure as in God's Son." His adversaries interpreted this to mean a voluntary and moral union in which God dwells in Christ as he does with his saints in grace, but in a far superior way. I seek to determine what Theodore meant by his ambivalent Greek phrase, for it can be rendered in two ways, "as in a son" and "as in His Son." I argue that the latter translation is preferable, because Theodore explains it in other extant passages and because it ought to be interpreted in light of Colossians 1–2. The sacred writer is speaking here of Christ as being God's Son in whom the heavens and earth are bound and recapitulated and in whom the divine *plerôma* dwells "in a bodily way." This leads to the question of how the assuming Word and the assumed humanity can function as "one." I argue that the answer is found in Theodore's analogy likening the union of Christ's divine and human natures to that of the soul with its body. I do so in light of how Nemesius, an early contemporary of Theodore at Antioch, demonstrates how the soul relates to its body. So, while Theodore rejects Apollinaris's use of the analogy to express how Christ can have one nature, he believes that it suggests how Christ's two natures can remain integral on one level and be united as one on another level. This provides a context for grasping what he intends by his explanation. I also consider the role the Spirit plays in enabling Christ's human nature to be united to the Word and to be freely functioning in the union during his earthly life, especially in his role as the unique mediator of graces for others. I conclude with an expanded treatment of what seems to be Theodore's *communicatio idiomatum,* that is, his way of speaking about Christ's human and divine natures and their union in the ego of Christ's one common *prosôpon.* I then explore the full ramifications of how he likens the ways attributes can be assigned to each nature and to their common *prosôpon* to the similar ways one can refer to the union of the soul with its body as one person.

The aim of Chapter 8 is to spell out the principal charges raised against Theodore's orthodoxy. I first summarize the primary points advanced in the seventy-one excerpts and the creed contained in the *Acta* of the Second Council of Constantinople that were accepted as evidence of Theodore's heterodoxy. Because some have been incorporated into the conciliar anathemas, we possess some indication of what the fathers found objectionable in these citations, but even here there is no in-depth elaboration. We do, however, have at least hints of what troubled the fathers in the concise headings attached to some of the excerpts. To understand, therefore, the likely reasons why these passages from Theodore's works were thought to be heretical, I shall summarize the principal arguments that two modern-day theologians offer in agreement with the council's condemnation, and, for balance, two others who disagree.

The aim of Chapter 9 is to reassess the principal charges raised against Theodore's orthodoxy in light of the earlier chapters. I begin by citing passages where Theodore explicitly denies that he looks upon Christ as a mere man and lays bare the general parameters of his own thought by rejecting the position of his adversaries. I then review the major arguments for why he and his works have been condemned and address each in light of the wider systematic outlook proposed here. My concern is threefold: does an understanding of Christ's roles in salvation support Theodore's claim that he holds Christ to be more than a mere man? Does Theodore's manner of speaking about the union of Christ's natures fulfill what is traditionally required for a substantial unity of Christ's natures? And does Theodore's teaching fatally undermine the full unity that Cyril and others maintain must be present, especially by what appears to be his inability to state that the Word alone is the subject of all of Christ's human attributes and operations? This last question goes to the heart of the mystery of how Christ can be truly and fully human as well as truly and fully divine, especially in regard to what Christ knew in a human way and whether he was able truly to grow both in human freedom and virtue as well as be subject to the temptations and passions that all humans experience. I conclude by considering the specific charges leveled against Theodore's exegetical interpretations, especially that he has weakened, if not broken, the nexus between the Hebrew Scripture and the New Testament.

The concluding chapter considers the strengths and weaknesses of Theodore's approach, examining what ought to be the "correct" standard for appraising whether and to what extent Theodore's Christological formulations can be said to be orthodox or heretical, especially whether the traditional *communicatio idiomatum* suffices for this purpose. I consider Paul Galtier's proposition that Theodore's writings and person ought to be judged in light of all the conciliar Christological declarations, not merely on the basis of a *communicatio idiomatum* emanating out of the decrees of Ephesus and Constantinople II. Galtier believes it is necessary to assess Theodore's Christology also in light of the Council of Chalcedon (to which one can add that of Constantinople III's declaration). I also consider whether Theodore ought to have been condemned as a person.

The answers to these questions will reveal, I think, Theodore's brilliant theological mind working at a time when the Church fathers were initially formulating how best to profess who Christ is in a way that would defend Christ's full humanity as well as his divinity. Theodore's approach can be instructive for those today who approach Christ from a "low Christology" that regards Christ as a brother who, while being God, is entirely human, like all other men and women except in the matter of sin. For we live in an age where the emphasis on a historical critical perspective has focused attention upon the human Jesus. Finally, I conclude with a consideration of how Theodore's approach is also valuable for its insights into how the "body" plays a pivotal role within the salvation of humanity and the whole cosmos. It brings home how absolutely essential is the "body" in God's plan for the salvific union of all creatures with himself.

2. THEODORE'S METHOD OF INTERPRETING SCRIPTURE

I N ONE OF HISTORY'S MOST IRONIC TWISTS, Theodore of Mopsuestia and Origen stand out in patristic times as the two pre-eminent Christian scriptural scholars, yet they were also denounced as two of the most hated heretics of the period. In their own day they were recognized as the leaders of the two most respected—and often generally antagonistic[1]—traditions: that of Alexandria and that of Antioch. Though Origen will be mentioned in passing as a foil to Theodore, our principal preoccupation here is Theodore, whom José Lera described as "the most eminent representative of the School of Antioch, in its exegetical and theological tendencies," and whom H. B. Swete called the one who "stands out among ancient expositors of Scripture almost alone—that of an independent inquirer, provided with a true

---

1. There is not, of course, a rigid, polarized difference between these two patristic exegetical schools.

method of eliciting the sense of his author, and considerable skill in the use of it."[2]

My goal is not to repeat what others have uncovered about Theodore's exegetical method or, for that matter, about Antiochene exegesis in general. For those so interested, Albert Viciano's lengthy article furnishes a meticulous summary of the prodigious scholarly research that has already been published in both areas.[3] I have rather a twofold purpose: (1) to determine, as completely as possible, what factors have most influenced Theodore's literal, historical, and rational emphasis in exegesis, particularly from his early rhetorical education, his scriptural training under his famed teacher Diodore, his own temperament, and the development in his outlook, especially as regards inspiration; and (2) to expose his understanding of typology, as he has used it to explore the theological significance of how Adam and Christ's humanity serves as the heads of humanity and creation, as well as the bonds of the universe and the "images of God."

Let us begin with key passages from Theodore's extant works that explain why he interprets a passage as he does. I shall then turn to the influences on Theodore's exegesis, namely, his rhetorical education as a youth and his scriptural training under Diodore at his school at Antioch. His training under Diodore will reveal what was characteristic of the Antiochene tradition that Theodore inherited, especially its commitment to a "his-

---

2. Lera, "Théodore de Mopsueste," 386–87; [H. B. Swete], "Theodorus," in *Dictionary of Christian Biography, Literature, Sects and Doctrines,* ed. W. Smith and H. Wace (London: J. Murray, 1877), 947. Although there is no author listed for the article, it was undoubtedly written by H. B. Swete.

3. For a summary of the various theories concerning Antiochene methods of interpretation, see Albert Viciano, "Das Formale Verfahren der Antiochenischen Scriftauslegung: Ein Forschungüberblick," in *Stimuli* (Munich: Aschendorff, 1996), 370–405. Viciano treats the publications that deal with the Antiochene exegesis up to 1996. He highlights the different schools of thought that have developed between the classical philology of Christoph Schäublin, *Untersuchungen zu Methode und Herkunft der Antiochenischen Exegese,* Theophaneia 23 (Cologne: Hanstein, 1974), and Manlio Simonetti's opinion that the origin of the Antiochene exegesis is to be sought in Christian, Jewish, and pagan sources. Viciano sides with Simonetti, believing that Theodore's theological outlook was the motivating factor in his use of his classically rhetorical principles. He also notes (209) that Schäublin was in dialogue with Simonetti and has accepted some of his (unspecified) observations.

torical" kind of interpretation and its outspoken opposition to Origen's allegorical method. I shall also consider whether and to what extent Jewish, Stoic, and Aristotelian concepts influenced Theodore.

In the second section of this chapter, I shall analyze Theodore's understanding of typology and his main criteria for judging what is a true type (in contrast to an allegorical interpretation), as well as his viewpoint on *theoria* and an accommodated sense in exegesis. All of this will prepare us for the following chapters, which look at how Theodore regards Adam's roles as the head of human mortal existence, as the bond of the universe, and as God's image as typifying the roles of Christ's humanity as the head of an immortal existence, as the one who recapitulates the universe within himself, and as the perfect visible "image of God." I am most interested in the kind of relational bond that Theodore sees uniting a type to its archetypal fulfillment. This will be particularly germane when we address what Theodore proposes by a "common *prosôpon*" and by his union of Christ's natures as an "indwelling of good pleasure as in God's Son."

Theodore's Own Statements

Several passages in Theodore's extant writings explicitly affirm how and why he exegetes a passage as he does. "Our purpose, therefore, in this book, with the help of the omnipotent God, is this: that in explaining [these] words, we do not omit anything of those matters that are difficult for others. Nor will we tarry over those evident to all by a simple reading. Indeed, when we comment on any book, our intent is not to introduce any superfluous words into our exposition, as we will [not] now do, insofar as we can. For we think that the task of an interpreter is this: to explain words that are difficult for most, while the task of the preacher is, after reflection, to speak about those matters that are clear."[4]

Theodore is also firmly convinced that the Scriptures have been written with the declared intent of revealing God's will or at least hinting at it: "For this reason the divine books also used words in an equal way in what they intend and at what they hint" (13/8). He is adamant on this point, insist-

4. *TJA*, 4/2. The left number is the Syriac page, the right, the Latin translation. This system will be followed throughout this chapter.

ing that it is not what one thinks is important but what the text actually discloses. In commenting on the passage in which Jesus is said to have loved John more, Theodore remarks: "But each one may think as he wants to about this. For it is not according to how I think, that we [ought to] judge [such] a human issue" (5/2). Rather an exegete's task is first and foremost to respect the text itself and to express its meaning in as brief and exact a way as possible. "Likewise in my interpretation of the psalm, I will also fully respect the substance of the text, being anxious only, as [is] my custom, to voice the exact sense that a word possesses and also [do so] briefly."[5]

An example of how Theodore exegetes a text is his commentary on what the Gospel of John means when it affirms that Jesus and the Father are one. While an interpreter ought to be fully aware of how a word is used in other passages, he must seek its meaning in its own context: "Therefore, because it is evident that [the word] 'one' is spoken of in many ways, being spoken of as both a [unity of] likeness and as a [unity of] agreement, one is not to ask whether or not this is said in this or in another place. Rather one ought to inquire into this [as to] how or in what sense it is spoken of here: whether as an equality or in some other way. The context in which it is [now] spoken [here] also indicates that one ought, above all, to trust the meaning of what is [actually] said—that he said that he is 'one' in the sense of [their] power [being one] and that he can prevail over all. This is discerned by interpreting the words."[6] One should note here that Theodore uses the same word, "exact," to express the relationship between a text and its meaning and the ways that Christ's outward human and divine actions reflect his human and divine natures.

Theodore also notes how Scripture frequently employs comparisons to demonstrate the suitability of one thing to another: "Nevertheless, who does not know that [the word] 'as' is spoken of in an illustrative way when it compares one thing to another. For if it is, in fact, spoken of thus, it is

5. Theodore of Mopsuestia, *Fragments syriaque*, 189:14/190:18. All translations are mine and are based on the Syriac. The translator and editor, van Rompay, notes that the present text is corrupt here.

6. *TJA*, 215/153.

also confirming the suitability[7] of what is said by this relationship. Indeed this usage is frequent in Scripture" (35/24). As we shall see later, this has a special application for understanding the analogies Theodore uses to suggest the kind of union he is proposing for Christ's natures. He clearly points out that it is not necessary to elaborate on all the details of a comparison—a point that is significant when he likens the union of the soul and body within a person to the union of the divine and human natures in Christ's common *prosôpon:* "Because it is clear that these things were said by the Lord by way of illustration, it is not necessary for us to speak of the whole illustration. . . . [but rather showing] what is the force of the words [as to] how the Scriptures are to be understood" (26/25). In other words, one must attend to the point that Theodore considers important and not struggle to apply his analogy in every detail.

As the following quotation indicates, Theodore notes that, although he is reluctant to respond directly to opposing interpretations, he is forced by these to clarify his position: "For we believe this is the task of an interpreter: to explicate the true meaning of a thought not only by what is said but also by refuting contrary conjectures" (28/19). This point needs to be somewhat qualified, however, by Theodore's refusal to make the refutation of adversaries his primary concern. His focus is on the text itself: "[These adversaries] raise many other objections to this [position]—which we can refer to and refute one by one; but there is not time. For our intent is to interpret the texts, not at all to refute heresies" (209–10/149).

Sources of Theodore's Exegesis

My purpose here is to determine not so much the sources of Theodore's exegesis but the influences that appear to have shaped the evolution of his thought. It is more concerned about why Theodore interpreted scriptural passages as he did, and whether he is consistent in his method of exegeting a text.

Theodore believes that his systematic outlook regarding God's plan of

---

7. I think that the Syriac word in *TJA,* špî´çwt͗ (abundance), ought to be replaced by the špî´rwt͗ (suitability). The latter makes better sense in the present context.

salvation is present in Scripture. He is sure that one can discern God's intent in a particular text by means of a literal and rational interpretation of what a sacred writer actually wrote. He also believes that one is able to derive theological meaning from a close examination of the types that he is convinced God established within the Scriptures between two historical persons, events, actions, traditions, etc. For him, the type and its archetype illuminate the spiritual meaning of each other in God's plan for salvation. This is important because the ways that Adam serves as a type of Christ's human nature illumines the salvific roles of Christ's humanity and vice versa.

Rhetorical Education

As a youth, Theodore was probably educated at the school of the celebrated Sophist teacher Libanius (314–ca. 393). Libanius's school was founded at Antioch in 354, around the time that Theodore and John Chrysostom were born. It quickly attained a reputation as one of the most elite rhetorical schools in the empire, its graduates excelling as successful leaders in the civic, political, and commercial life of the Roman-Byzantine Empire.[8] As one would expect, this schooling shaped Theodore's early thinking. How profoundly it influenced his grammatical analysis and rhetorical interpretations, particularly in his earliest works on the Psalms and the twelve Minor Prophets, is thoroughly explored in studies by Christoph Shäublin, Frances Young, and John O'Keefe.[9]

8. Such schools as Libanius's were one of the principal agents for the spread of the Hellenistic culture throughout the then-known world. Libanius is also famous because many of his writings have survived and provide us with valuable information about the political, social, economic, and educational life at Antioch throughout the second half of the fourth century. For a study that has made extended use of Libanius's writings, see A. Harrent, *Les Écoles d'Antioche* (Paris: Thorin, 1878), and for a summary of the social significance of Libanius's letters, see Glanville Downey, *A History of Antioch in Syria from Seleucus to the Arab Conquest* (Princeton: Princeton University Press, 1961), 373–79.

9. Schäublin, *Untersuchungen,* esp. 84–155; Frances M. Young, "The Rhetorical Schools and Their Influence on Patristic Exegesis," in *The Making of Orthodoxy: Essays in Honor of Henry Chadwick,* ed. Rowan Williams (Cambridge: Cambridge University Press, 1989), 182–99; and also Young's *Biblical Exegesis and the Formation of Christian Culture* (Cambridge: Cambridge University Press, 1997); John J. O'Keefe, "'A Letter That Killeth': Toward a Reassessment of Antiochene Exegesis, or Diodore, Theodore, and Theodoret on

Theodore's early education probably passed through three stages. The first, lasting seven years, emphasized reading, writing, and arithmetic' the second stage, lasting three to four years, grammar, etymology, exegesis, history, and dialectic.[10] The climactic third stage would have stressed rhetorical, literary, and sophistical principles of composition, the technical skill in speaking from a text and in the art of improvising, and training in logic and the virtues.[11] What is striking here is the lack of formal philosophical schooling other than in logic and ethics. This is understandable when one considers that the two schools of rhetoric and philosophy had divergent goals, which created a certain tension between them. The philosophers looked upon the rhetoricians as so concerned with technique that they valued form over substance. The rhetoricians countered that their approach was more relevant for the virtues for everyday life than the philosophers' airy abstractions.[12]

There are many similarities between the rhetorical principles of the schools and the Antiochene exegetical method as practiced by Theodore. The schools emphasized discerning the historical context of a work, establishing a text's reliability and its author's principal intent and argument,[13] ascertaining the significance and force of an author's punctuation and sentence structure, and employing a precise style and a methodical examination of other passages related to the one under consideration[14]—all charac-

the Psalms," *Journal of Early Christian Studies* 8, no. 1, 83–104. See also [Swete], "Theodorus," 947.

10. See Harrent, *Les Écoles d'Antioche,* 74–82.

11. Ibid., 83–102.

12. Ibid., 224–26.

13. Schäublin, *Untersuchungen,* 84, sums this up well: "Each book [of Scripture] should be understood and interpreted on the basis of a particular historical situation [that is] to be recognized by the exegetes." My translation.

14. See Josef Martin, *Antike Rhetorik: Technik und Methode* (Munich: Beck, 1974). Theodore believed that a text had only one aim. This led him to oppose on principle all those who would interpret a Psalm as containing a reference to Christ, even in those instances where the gospel affirms that Jesus is said to have referred to the words of the Psalm, such as Psalm 21 (or, as in most versions, 22). While Theodore is reluctant to find Christ mentioned in the Psalms, we do have the instance where in his commentary on Psalm 44 (45) he refers particular verses to the Word and others to Christ *qua* man. What is interesting here is that he affirms the presence of only one *prosôpon,* as seen in his section 8b: "But also because [the verse] 'Therefore God, your God, has anointed you' does

teristics of Theodore's exegesis and often spelled out in the prologues to his works. Moreover, Theodore's rhetorical training may have taught him to weigh the significance of individual words in a sentence, to paraphrase a sentence to clarify its thought, to compare the meaning of a word in context with its meaning in other contexts, and to be in all things brief. Theodore used all of these practical tools to unlock the literal meaning of scriptural passages that he believed contained God's inspired message.[15]

H. B. Swete has also studied Theodore's grammatical method of exegesis. Although he does not associate this with Theodore's rhetorical training, his analysis is valuable in reinforcing how Theodore consistently interpreted Scripture and for demonstrating Theodore's use of these practices: "the precision with which he adheres to the letter of the author. . . . his readiness to press into service of the interpreter those minor words which are commonly overlooked . . . his attention to the niceties of grammar and punctuation . . . his keen discussion of doubtful readings . . . [and] his acuteness in seizing on the ἰδιώματα of Scripture . . . in bringing out the points of a parable or discourse."[16] Other scholars who have argued that Theodore derived his method of exegesis from the methods used in the rhetorical schools support Swete's analysis. They have also demonstrated the precision of Theodore's examination of words and the kind of personality he had. In Swete's words, "The more difficult or obscure arguments are worked out in detail, with varying success, but for the most part with a genuine effort to grasp the mind of the Apostle."[17] In brief, Scripture is the sourcebook for Theodore's understanding of truth, while his rhetorical training provided him the tools that he needed to determine the inspired meaning of the sacred writer.

---

not apply to God the Father. It is clearly then to be reckoned that these things are said of Christ in a way so wondrous to us. He both divided the natures and demonstrated the unity of the [one] person (prosôpon)." The text is found in Theodore of Mopsuestia, *Commentaire sur les Psaumes*, 289. See too Rowan Greer's interpretation of this Psalm in *Theodore of Mopsuestia*, 256–58. I am grateful for his alerting me to this text.

15. This is a personal summary of what I have digested from the works noted above that treat the question of how much Theodore's rhetorical training affected his outlook.

16. [Swete], "Theodorus," 947. See also Swete's detailed analysis in *TEP* 1:lxv–lxxi.

17. *TEP* 1:lxviii.

Diodore's Influence

After leaving Libanius's school and finally resolving to remain a monk, Theodore undertook his religious and scriptural studies under the renowned exegete Diodore, who is now generally considered the true founder of the so-called School of Antioch.[18] While Diodore shared the same general classical and rhetorical background as Theodore, he would in turn have taught Theodore what he learned from his teachers and his own experience about how to apply rhetorical training to the Antiochene tradition, as reflected in the writings of such Antiochenes as Diodore, Eusebius of Emesa (ca. 300–ca. 359), and Eustathius of Antioch (early fourth century), who wrote his "Witch of Endor" to refute the allegorical method of Origen (d. ca. 254) because it undermined the historical character of Scripture. Theodore may have also been aware of the writings of Lucian of Antioch (d. early fourth century), a formidable scriptural opponent of the allegorical method of Origen,[19] and perhaps also of the thought of Theophilus (late third century), who sought in his writings to explain the Christian message to a pagan world.

Whatever the other influences on Theodore, Diodore without doubt had the greatest impact in instilling the principles of the Antiochene tradition. He would certainly have imparted to Theodore a commitment to a literal, historical, and rational exegetical method, and would have emphasized the sharp distinction between a transcendent and a created nature. This is clearly evident from even a superficial comparison of Diodore's *Commentary on the Psalms* with what survives of Theodore's commentary.[20] The same can be said of the similarities between Diodore's and The-

18. This was not a "school" in the modern sense of the term but of a gathering of like-minded scholars who shared general exegetical and theological principles.

19. Regarding the origin of the Antiochene exegesis, Manlio Simonetti, "Exegesis, Patristic," thinks that "its remote exegesis must not be seen in Lucian of Antioch . . . but in the above-mentioned interest in the literal appreciation of Scripture, seen in Syria and Palestine in the course of the fourth century" (*EEC* 1:309–10).

20. In his study of the most likely influence of Diodore on Theodore's exegesis of the Psalms, O'Keefe believes that "The Psalms commentaries of Diodore and Theodore contain more than superficial similarities. Even a casual reading of the texts reveals the

odore's defense of Christ's complete humanity, though Diodore referred to it as a Word/flesh kind of union. In regard to his Christology, Theodore would have learned from Diodore the need to be circumspect in defending Christ's humanity. For a ominous cloud hung over Antioch because of the condemnation in 268 of Paul of Samosata, for a time the bishop of Antioch, who apparently taught that Christ was a mere man. Antioch was also under suspicion because of its reputation in the fourth century as a major center of Arianism. As we shall discuss later, Theodore sought to strike a fine balance between those, like Paul, who overemphasized the humanity of Christ and those, like Apollinaris (ca. 315–d. before 392), who undermined it by his insistence that the Word supplanted Christ's rational human soul (nous). J.N.D. Kelly understood the latter position to mean an organic unity wherein the Word influenced Christ's human nature "on the biological, physical and spiritual levels."[21]

Exactly how Diodore influenced Theodore is difficult to say. Theodore must have begun his studies with him as a young adult, either in his late teens or very early twenties, around 370.[22] By this time Diodore had achieved considerable fame as a scriptural scholar and theologian who wrote courageously in defense of Christianity against the attacks of Julian the Emperor when Julian resided at Antioch in 362–63. These defenses probably constitute Diodore's lost polemics against the pagan philosophical thought that dealt with God, nature, and matter.[23] Theodore would probably have been familiar with Diodore's theological opinions on these topics (which may have contributed to Theodore's negative attitude toward philosophy). We do not know how long Diodore would have instructed Theodore, for Diodore was exiled in 372 and probably did not return to Antioch until around the time that he became the bishop of Tarsus in 378.[24] But even if

---

dependence of the pupil on the teacher" ("'A Letter That Killeth,'" 97. For other specifics, see 85, 88–89, 93, 96, and esp. 97–101).

21. Kelly, Early Christian Doctrines, 294.

22. Swete, TEP, suggests 369 as the time that Theodore began to study under Diodore (1:lix).

23. These are Diodore's lost works "On Nature and Matter" and "On God and the False Matter of the Greeks."

24. According to Swete's "Theodorus" (936), some source (which Swete does not

Diodore was not teaching at his school at this time, his theological outlook and spirit would have permeated whatever training Theodore received.

Theodore's years of training at Diodore's school during the 370s were tumultuous.[25] From the time of the Council of Nicaea in 325 until 378, the Church at Antioch was frequently convulsed by the Arian controversy, at one time having four factions that vied for ecclesiastical control: the Eustathians (later known as the Paulinians), strict defenders of Nicaea; the Meletians, who, though Niceans in spirit, were reluctant to use the term *homoousion*, perhaps because it was not a scriptural term (Diodore, John Chrysostom, and Theodore belonged to this party); the Arians, who asserted that the Word was a divine creature and thus denied that Christ is God; and the Apollinarians—named after Apollinaris, who taught at Antioch in 373.[26] Theodore was certainly conscious of all these controversies, but he was personally most involved against Apollinaris's Christology, especially as enunciated in Apollinaris's *Logos Syllogistikos*, which attacked Diodore.[27]

Theodore's first published work was his commentary on the Psalms, probably written while he was still at Diodore's school, judging from a later statement in which Theodore expresses misgivings about his youthful work on the Psalms.[28] His next work was his commentary on the twelve Minor Prophets, probably published immediately after his works on the Psalms. While Theodore may have been separated from Diodore when he wrote these works during the 370s, he appears to have rejoined his teacher in Tarsus sometime after his ordination as a priest in 383, and remained

---

cite) affirms that "Theodore appears to have left Antioch while yet a priest and betaken himself to Tarsus" (936) to be with Diodore.

25. For a fuller treatment of this period between 358–78, see Downey, *History of Antioch*, 398–413.

26. Grillmeier, *Christ in Christian Tradition*, 1:318–19. Athanasius indicates in his *Tome to the Antiochenes* (362) that there were four factions vying for control in Antioch.

27. Charles Kannengiesser, "Apollinaris," *EEC* 1:58–59. Apollinarius was eventually condemned at 378 at Antioch, in general terms in the first canon of the First Council of Constantinople in 381 and by an imperial decree in 388.

28. [Swete], "Theodorus," quotes Hesychius, with the reservation that "if we may trust him, Theodore promised to burn his commentary on the Psalms but craftily hid it" (935). See as well *TEP* 1:lix–lxiii, for the division that Swete proposes for the various periods of Theodore's literary works.

with Diodore until Theodore became the bishop of Mopsuestia in 392, when he is said to have been consecrated a bishop so as to be endowed with the episcopal status the Macedonians wanted in the person who would confer with them over the question of the divinity of the Holy Spirit. This suggests that Theodore had achieved a reputation as a biblical theologian by this time, perhaps because of his Christological work *On the Incarnation,* written against the Apollinarians. In a subsequent apologetical work against the Apollinarians, Theodore mentions that *On the Incarnation* had been published around the mid-380s. Another of Theodore's extant works, his *Commentaries on the Minor Pauline Epistles,* appears to have been written sometime in the first two decades of the fifth century. The publication dates of his other writings remain unclear, though his *Catechetical Homilies* may have been written in the mid-380s or 390s.[29]

The Source of the Antiochene Exegetical Tradition

A comparison of Theodore's exegesis with what Diodore employs in his surviving works reveals that both emphasized a literal, historical, and rational method of interpretation and that both rejected Origen's allegorical method. While Diodore doubtless had an impact on Theodore in these two areas, the approach predates Diodore. Lucian, Eusebius of Emesa, and Eustathius of Antioch also manifest these characteristics. One can only speculate as to the source from which these Antiochenes derived their hermeneutical emphases. One can indeed argue that the Antiochene exegetical approach was sculpted by the rhetorical schools, the cultural rational outlook molded either by Aristotelian thought or by an earlier oral Syriac tradition conversant with the major conservative rabbinical schools in Palestine and Babylon, or a combination of all of these. Rudolf Bultmann speculates that the Antiochene emphasis on *historia* may stem from the early Christians' view of their religion as historical.[30] By this he appears to

29. For a closer study of this topic, see J.-M. Vosté, "La chronologie de l'activité de Thédore de Mopsueste au II Councile de Constantinople," *Revue Biblique* 34 (Jan. 1925): 54–81.

30. Rudolf Bultmann, *Die Exegese des Theodor von Mopsuestia,* ed. H. Field and K. Schelke (Stuttgart: Kohlhammer, 1984), 126.

mean that Christianity justifies its beliefs and moral convictions by relying on a sacred, inspired work that recounts how God has intervened in the history of salvation and has revealed in the scriptural narrative what will truly come to pass in the future life.

Whether Bultmann is correct or not, the Antiochenes did make *historia* a central tenet of their exegesis, believing that what God has actually revealed in the scriptural narrative (or in an event) is his will. They were convinced that since God has inspired a sacred writer, every word, phrase, clause, and sentence of what he has written ought to be carefully heeded as truly revealing God's inspired message. One must, therefore, pay attention to what the sacred author actually intended to affirm in what the text affirms and be ready to justify this in a strictly literal and rational way. This view is substantiated in Diodore's prologue to his *Commentary on the Psalms,* where he declares that *theoria* and *allegoria* differ from each other on the basis of *historia,* by which he meant not "history" as such but Scripture's narrative account: "We do not object to *anagogē* [a search for a higher meaning][31] and a more lofty *theoria* [seeing the actual spiritual fulfillment of a text]. . . . For *historia* [a narrative text] does not exclude a more lofty *theoria*. Rather it is the basic substructure for higher insights. This alone must be held to, lest *theoria* be ever looked upon as subverting that upon which it is founded. For such would no longer be *theoria* but *allegoria*."[32]

The Antiochenes also believed that whatever Scripture is affirming, whether it be a religious or secular kind of assertion, is a revelation of truth.[33] If so, we can grasp why the Antiochenes were so strenuously op-

---

31. The word *anagogē* literally means to refer one thing to another but connotes here what the English word "anagogy" signifies today, the discovery of a spiritual or mystical meaning for a text. For a translation of Diodore's "Preface," see Karlfried Froelich, trans. and ed., *Biblical Interpretation in the Early Church,* Sources of Early Christian Thought (Philadelphia: Fortress, 1984), 87–94, 21–22.

32. Jean-Marie Olivier, ed., *Diodori Tarsensis Commentarii in Psalmos,* Corpus Christianorum, Series Graeca 6 (Turnhout: Brepols, 1980), xcii.

33. For a study of how, in the pre-critical world, the text presented itself directly to the reader as the true word of God but in the post-critical worldview became a second-level language that pointed to the truth present in the history contained behind the text, see Hans Frei, *The Eclipse of the Biblical Narrative* (New Haven: Yale University Press, 1974).

posed to Origen's allegorical methodology. His spiritual interpretations would have been regarded as ahistorical. The fundamental question for the Antiochenes therefore becomes, what did God in fact intend to reveal in his Scriptures? This is not what the exegete might or ought to imagine but what one can reason, in a serious, critical way, to be a sacred writer's intention as expressed in his actual choice of words. The crucial question, then, is whether one's interpretation is what God intended to be derived from the text and, if so, how one authenticates it.

The Ramifications of Inspired Scripture

Christian inspiration can perhaps be defined as the infusion of the Holy Spirit into the writers of Scripture such that the Scriptures can be embraced by readers as the Word of God. For the fathers, inspiration was in practice identified with infallibility, and the text itself with revelation. This meant that they regarded the sacred writer as a secretary, much as Muslims believe that the Koran is God's factual word. As Dimitri Zaharopoulos notes, the fathers, like Origen, were convinced that "In the Bible there is nothing without purpose, not a syllable, not an iota, not the smallest dash."[34] In this way they regarded Scripture as a sourcebook of knowledge of revealed truth. "The fathers as a whole insisted so much on the divine action in the composition of our Bible that they came to view inspiration as being a mechanical dictation of truths into the scripture. . . . Divine inspiration of the Bible was generally held by the fathers to require belief in the truth of all its assertions on matters not only of religious doctrine and ethics, but also of cosmology, astronomy, history and biology."[35] As Zaharopoulos further notes, the fathers' complete silence on this point indicates how widely this opinion was held; only Marcion and the Manicheans challenged it seriously.

As I shall discuss at greater length below, Theodore later evolved in his understanding of inspiration. But it is easy to see why he was so insistent on emphasizing what the text in fact states in a literal way and why he was so resolved to make use of grammatical and rhetorical principles to deter-

---

34. Dimitri Z. Zaharopoulos, *Theodore of Mopsuestia on the Bible: A Study of His Old Testament Exegesis* (New York: Paulist Press, 1989), 79. The quotation is taken from Origen. For a further treatment of this, see Kelly, *Early Christian Doctrines*, 61–62.

35. Zaharopoulos, *Theodore on the Bible*, 81–82.

mine the author's true intentions. If the author's statements are a true expression of God's will, then it becomes of paramount importance to deal with the original text and to understand what words meant both in their context and also in other contexts. This requires a knowledge of the author's purpose in writing and the specific historical setting in which a particular work was written. To establish all this, one had to rely on a rigorous application of reason to justify one's answers in an objective way, and not by the imaginative subjective musings of the allegorists.

Reaction to Allegory

Reliance on allegory as an exegetical tool had grown among Christians from the time of Origen's death (254?). But throughout the fourth century there occurred a strong counterreaction at Antioch to allegorical interpretation in scriptural exegesis.[36] While the Antiochenes accepted Origen's critical approach to establishing an original text, they resisted his conviction that the number of inconsistencies, contradictions, and ambiguities discernable in the Scriptures necessitated an allegorical interpretation. For the Antiochenes, these inconsistencies and ambiguities only meant that God had implanted spiritual meanings in the text that could not be discerned in a merely literal reading. But how does an exegete verify an allegorical explanation when the meaning is not specifically revealed by God? They would also have bristled at the three levels of interpretation that Origen put forward: the literal, the moral, and the spiritual. Origen likened these to the human body, soul, and spirit, principally because he presumed that a literal reading of the body of the text pertained to the lowest level at which the "rudi" or the simpleminded read Scripture.

For the Antiochenes, therefore, to search for God's will by means of an allegorical interpretation meant that an exegete was not confronting the actual meaning God had revealed but was allowing his subjective imagination free license. In other words, the Antiochenes held that there was a re-

---

36. The Antiochenes differed too over what was the inspired Hebrew Testament text. While the Alexandrians followed the Septuagint, the Antiochenes accepted the Jewish canon.

lational bond between God's actual intent and its verbal expression. This position is also reflected in the revealed way that the transcendent Word manifests himself through Christ, his visible image. The source of allegory further incensed the Antiochenes. They seemed truly scandalized that Origen had rejected close literal interpretation of a text in favor of a pagan, Stoic methodology in seeking the meaning of the inspired word of God in sacred Scripture.[37] Theodore charges Origen with using a method that the Stoics had invented so as to discern meaning in their pagan myths: "But to twist the entire account or change the text of Scripture, how is this not complete insanity and manifest wickedness?[38] . . . [so as to] introduce [ideas] that have no [connection] and no agreement with what is written and use the words of the divine Scriptures in an unusual way to seduce and ruin many. . . . But whenever they speak of 'the allegorical interpretation,' I also say that it truly originates with the pagans who have invented these to abolish their myths and the real facts in the divine Scriptures" (8/11). This rejection of allegory mirrors that of earlier Jewish rabbis against Philo and raises the question of whether the Antiochenes originally followed the Jewish method of exegesis.

Theodore also takes the allegorists to task for their belief that Scripture contains more than one revealed message: "One ought to learn the real sense of what is written. . . . there is only a single sense in all of the divine scriptures" (13/17–18). In other words, Theodore strenuously objects to the opinion that every line of the Scriptures contains a spiritual meaning that can be other than the literal. For if this were true, then there would be no limit to the number of possible interpretations. Furthermore, he cen-

---

37. Origen's method can provide insightful, spiritually rich interpretations, as for instance in St. Augustine's treatise on John's Gospel, in which Augustine offers, in the Antiochene sense, an allegory but calls it a type: "A woman came. She is a form of the Church not yet justified, but now about to be. . . . that woman who was acting as a type of the church. . . . Let us acknowledge ourselves in her and in her give our own thanks to God. She was a figure, not the reality. For she also foreshadowed the reality, and the reality came to be. She found faith in Christ, who was using her as a figure for us." Augustine, "In Johannis Evangelium Tractatus CXXIV," in *Aureli Augustini Opera*, part 8, Corpus Christianorum, Series Latina 36 c. 2 (Brepols: Turnhout, 1954), tract. 15:10–12, 154. My translation.

38. Theodore of Mopsuestia, *Fragments syriaque*, 13/17.

sures Origen for deliberately undermining Scripture, charging that he is "aware that he was greatly dishonoring the divine Scriptures by suppressing their narrative accounts and making these appear to be deceitful and fallacious like those of the pagans" (11/15). Theodore is even more outspoken when he contends that "This is a thing he should never have done—to delight in being diligent for this interpretation that is full of madness and pagan blasphemy—if he had learned the true sense of what is written and if he had inquired into what is the meaning of each of the words. So he could know that there is one sense in all the passages of divine Scripture and he could [thereby know what is] the invincible truth of the teaching of the church" (13/17–18).

These passages indicate that the Antiochenes were among those who raised the cry, what has Athens to do with Jerusalem? While the Antiochenes employed rhetorical principles to determine the literal meaning of a text, their attention was centered on using these principles to elucidate the text itself. They would have considered these rhetorical principles tools for discerning the intent of an author. But Theodore objects to allegory not only because it relies on subjective imagination rather than the narrative text but also because it distorts Paul's definition of allegory in Galatians 4:24:

> Those who are very zealous to reverse the meanings of divine Scripture and appropriate all that is found there [to their own way of thinking and] in fact make up their own foolish fables and posit the name "allegory" to [cover] their own foolishness, abuse this word of the apostle, as if they were empowered to put aside all the senses of divine Scripture because they rest [their case] upon the Apostle's use of "through an allegory." They do not understand how much difference there is between what is said by them and by the apostle on this point. For the apostle does not destroy the historical narrative. Nor has he detached what has been done a long time ago. But he asserted those things as they were then done and employed the historical narrative of what had occurred to [bring out] his own meaning. . . . For the fact he said "just as" shows, to be sure, a likeness. But a likeness cannot happen if facts are not present. . . . However, the division of times will be useless, if there would not be a factual content. But the apostle says that [that has to be] so. Indeed these (allegorists) do everything contrariwise, wanting the whole historical narrative of the divine Scriptures to be

in no way different from nocturnal dreams. . . . If indeed they teach these things about Scripture, what they call "allegory" is necessarily manifest foolishness because it is also proven to be wholly superfluous. . . . For this reason he said "what is said through an allegory," calling an allegory that comparison whereby facts from the past can be compared to what is [now] at hand.[39]

If this speculation is correct, then the Antiochenes, especially Theodore, were realists in an Aristotelian sense. They believed that the real did not exist in a Platonic world of ideal forms and ideas but in the specific, concrete reality that one confronted in life. For them, a true exegete must respect the actual text that God's Spirit inspired its author to write. The author's intent is to be determined by solid rational arguments, not in brilliant imaginative possibilities that one's mind can conjure up. Swete aptly characterizes the underlying difference between Origen and Theodore as scriptural exegetes: "Origen approaches the sacred text as a seeker after truth; Theodore, as one who has already found the key of knowledge and who, thus furnished, proceeds to unlock the treasures of S. Paul's teaching with almost entire confidence in the result."[40]

Origen, of course, developed his allegorical method so as to deal reasonably with textual problems. Their presence in the Scriptures raises a really serious problem for those who hold for a verbal kind of inspiration that can be discovered through rational exegesis. For how does one explain the problematic texts in a way that makes sense as God's will? Theodore takes up the challenge in his partially intact treatise "Against the Allegorists." Here he explains a number of passages that reveal how a literal, historical, and rational methodology can give truly meaningful answers to passages that seem unintelligible in their literal sense.[41] He argues that since it is possible to interpret these passages in a meaningful way, why should anyone resort to what they rashly presume are providentially placed spiritual meanings within a text? This, he argues, is to yield to deception.[42]

---

39. *TEP* 1:73–79.
40. Ibid., 1:lxxvii.
41. See Theodore of Mopsuestia, *Fragments syriaque*, 3–7/4–10.
42. Ibid.

Possible Jewish Influence

Agreeing with Heinrich Kihn, Rowan Greer sees the influence of a Jewish exegesis on Theodore.[43] Schäublin dismisses this possibility, convinced that Theodore's rhetorical training as a youth is sufficient to explain his interpretations. To substantiate his opinion Schäublin notes that Theodore was neither raised in a rabbinical tradition nor conversant with Hebrew.[44] While it is arguable that the Antiochenes derived their literary vocabulary and methods from their rhetorical teachers, there are in fact unmistakable similarities in exegetical methodology and theological outlook that suggest some Jewish influence on Antiochene exegesis.[45] Like all the other Antiochenes, Theodore chose to follow the list of inspired works contained in the Hebrew canon rather than the forty-six books found in the Septuagint, the way most fathers did. Zaharopoulos notes that Theodore's "remarks afford evidence of his awareness that the original Hebrew text should be the basis for a faithful interpretation of scripture."[46] Yet, although he was keenly sensitive to the need to adhere to the original text in order to discern its inspired literal meaning, he had to rely on the Greek text of the Septuagint—doubtless because he was unable to read Hebrew. In those passages where the Septuagint was unclear, however, he turned for assistance to the Greek versions of and commentaries on Hebrew Scripture by the famed Jewish scholars Symmachus, Theodotion, and Aquila, whose names appear repeatedly in the index of Devreese's edition of Theodore's *Commentary on the Psalms*.[47] Theodore seems to have relied upon these comments, at least in his earliest writings, as useful tools for ferreting out the meaning of the LXX.[48]

43. Greer, *Theodore of Mopsuestia*, 93.

44. See Schäublin, *Untersuchungen*, 28–30, esp. 29, and also 173.

45. Frederick McLeod, "Judaism's Influence upon the Early Syriac Christians," in *Religions of the Book*, ed. Gerald S. Sloyan (Lanham, Md.: University Press of America, 1996), 193–208.

46. Zaharopoulos, *Theodore on the Bible*, 57.

47. For references to the number of times that Theodore refers to Aquila, Symmachus, Theodotion, the Septuagint, and the Hebrew text of the Psalms, see the index in Robert Devreese's edition of Theodore's *Commentaire sur les Psaumes*, 564, 566–67, 570–71.

48. For a treatment of Theodore's attitude toward the Septuagint and Hebrew Scriptures, see Greer, *Theodore of Mopsuestia*, 98–102.

Theodore also practices a "literal" and a "practical" interpretation that is somewhat similar to those employed in the Jewish Talmud. For Talmudic scholars, a "literal" reading aims at establishing the basic meaning of a text, including what is narrated in figurative language. What is derived from this is then to determine how to respond in a "practical" way to a specific situation. We see this in Jewish midrashic interpretations, which are meant both to comment and to elaborate on the literal text. Theodore's writing manifests similar traits, though he may be merely reflecting what he found in the Scriptures, especially in Paul, regarding the meaning and the practical implications of Christ *qua* man as the bond of the universe and the "image of God."

While the methodological approaches outlined above are exhibited in Theodore's work, his theological views are also similar in some respects to the Jewish. For instance, Theodore shared an active sense of time with the rabbis that seems to underlie the negative attitude both had toward allegory. Another common trait is their esteem for the Hebrew Scriptures as inspired by God and therefore to be taken seriously as revelations of how God has manifested himself to his chosen people in history. Though Theodore has been roundly criticized for not stressing the close bond between the Jewish and Christian Scriptures, and particularly for his willingness to admit only a few messianic prophecies in the Hebrew Scriptures, he nevertheless saw an important typological nexus between the two testaments. In addition, both Theodore and the rabbis insisted on the unbridgeable gulf between a transcendent, totally other Creator and his creation.[49]

There are stylistic similarities as well. For instance, Theodore and the rabbis compare words and ideas from different biblical passages in order to gain insight into other meanings present in particular passages. They also use paraphrases, which the Jews call targums, to bring out a meaning in a way that an exact translation cannot. And, as I shall discuss later, both the rabbis and Theodore approach concrete and abstract natures as interchangeable.

If these similarities suggest Theodore's dependence on Jewish writing,

49. See Bradley Nassif, "'Spiritual Exegesis' in the School of Antioch," in *New Perspectives on Historical Theology: Essays in Memory of John Meyendorff,* ed. Bradley Nassif (Grand Rapids: Eerdmans, 1996), 346.

how do we reconcile the sharp antipathy that seems to have existed at Antioch between the Christians and the Jews, who formed a sizeable and wealthy segment of the population?[50] This antagonism is exemplified in the eight homilies in which John Chrysostom chided Christians who were attracted to Jewish ceremonies.[51] John was reacting to Christians who were fascinated by Jewish rituals and were going to the nearby shrine of the Maccabean martyrs in the hope of achieving cures for various maladies. Christians were also drawn to the judicial tribunals of the Jews, which were much more even-handed than their own. In spite of these and other possible grounds for hostility, the Antiochene reverence for the Hebrew Scriptures may have led them at times to confer with certain Hebrew teachers over disputed or ambiguous passages. Moreover, their engagement in polemical argument with Jewish writers may have helped them to enlarge their own understanding of literal and historical methodology. It is also possible that the apparent Jewish influence may simply be the result of Theodore and the other Antiochenes' sensitivity to the exegetical method their Jewish adversaries employed to interpret the Hebrew Scriptures, or, as Greer believes, that the source of Theodore's exegesis "must lie in the spirit with which Theodore approached Scripture. . . . because he had an understanding of the way of thinking implicit in the Bible," and that "it is necessary to realize that in great measure [Theodore's] exegesis was determined by Jewish ideas of the subject."[52]

Still, because of the antipathy between the Christian and Jewish communities at Antioch, any direct linkage probably antedates the late fourth century. As such, it may have been part of the Antiochene tradition from the first centuries or have come from an early Syriac source that reflects

50. For a study into how Christians and Jews related to one another in the first four hundred years, see Wayne A. Meeks and Robert L. Wilken, *Jews and Christians in the First Four Centuries of the Common Era* (Missoula: Scholars, 1978).

51. Robert L. Wilken argues persuasively in his *John Chrysostom and the Jews: Rhetoric and Reality in the Late Fourth Century* (Berkeley and Los Angeles: University of California Press, 1983) that a large part of the Jewish population at Antioch was well educated, wealthy, and influential. So, while the Antiochenes were set in their scriptural methodology at this period, they were doubtless involved in friendly as well hostile exchanges with the rabbis in Antioch.

52. Greer, *Theodore of Mopsuestia*, 110, 86.

the approach of the conservative Jewish rabbis who taught at the School of Babylon or that of Palestine. There is some direct evidence of Jewish influence in Theophilus. In "The Use of Stoic Cosmogony in Theophilus of Antioch's *Haexaemeron,*"[53] Kathleen McVey argues that when Theophilus describes the generation of the Logos through Sophia, he must have used a Hellenistic Jewish source that remained close to its Stoic roots. McVey concludes from this that there was undoubtedly considerable eclecticism in the evolution of a Christian biblical methodology. We must be careful about drawing general conclusions when more particulars remain to be established. But even if all these similarities with a Jewish methodology are superficial likenesses, they are nevertheless characteristic of Theodore's exegesis.

Possible Stoic and Aristotelian Influences

The Church historian Sozomen informs us that John Chrysostom, in his youth, "learned rhetoric from Libanius and philosophy from Andragathius."[54] Since Theodore probably studied at the same time as John, he was probably also exposed to philosophy. But what kind of philosophy did Andragathius teach? Logic and the meaning and value of the virtues were taught in the schools of rhetoric; is this what Sozomen is referring to? The stress on logic and virtue as pertaining to philosophy also fits in with the prevailing Christian view of philosophy as broadly providing a systematic outlook on the meaning of life and the moral ways to live. In this sense, one can speak of a Christian philosophy. But even granted this, we must deal with passages where we find Theodore consistently negative toward classical philosophers. This negative attitude may have been further sharpened not only by his belief that the Scriptures provide answers to the fun-

53. Kathleen McVey, "The Use of Stoic Cosmogony in Theophilus of Antioch's Hexaemeron," in *Biblical Hermeneutics in Historical Perspective: Studies in Honor of Karlfried Froelich on His Sixtieth Birthday,* ed. M. S. Burrows and P. Rorem (Grand Rapids: Eerdmans, 1991), 32–58.

54. Sozomen, *Historia Ecclesiastica,* trans. Chester D. Hartranft, *NPNF,* 2d ser. (1890; reprint, Peabody, Mass.: Hendrickson, 1994), 2:399. For a treatment on this point, see McLeod, *Image of God,* 117–21; and Chrysostomus Baur, *John Chrysostom and His Time,* trans. M. Gonzaga (Westminster, Md.: Newman, 1959–60), 1:306–12.

damental questions of life but also by the fact that the most important philosophers of his day were ardent defenders of paganism.

While it is true that in the past some thought that the Alexandrians were influenced by Platonism and the Antiochenes by Aristotelianism, this has turned out to be basically a superficial view, even while true in some narrow respects. In his analysis of Theodore's philosophical roots, Richard Norris Jr. has pointed out Stoic and Platonic elements.[55] Regarding Stoicism, Ulrich Wickert believes, as we shall see, that Theodore's idea about Adam being the bond of the universe shows Stoic influence. But the issue is whether this flows from Theodore's assimilation of Stoic ideas, or indirectly through Paul, or from Stoic ideas present in the culture. If we may judge Theodore's own attitude, he appears negative toward Stoicism when attacking Origen for turning to the allegorical method by which the Stoics explained the presumed wisdom of such Greek classics as Homer. For his part, Theodore was convinced that such an interpretation was contrary to a Christian literal and rational approach to Scripture.

As for Aristotle's influence on Theodore, one is hard pressed to find evidence of it in Theodore's writings, other than what may have come to him through his rhetorical education in logical reasoning and the meaning of the virtues. It is true that Theodore was dedicated to seeking out the real and the historical, but it is hard to argue from this to Aristotelian influence. On the contrary, there are prominent differences between Aristotle and Theodore, such as that regarding the soul's immortality and Aristotle's distinction between a concrete and an abstract nature. Theodore's emphasis upon justifying one's own interpretation by logic may be explained simply as his own habitual way of thinking and speaking about God, heightened by his early rhetorical training, with its rational and logical emphases.

Theodore's Temperament

Even granting the influences on Theodore of his rhetorical education, his training under Diodore, his immersion in the prevalent framework of

---

55. Norris, *Manhood and Christ* 1–67. Norris believes that "Theodore is not a Neo-Platonist: and this fact is nowhere more evident than in his emphasis on the practical as opposed to the contemplative reason" (136).

the Antiochene tradition, and possibly his exposure to Jewish and Stoic thought, one must also allow a prominent role for Theodore's own temperament and the evolution in his thinking. Thanks to Facundus, we possess an excerpt where Theodore writes to a certain Cerdo: "You wonder above all about those things written in the Psalms which we wrote before all the rest [of my works]. As regards this, we did not exercise as much care as ought to have been. For we suffered from a lack of writing skill, as it happens, when beginning [to write] whatsoever."[56] This certainly indicates a change in Theodore's outlook, which is not unusual as a person grows older and his thinking evolves. The fundamental problem that a scholar faces in tracing the development of Theodore's method of exegesis is that it is difficult to determine when all of his extant works were written.

That Theodore is credited with having fine-tuned Antiochene exegesis also suggests the evolution of his thought, one that is unlikely to have arisen merely from a deeper application of grammatical and rhetorical principles. In addition, when we compare Theodore's interpretations and his literary styles with those of John Chrysostom and Theodoret, we discover some major differences in the ways Chrysostom and Theodoret were, for example, more sympathetic to the application of allegory and have a notably different view of the "image of God."[57] This suggests that besides there being some flexibility in the ways the Antiochenes applied their principles, Theodore was an independent thinker. This is exemplified in his exegesis of the Book of Job, which he thinks is based on a pagan story, and in his adamant exclusion of the Song of Songs from the canon of Scripture. Zaharopoulos explains why this is so meaningful: "Theodore has a significant place in the history of biblical studies, and it matters little if his attempts to investigate the book of Job critically for the purpose of determining the date and origin of its component parts have been considered neither traditional nor pious. For the first time in the history of the church a book of the Bible was expounded from the perspective of a critical method by a scholar."[58]

56. Facundus of Hermiane, PL 67:602.
57. For a treatment of these differences, see McLeod, *Image of God*, 60–61, 78–80.
58. Zaharopoulos, *Theodore on the Bible*, 45–46.

It is a bit of an exaggeration to claim that Theodore was a forerunner of the modern historical critical method. While he could admit that the Book of Job was based on an earlier tradition, he did not have the tools to pursue this in a solid, rational way. Nor could he detect the different traditions reflected in the Hebrew historical books or the very intricate literary structures that Luke and John wove into their works. Still, Theodore comes closer than any of the other fathers in this respect. While he may have become aware of the complexity involved in asserting that the Bible is inspired, he seems oblivious of how difficult it is to assert where and when God has inspired a sacred writer. He seems to have allowed that the sacred writer has a role to play in voicing God's revealed Word. But he would have been dumbfounded by those who questioned where the inspiration is to be found: whether among those who had begun or promoted or put into writing a tradition, or whether it was the redactor or the very community itself. If he were sensitive to this issue, he would have to confront a serious problem, one that would call into question his conviction that God's inspired message is identified with the intent of the sacred writer.

Theodore's Thinking about Inspiration

One area in which we can see the evolution of Theodore's thought is his understanding of inspiration. In his youth, he apparently held for a verbal inspiration, where God was the author and the sacred writer (or redactor) his secretary. Theodore initially looked upon the Holy Spirit as the one dictating, as it were, divine revelations. As Zaharopoulos puts it: "Revelation is an illumination of mind imparting inspiration in propositional form."[59] This means that Theodore makes no distinction between revelation and inspiration, with the result that the sacred writer has no personal role in what he has written: "Because, however, we are about to interpret the book of creation, the one that the blessed Moses wrote for us not according to his own original thoughts but as something he learns from the Holy Spirit about those matters which up to that time were not yet known to human beings."[60]

59. Ibid., 47.
60. *TFS,* fol. 23b/8-9. The number on the left side of the slash is to the Syriac text, and on the right to Sachau's Latin translation.

Theodore is clearer about this kind of inspiration when commenting on Psalm 44 (45). Theodore says of the psalmist: "He calls the Holy Spirit the recorder, because the things [stated] in the ink have been impressed [there] by the Spirit. For the Spirit, just like the very best writer—that is, the recorder—fills the heart with thoughts of revelation by way of the ink; for He grants to the tongue [the ability] to speak loud and clear what remains and to arrange the letters to [fit] the ideas and articulate them distinctly for those who are willing to receive the benefit which [flows] from them. Therefore He wills that the tongue speak loudly and clearly not its own thoughts but those of the Spirit's revelation."[61] We see the same view expressed in the following statement: "The vision of Abdia (Obediah). He does not alter this (that is, the word of the Lord) [but acts] in conformity with [its] power. For he calls the word of the Lord the activity of God whereby the prophets have received the revelations of things to come by a spiritual grace. He calls the vision to be the same as a divine revelation whereby it comes about that they receive knowledge of unclear matters. For when the prophets received certain messages in an unspeakable manner through a spiritual activity upon one's own soul and heard the teaching of future things as if by someone speaking according to an operation springing up in them by the Holy Spirit."[62] In other words, Theodore is asserting that the Spirit imparts into the sacred writer's mind the words God wants revealed.[63]

Evolution in Theodore's Thinking

Theodore clearly appears to have evolved in his thinking, for he came to regard inspiration in a more flexible way. The "word" imparted by the Spirit is a spiritual force "according to which the one instructed thinks that he is being taught by some voice about what is binding."[64] In other words, the Spirit arouses thoughts and images within the depths of the sacred writer's mind. It seems to the writer that the Spirit is speaking directly to him.[65] This highlights why an exegete has to examine the individual words in Scripture

---

61. Theodore of Mopsuestia, *Commentaire sur les Psaumes*, 282.
62. Theodore, PG 66:308C.
63. See Zaharopoulos, *Theodore on the Bible*, 86, for a fuller treatment of this point.
64. Theodore, PG 66:404B.
65. See Zaharopoulos, *Theodore on the Bible*, 78–82.

and scrutinize each peculiarity of grammar and expression. However, Za-haropoulos believes that by the time Theodore wrote his commentary on the minor Pauline epistles in the early decades of the fifth century, he had evolved in his thinking about inspiration: "This flexibility of the part of Theodore, which can be explained as a modification of his original conception of inspiration, can only be discovered in his later writings; in all of his earlier works he adheres to the doctrine of plenary and verbal inspiration."[66]

A sign of the change can be seen in Theodore's willingness to criticize the style and ambiguities in the letters of Paul. Had he believed every word inspired by the Holy Spirit, he should have been more circumspect and approving. Instead, he remarks in his commentary on Galatians 5:13: "and when someone fully considers those things [present] in the epistle as well as those things outside [its] examination, whether [these are] said to the Galatians or to adversaries, he will discover that [the matter] is dense and illustrated by a variety of senses with (Paul) saying now these points and now indeed those. These [readers] are rightly upset. For they come across many points that frequently state everything in a summary way, with (Paul) expanding upon the meaning nowhere."[67] Zaharopoulos summarizes the development thus: "It was especially in his writings dealing with the New Testament that Theodore gave the human factor such prominence that we cannot credit him anymore with a traditional view of inspiration. The autonomy of the authors was explicitly emphasized. Thus in his commentary on the epistle to the Galatians he criticized Paul's style and diction as abrupt and obscure, and blamed Paul for a passionate indignation against his adversaries that had caused the textual abruptness."[68]

Another indication of Theodore's changed view of inspiration is his realization that God complements his revelation with other passages. This is exemplified in the prologue to his commentary on John's Gospel. He notes that the Synoptic writers' portrayal of Christ needs to be supplemented in order to bring out Christ's divinity clearly. In his prologue to John, Theodore explicitly states that John added to and complemented what the three other evangelists had omitted, especially on the subject of the divinity of

66. Ibid., 82.   67. *TEP* 1:93.
68. Zaharopoulos, *Theodore on the Bible*, 88.

Christ. Mark, Matthew, and Luke described only what they could recall.[69] Evidently Theodore had concluded that the limitations of the sacred writer has to be taken into account when interpreting to what extent the Spirit's inspiring power expressed itself. As Zaharopoulos notes, "In Theodore's commentaries on Pauline letters the autonomy of Paul was so carefully safeguarded that there seems to have been only limited room for divine intervention."[70] All of this suggests that Theodore was becoming aware of the distinction between inspiration and revelation.

Theodore's Typology

Let us now turn to a key theological and methodological "tool" that Theodore employed to reveal the scope of Christ's humanity's integrated roles in salvation. It is not clear how and when Theodore became aware of the fundamental role that scriptural typology could play in understanding God's plan for the salvation of all creation. While he firmly rejected an allegorical interpretation of Scripture as an arbitrary imaginative method, he did recognize within the two testaments the special kind of relationship that God established between two persons, places, acts, events, and things. He was no doubt influenced by what his mentor Diodore taught him and, above all, by what he discovered in Paul's Letter to the Hebrews. Paul acknowledges, for instance, that Adam and Moses were true types of Christ, Sarah and Hagar types of the Jewish and Christian covenants, and the sacraments of baptism and the Eucharist types of Christ's death and the future immortal life.[71] Theodore seems also to have been influenced by the

---

69. See *TJA*, 7–9/3–5.

70. Zaharopoulos, *Theodore on the Bible*, 78; see also 90–94.

71. Jean Daniélou, *Sacramentum Futuri: Études sur les Origines de la Typologie Biblique*, Études de Théologie Historique (Paris: Beauchesne, 1950), observes that Theodore's typology deals almost exclusively with the New Testament. He is judging, it seems, from what he found in Theodore's *Catechetical Homilies*. He states his view thus: "what actually strikes us, when we compare Theodore to St. Cyril of Jerusalem, and, even more, to St. Ambrose, is the almost complete absence of any typology borrowed from the Old Testament. There is only one exception . . . the theme of Adam appears several times . . . but we must make it clear that Theodore is concerned more with the relation of things visible to the invisible than with the relation of things past to things to come, which is the true bearing of the word . . . the sacraments are for Theodore also a ritual imitation of the historical actions of Christ. . . . But it is obviously artificial, for ex-

way the Letter to the Hebrews describes at length how the Christian liturgy was a true type of the heavenly reality, in contrast to the empty Jewish rituals. Theodore called the ability to discern the presence of the real relation God established between these types and their fulfillment *theoria*. By examining how Paul and others made use of a type, Theodore was apparently able to derive his criteria for establishing a true type and distinguishing it from an allegory.

Fortunately, Theodore's commentary on Galatians 4:23 is extant. He explains there that when Paul compares the slave/free relationship between Sarah and Hagar to that between the Jewish and Christian covenants, he is actually describing a type, not an allegory.[72] Paul confirms that each "element" is historical (that is, present in the scriptural narrative) and points out how Sarah's superiority over Hagar—her being a free person and Hagar a slave—images to a lesser, inferior degree the complete superiority of the New over the Hebrew Testament. For Paul, Hagar symbolizes the old covenant, which adheres slavishly to the law, while Sarah represents the new covenant, based on faith. Sarah fulfills what Hagar can only hope for. So too Isaac, the son of Sarah, typifies Christ, while Ishmael, the son of Hagar, is a true type of those who reject Christ. Paul's controlling point here is to show how the Christian covenant is the fulfillment and completion of the Jewish law. Theodore understands these typical relationships as prophetically inspired and thus indicating what would come to pass in the future, when Christ establishes a new covenant between God and his chosen people. This fulfillment has been always destined insofar as God as the Lord of history has willed it to be thus. This concept is embodied in Theodore's *Commentary on Jonah:* "Therefore one discovers that some things from the Old [Testament] are a certain type of the later [New Testament] as they

ample when he tries to establish a comparison between the deacons who accompany the offertory procession and the Roman soldiers who accompanied Jesus to Golgotha" (13–14). The reference to the deacons is found in Theodore's *Catechetical Homilies*, 15:25 (see *THC*, 504/505). It needs to be noted, however, that in this passage Theodore is actually comparing the deacons to the invisible powers mentioned in Heb. 1:14.

72. For a further treatment that develops Theodore's thought, see Robert J. Kepple, "Analysis of Antiochene Exegesis of Galatians 4:24–26," *Westminster Theological Journal* 39 (1977): 239–49. Kepple concludes that, while allegory and typology are logically distinct, they nevertheless belong to the opposite ends of the same continuum.

have a likeness to the latter and are then later necessarily (*chreian*) produced in [their] proper times, while clearly falling very short of these."[73]

First, Theodore required that a true type had to be acknowledged as such in Scripture. For, as Scripture is the inspired word of God, this provides him with the certainty that the relationship between type and archetype exists, for God guarantees it as true.[74] It is known as such because God's Spirit inspires the sacred writer to discern a future reality. In his *Commentary on Nahum,* Theodore affirms this when speaking of how the prophet knew what was to be: "(God) produced a sudden conversion of the (prophets') mind so that at the same time they might also receive, by such a presentation, knowledge of future things with a greater reverential fear. He called this, therefore, 'an assumption,' when the grace of the Spirit having laid hold of the mind of the prophet turned it to a revelation of what has been received."[75] Theodore maintains that it is this that distinguishes a type from an allegory. For an allegory's meaning is derived not from within Scripture but from the imaginative speculations of the exegete. This indicates, moreover, that the type and its archetype (or its antitype), which constitute the two ends or poles of a relationship, must both be historical realities related in the Scriptures.[76] The antitype usually expresses a reality that has already come to pass. But in the case of sacramental types, the goal has been already achieved for Christ in the flesh. However, those who receive baptism have not yet attained in their earthly life its full promise but are assured that it will also certainly become theirs as long as they

73. Theodore #62 and 64, PG 66:320. See also Theodore of Mopsuestia, *Commentaire sur les Psaumes,* 2, where Theodore is speaking about what leads to beatitude and insists that dogma and experience both be present. This can be said to be true also for a type and its archetype.

74. Zaharopoulos, *Theodore on the Bible,* discusses this need for a New Testament proof-text (185).

75. Theodore, PG 66:404.

76. John Chrysostom distinguishes a type from an allegory because both the type and archetype are public events. He remarks, apropos of Paul's reference to "allegory" in Galatians 4:21–31: "(Paul) called this type an allegory in a misuse of language. What he is affirming is this: the *historia* itself not only manifests what is apparent but also proclaims publicly some other points. For this it has been called an allegory. But what has made it public? Nothing else than everything that is now present" (PG 61:531–32). My translation.

remain faithfully united to Christ's body. So, in one sense, the sacramental goal in fact exists, but in another sense it is not yet fully attained by those who are still living an earthly existence. In other words, the kind of strict relationship that obtains between the life of a baptized person and its heavenly fulfillment is a real ontological one, similar to the way an active potency is related dynamically to its actual fulfillment.

Theodore adds one more criterion to those outlined above that we will examine in the following three chapters. The type must not simply foreshadow the existence of its archetype but must also image the future realities. In this Theodore was doubtless influenced by Hebrews 10:1: "The Law contains the shadow of goods to come and does not itself image (icon) the realities." Theodore considers the Jewish rituals empty shadows that simply confirm the existence of another reality but do not allow one to know much more about it.[77] In his homily "On Baptism," Theodore explains how a ritualistic kind of "shadow" differs radically from the "image" present in a real type: "The shadow points to the proximity of a body because there cannot be a shadow without a body. But it does not describe the body that it points to—something that an image can [do]. For when one sees the icon, one does know this from what is depicted because of its correct likeness, if by chance one knows what is depicted by the shadow. But one can never know whose it is because the shadow has no representative likeness with the body from which it has come to be."[78] The type, of course, truly images its reality but always in an inchoate, imperfect, and inferior way.

Besides merely foreshadowing the existence of another reality, Jewish rites lack an inner relationship to what they point to. They are simply shadows of reality. No inner dynamic force impels them toward fulfillment, as happens between a potency and its realization in act. This will be seen more clearly in the next chapter, in the discussion of how the sacrament of baptism reaches its fulfillment.

One more example will suffice to indicate how a type can be said to image its reality.

77. Robert Devreese, "La méthode exégétique de Théodore de Mopsueste," *Revue Biblique* (April 1946): 90–91.
78. *THC*, 324–26/325–27; *CH* 12:2. See also the following pages, *THC*, 326–33.

Adam was created first among all human beings, and afterward God took a small [part] from him and formed the woman whom He also united to him in perfect love by means of [an act of] conjugal intercourse, as it is said: "both are one flesh." From this [origin], the whole human race began its existence. So also in a [similar] way, Christ in the flesh was the first one born through a spiritual birth; whether in fact because he was the first of all to rise, or by a type, as he was the first to have received through [his] baptism a [new] birth by means of the grace of the Spirit whereby He has fulfilled the fact and the type. God, therefore, took a portion of this grace and gave it in this way to others in order that they might share in this (grace). He made everyone a sharer in the Spirit by whom we are reborn in a spiritual way. And since we possess a natural union with him [Christ's humanity] by a similar birth, so also we receive by his means a family relationship with God the Word. It was not one of conjugal intercourse but one of faith and perfect love that unites all the believers to Christ our Lord.[79]

Just as Adam was the first born to a mortal existence, and just as Eve received a share in his life when she was taken as a portion from his body, so is Christ the first born of an immortal existence, and those who are members of his body share a portion of the grace he has received. These types are verified in Scripture, indicating that Adam and Eve are historical figures, as are also Christ's humanity and all those united to him. There are likenesses as well between Adam and Eve as types and between Christ's humanity and the members of his body as archetypes, although Adam's typological role is far inferior to that of Christ's fulfillment as the archetype. Because Scripture contains these elements, the relationship between them is guaranteed.

While Theodore is restrained in the number of true types that he clearly recognizes in Scripture, in one instance he develops his typology at considerable length, almost to the point of turning it into an analogy. We find this amplified in his commentary on 1 Corinthians 10:2–4: "The sea is a type of baptism in the water, the cloud one [of baptism] in the Spirit. . . . All have drunk the same spiritual drink for they drank of the spiritual 'Rock' that had followed them; and that 'Rock' was Christ."[80] Theodore,

---

79. *TJA*, 80–81/57.
80. Theodore of Mopsuestia, *Pauluskommentare aus der Griechischen Kirche,* ed. Karl

then, regards Moses as a type of Christ the Savior and adds in his commentary elements not found in the present Scripture passage but mentioned in other places: the wand becoming a type of the cross, Pharaoh becoming a type of the devil, the Egyptians becoming a type of the demons, the manna becoming a type of divine nourishment, the water from the rock becoming a type of the blood of the Savior, and the crossing of the Red Sea becoming a type of partaking of the divine mysteries through baptism. All these types, and their antitypes, are historical realities. They resemble their realities in recognizable ways sanctioned by Scripture. They have been foreordained by God, who is the One who assures that they will be fulfilled.

Theodore's typology raises a question about his conviction that a text has only one true inspired meaning—one that is to be obtained directly through a literal and rational interpretation. Theodore himself sees no problem here, because Scripture itself witnesses to the presence of types. He has discerned how they provide insight into the fuller meaning of a text and, as we shall see in the next three chapters, enrich our theological understanding of Adam's and Christ's roles in salvation. A typological interpretation as practiced by Theodore appears to be what Scripture scholars today refer to as a *sensus plenior*, a text containing a fuller meaning beyond its literal sense—that is, a double sense, a literal meaning and a fuller spiritual meaning that surpasses the original intent of the biblical author. For Theodore, nevertheless, care has to be taken in assigning types. If any of his four criteria is missing, then he considers the relationship to be merely an allegory. A true type must possess a literal meaning that has an essential relationship to a fuller meaning that God himself has ordained and explicitly affirmed in the Scriptures. In one sense, the literal meaning of a type is different, but in another it is the same, only in a completed sense.

Accommodated Sense

As we have seen, Theodore regards a type as a reality that has a relationship with another reality whose existence is acknowledged in the New Testament, primarily by Paul. But what of those passages where a scriptur-

Staab, 2d ed. (Münster: Aschendorff, 1984), 185–86. The catenae for Theodore are found at 113–212.

al passage is explained in an applied sense different from what the Scriptures approves? For Theodore, such cases are examples of an "accommodated" use of Scripture.[81] Theodore affirms this as follows: "This (verse) indeed is present in a psalm. He employs this testimony not as something said prophetically but as we ourselves are frequently wont to do [when] employing scriptural testimonies in [our] ecclesiastical speech."[82] Yet the similarities are nevertheless close enough that one can point out how appropriate they are to this new, later situation. Preachers frequently accommodate scriptural verses to a particular setting, as when they use the account of Jesus' conversation with Martha about Lazarus's death at a funeral mass. This, however, is not an interpretation that has been truly prophetically implanted and intended by God.

'Theôria'

The relationship between a type and its antitype or archetype brings us to a consideration of what Theodore means by the term *theôria*. The Greek root denotes a "viewing" or a "contemplation" or an "act of discerning." As such, *theôria* is the ability to see the bond that God has established to unite the type and its archetype in a dynamic causal kind of relationship. Simonetti sees the influence of Eusebius of Emesa (ca. 300–d. before 359) on Diodore for the development of the Antiochene *theôria*. For Simonetti, *theôria* is "the possibility of seeing some Old Testament episodes as typological and prophetic anticipations of the facts of Christ and the church."[83] Bradley Nassif defines it more expansively: "*Theôria* is actually the investigation of the objectively verifiable but hidden meaning of Scripture. . . . that meaning which one arrives at through the study of history and doc-

---

81. For references in Theodore to an accommodated sense, see Devreese's index in Theodore's *Commentaire sur les Psaumes*, 563. Theodore affirms his meaning in his commentary on Romans 3:12 (*Pauluskommentare*, 117): "(Paul) was using the citation not as if it was being said in a prophetic way, but as adapting in a summary fashion the very things that David said about those who have fallen. Thus just as even today in our ecclesiastical discourses we also make use of citations which our reason can harmonize with what we are presently affirming." My translation.

82. *TEP* 1:166. See also Theodore's commentary on Rom. 3:12 (*Pauluskommentare*, 117) where he justifies accommodation as being based on God's foreknowledge.

83. Simonetti, "Diodore of Tarsus," *EEC* 1:236.

trine, a typical-mystical meaning based on reality and relating to the dogmas of the New Testament, improvement of the ethical life, and life after death."[84] Julian of Halicarnum includes another important element: "*Theôria*, however, as it has pleased the erudite, is considered to be the perception of those more potent realities [found] generally within either brief forms or causes."[85] Julian has caught, in my opinion, an insight into one of the relationships that Theodore discerns between a type and the fuller reality it images: that it is a causal one.

Doubtless influenced by Paul, Theodore looked upon *theôria* as the intellect's capability to discover a real fundamental spiritual relationship between two texts. It is the mental ability to detect within the historical (bodily?) elements of a text another higher or more sublime "reality" to which the present text points as its own fulfillment. Greer adds another critical element; a type is moving toward a goal: "[Typology] sets those realities against an historical background. And by 'historical' is simply meant the view of life which sees things in terms of events moving towards a goal of some sort."[86] Underlying this view of history is the belief that God is directing historical events to their ordained end. In other words, "historical" here does not signify simply an event that actually took place but one related in the scriptural narrative that fits in with God's plan for salvation. We discover this exemplified in Theodore's commentary on Hebrews 9:1: "He begins here to state how the things [signified] in the Law are symbols and types of those things [signified] in grace and how in those former things it is possible to discern the same things that have been foreordained, also having shown at the same time by the juxtaposition how much is the preeminence of these latter things."[87]

Our interest here is not in how Theodore might have looked upon *theôria* in general but how he conceived its role in establishing the typological relationships between Adam and Christ and between the sacraments of baptism and the Eucharist and their future fulfillment. Paul possessed this

84. Nassif, "'Spiritual Exegesis,'" 346.
85. The text reads: "theoria est autem, ut eruditis placuit, in brevibus plerumque aut formis aut causis earum rerum quae potiores sunt considerata perceptio."
86. Greer, *Theodore of Mopsuestia*, 94.
87. Theodore, *Pauluskommentare*, 208.

kind of *theôria* when he was inspired prophetically to discern the relationships between these two sacraments. The same would be true for Theodore and those who recognize what God has confirmed in Scripture. In practice, Theodore would consider a person endowed with *theôria* as being able to distinguish a true type from an allegory and an accommodation. Because it is very difficult to determine who has been truly prophetically inspired, Theodore insists on the need for a rational justification of what is proposed. He may be conservative, but he avoids the pitfalls of those who regard any superficial resemblance between Jewish prophecies and events in Jesus' life to be truly messianic. He does not reject, therefore, the existence of a connection between the Old and New Testaments, especially as they both have been accepted by the Church as divinely inspired and as the New Testament does approve of some messianic prophecies. But he wanted to be assured that there does really exist a linkage in a specific case. He regarded *allegoria* as an "arbitrary exegesis," for the nexus between a text and its meaning has not been authenticated. He would probably have looked upon the allegorists as exegetes who lacked *theôria* because they were unable to distinguish a true spiritual relationship from one that imposes an imaginary and arbitrary relationship.[88]

Theodore does not deny that there can exist a deeper spiritual meaning in Scripture. He differs from Origen in regard to how it is known and used in a highly qualified and restricted way. Both agree that a text may contain a meaning that transcends the literal. Theodore argues that this sense must be acknowledged by God as being present between two realities and can be objectively justified by critical reason. If this is established—for example, that Adam is a type of Christ—then an exegete can expect to discover real similarities between the two figures, but with Christ's humanity bringing these likenesses to fulfillment. Gifted with *theôria*, Theodore was able to elaborate upon the spiritual relationship and the likenesses present in both.[89]

88. See Heinrich Kihn, "Über 'Theôria' und 'Allegoria' nach den verloren hermeneutischen Schriftender Antiochener," *Theologische Quartalscrift* 20 (1880): 531–82. 536. See also Nassif, "'Spiritual Exegesis,'" 343–77.

89. Nassif, "'Spiritual Exegesis,'" 369.

If this analysis is correct, Theodore's typological thinking indicates a realm in which his exegesis has evolved from his understanding of how God reveals himself in Scripture and not from what he acquired from his rhetorical education. He relies upon the nexus that Paul saw in an inspired way as existing between Adam and Christ. In this way he is able to find theological meaning in his exegesis and synthesize it in a systematic way with regard to the role of Christ's humanity within salvation. As the Scripture scholar John McKenzie has pointed out, typology is not simply an exegetical tool but a source of theological interpretations of the special relations that God has foreordained between certain historical realities in the Scriptures: "Typology in the genuine sense arises from an inner and organic connection between the OT and the NT; the task of the modern biblical theology is to define this connection."[90] He also calls attention to the fact that God has instilled within salvation history certain types that are destined to develop, grow, and be fulfilled at a later time: "This understanding is developmental rather than prefigurative. It suits historical and critical interpretation."[91] We shall soon see how this applies to the roles Theodore has ascribed to Adam and Christ's humanity in salvation.

Summary

We are now in a position to summarize how Theodore approached a text. He wanted to determine the sacred writer's intent in a passage that he revered as the revealed word of God. This meant, first of all, that he had to be sure that his text was authentic and that every word and grammatical detail was examined carefully. He did concede that a literal interpretation can embody both a metaphorical and a typical meaning and that other, similar passages could contribute insights into the text at hand. Admittedly he approached a text with questions that reflected his theological stance toward such fundamental issues as the value of allegory and the preservation of Christ's full, integral humanity. But he believed that his interpretations were solidly based in Scripture; he was a realist who wanted to deal in

90. John L. McKenzie, *Dictionary of the Bible* (London: Geoffrey Chapman, 1965), 904.
91. Ibid.

facts. While one can dispute some of his interpretations, his answers can be rationally justified as possible, though perhaps not always likely, explanations. This is not to minimize his insights, especially, as shall see, into the roles of Christ within salvation. Perhaps influenced by his rhetorical training, Theodore sought to state his interpretations as briefly as possible and not to expand his answers unnecessarily.

Two final points need to be made. First, Theodore could apply the Antiochene principles in his own original way, which differed notably from Diodore, John Chrysostom, and Theodoret. This is demonstrated in his unique interpretations of the "image of God" and the "divine pleroma." Swete comments on the extent to which Theodore was willing to proceed in his exegesis: "But where the Church had not spoken, he conceived himself free to speculate or to reproduce the speculations of his school, little dreaming that in these wanderings of his restless mind across the frontier of ascertained truth he was treading on dangerous and hereafter to be forbidden ground."[92] Second, from those writings that come down to us, we see that Theodore did not consider the Christological question about the unity of Christ's human and divine natures from a philosophical perspective. He had little or no background, and less interest, in addressing the unity of Christ's natures from a metaphysical point of view. He sought, as always, his answers from what the New Testament affirms as true. This means that his scriptural language describing the roles of Christ's humanity in salvation and the union of Christ's two natures should be evaluated in light of the scriptural passages from which his words have been drawn, and in light of his understanding of the typological relationship he saw existing between Adam and Christ. We turn now to consider how Theodore applied his exegetical principles to interpret Christ's salvific role as the head of his body, the Church. His response to this issue will further clarify his hermeneutical convictions.

92. *TEP* 1:lxxxvii.

3. THE ROLE OF CHRIST'S "BODY" IN HUMAN SALVATION

I N THE LAST CHAPTER we established how Theodore equates God's revealed message with what the sacred writer has intended by his words. An innovative, systematic biblical theologian, Theodore at the same time was an exegete who revered the text and remained as faithful to it as he could. We want now to consider how Theodore interpreted the Pauline passages concerning the roles that Christ's "body" plays in the salvation of human beings and the universe. Paul uses the term Christ's "body" in an ambivalent way. It may denote Christ's physical body: "We eagerly await our Savior, the Lord Jesus Christ, who will change this lowly body of ours making it conformed to his glorified body according to his power to subject everything to himself" (Phil. 3:20b–21). Paul also identifies Christ's Church as his "body": "For the husband is the head of his wife, even as Christ is also the head of his church; and he is the savior of his body" (Eph. 5:23). Two questions thus need to be addressed: what relationship does Theodore envision existing between Christ's physical body and the "body" that constitutes his Church, and what role does this twofold sense of "body" actively play in salvation? The answers to these questions will clarify how Theodore conceived of the mediating role of Christ's humanity in the history of human salvation.

Before entering into the question of Christ's role in salvation history, we need first of all to delve into how Theodore actually conceived of salvation. Following Paul, Theodore speaks of it as a "journey" from the present mortality and mutability to a future state of immortality and immutability, with Adam and Christ acting in typical and archetypical ways as the heads of these two "states." We shall begin by looking at Theodore's teaching about the original created "state" and the effects that Adam's sin has had upon humanity and the rest of the cosmos. Then we shall look at the pivotal role that Christ's humanity plays in reversing the effects Adam's sin and fulfilling God's original intent. Just as Adam's fall had universal "bodily" effects, so did Christ, but in reverse. For the victory of Christ's human nature's over death achieved an immortal union with God not merely for his own humanity but for all human and all other created spiritual and material beings who are members of his cosmic "body." This will entail a brief examination of how Theodore regards Adam's "original sin" and the kind of new life that Christ has attained for those living an earthly life.

I shall then examine what Theodore means when he says that salvation is achieved by being united to Christ's "body." This will involve a consideration of the twin roles that baptism and the Eucharist play not only in joining us to Christ's "body" but also in providing those who are bonded to this "body" an experience of the future life here and now. We shall examine these questions through the lens of the controversy that arose between Wilhelm de Vries, on one side, and Ignatio Oñatibia and Luise Abramowski, on the other, over the spiritual effects of baptism and the Eucharist, according to Theodore, on the Christian's life. This approach will enable us to penetrate more fully the ways in which Theodore considers these sacraments types and make clear what he means theologically by such words as "participating" and "sharing" in the divine life. We shall explore another disputed question over what kind of "body" Theodore is speaking about. Is it, as Ulrich Wickert believes, primarily a metaphor, or something like the organic relationship between a physical body and its head? This question of the pivotal role Christ *qua* man plays as the head of his "body," the Church, will prepare us for Chapter 4, in which Theodore depicts Christ's humanity as recapitulating the created world within himself as the head of the "body" that all the universe forms in relation to Christ's humanity.

The Nature of Salvation

Theodore envisions salvation history as encompassing two states or ages: the present life of mortality that will continue until the end of time, and the heavenly, immortal, and immutable life, to which all the faithful will rise and which Theodore also calls one of "perfect justification."[1] The two states are clearly expressed in Theodore's statement that Paul "then says that you have come by [your] birth at baptism to a new life and have become a part of the body of Christ our Lord and that we wait to have communion with him and that he has now removed us from the life of this world and made us die to the world and the Law."[2] It is not clear where Theodore derived this emphasis upon two ages, whether immediately from Scripture, from Jewish apocalypticism, or possibly from Theophilus of Antioch.[3] Nor are we able to determine when he actually incorporated such a view of salvation into his systematic outlook.[4] We are concerned at the moment only with the fact that this is an important element in his theological synthesis.

Theodore's division of salvation history into two periods marks him as "singing outside the choir" of most of the Church fathers, who taught three stages of human existence: an immortal state at the beginning, a mortal state resulting from Adam's sin, and a future heavenly existence.[5] Theo-

---

1. *TEP* 1:29.   2. *THC*, 154–56/155–57; *CH* 6:13.

3. Greer observes: "That source [Theodore's division of salvation history into two states] is almost always Scripture" (*Theodore of Mopsuestia*, 75).

4. The concept of a "state" *(katastasis)* appears only once in Theodore's *Catechetical Homilies* (*THC*, 64/65; *CH* 3:9). Theodore actually holds for a quasi-third stage, an intermediate one that the baptized now enjoy as being in some sense immortal during their mortal life.

5. Regarding the question of whether Theodore held Adam to be originally mortal, see Theodore of Mopsuestia, *Replica a Guiliano Imperatore*, 137–40; *TEP* 2:332–36.

dore appears to have come to his position by applying Paul's typology likening Adam as the principal head of the first age to that of Christ as the head of the second age.[6] If so, he would have reasoned that if Christ *qua* man is the first to become immortal, then Adam had to be mortal from the very beginning of creation. Theodore does appear to concede that Adam, after his creation, had the possibility of not sinning and thus was capable of becoming immortal. But God foreknew that this would not happen and chose to make Christ—after he discerned that Christ *qua* human would freely live a life without sin—the one in whose human nature the Word would dwell at the moment of his conception: "For from the very beginning before the fashioning of the creation of the universe, You (Father) knew by Your inscrutable knowledge who I was going to become and even then You loved me in Your foreknowledge and set me up to be the Lord of all these blessings."[7]

Theodore does not develop, at least in his extant works, the possibility that Adam might not have sinned and therefore does not explore what would have been the ramifications of this. For Theodore is committed to deal with history as God actually intended it to be—salvation is to come through and in a sinless Jesus because of his human nature's "exact union" with that of the Word. Theodore therefore takes as fact the scriptural revelation that Adam is the head of all mortals existing in the present life and that all of humanity forms "one being" together with him. "By reason of our [common] nature, we are all also 'one.'"[8] All humans are "one being" because all participate in the same human nature as that of Adam and thus constitute one combined "body," with Adam as its head. This relationship between Adam and all other humans appears, however, to be much more than a simple general kind of union. For what Adam does as the head affects the whole "body" of all those who share in his nature. This is seen in the way his sin keeps all humanity mortal, changeable, and corruptible and allows death to become a reality that strikes everyone

6. See Theodore's *CH* 1:4; 13:19; 14:1; 16:30; 5:10, 10:17; 12:26; 13:5; 14:21, 25 in Tonneau's edition *(THC)*.
7. *TJA*, 322/230.
8. *TEP* 2:198.

without exception. "After the first human being was created by God, he became subject to death on account of sin as did all those born from him. For they have, in fact, received existence [from him] because they share a [common] nature with the first human beings. Since they can also give birth to [other] human beings, these too have rightly received a natural sharing with them. And thus because they have a common nature, they have also contracted [the penalty of] death imposed upon their nature."[9] In other words, since Adam as the original human being is mortal and destined to die, all those who are generated from him will also be mortal and die. Besides affecting all humanity, Adam's sin, as we will discuss at length in the next chapter, had a devastating impact too upon the harmonious unity of all created beings. "For on account of the malice of human beings, all creation, as I have said, was seen to be dissolved."[10]

The Effect of Adam's "Original" Sin

The universal effect of Adam's sin upon all creation raises a perplexing question about the meaning of Adam's "original sin." Does Theodore believe that the reason why each human being remains in a state of mortality is that a mortal nature causes one to sin, or that each human being sins freely, thus perpetuating the state of human mortality? He is somewhat ambivalent on this question, doubtless because Paul is, too. But Theodore is opposed to any notion of an "original sin" that has kept human nature sinful insofar as this would militate against his conviction that sin is a free act of the human will. Moreover, if Adam's "original sin" is a sin of nature, this would at least imply that Christ's humanity would also have been affected by sin and unable to serve as the sinless mediator. Such an outlook would destroy the close antithesis Theodore maintains actually exists between the sinful Adam, who is principally responsible for humanity's mortal existence, and the sinless Christ, who has achieved an immortal existence for all those united to his human nature. Theodore appears to have reasoned that just as Adam sinned freely, Christ likewise had to overcome by his own will power—and with the aid of the Spirit's grace—all the

9. *TJA*, 313/224.
10. *TEP* 1:267.

temptations put in his path. "For the man whom He assumed was like Adam who had introduced sin in the world. (God) abolished sin by that one connatural to him. He assumed a man like Adam who by his sinning received the sentence of death, so that this one might wipe away sin from us and abolish death."[11]

Theodore does not espouse a dogma of an "original sin" that all inherit as such at birth. He believes that human mortality "disposes" one to sin but does not cause sin. Since all humans, as a matter of fact, do freely sin, they are thereby bound to die—except for the assumed man Jesus; because he alone remains sinless throughout his life, he is not subject to death. Theodore thus realized why Christ had to be humanly free. We can understand, too, why he reacted so vigorously against Apollinaris's opinion that the Word replaced Christ's rational soul. For this would deprive Christ of his human free will and his role as the true sinless mediator between God and all creation. It explains too why Theodore maintains that Christ was unjustly condemned to death. Unlike all others, he lived a virtuous life that never strayed away from a complete dedication to God's will. In the fifth homily of his *Catechetical Homilies,* Theodore addresses the question why God rewarded Christ our Lord: "(God the Word) would abolish sin by one connatural with (Adam). . . . Because Christ our Lord had committed no sin deserving death, he accepted the death that was imposed upon him by the iniquity of the tyrant Satan" (*CH* 5:18).

While Theodore denies the existence of an inherited "original sin" passed on through a sinful human nature, he does concede that a mortal and mutable human nature is weak and thus disposed to yield to sinful temptations. "As long as we are living in this world in a mortal and changeable nature, it is now no longer possible [for us] not to have a movement contrary [to the will of God]" (*CH* 11:12). This instability affects even all those who are united to Christ through baptism: "but in this world—seeing that we share in these mysteries in hope—it is nevertheless possible to fall again because we possess a changeable nature" (*CH* 1:6). In other words, a mutable nature is disposed to sin: "since we are mortal ac-

11. *THC,* 124/125; *CH* 5:17. Subsequent parenthetical references give the number the homily and the section where the passage can be found.

cording to the present life, a disposition to sinning accompanies [our] mortality in some way.[12] . . . since we can in no way [act otherwise] on account of the weakness present in us through mortality and since we would not suffice [on our own] to advance in a direct way to perfect virtue."[13] This is true even for those who know the law perfectly. They too are powerless: "Therefore he wants to say in this passage that it is impossible to be justified by the works of the Law because we are mortal by nature, even though we very much desire virtue. But we cannot, generally speaking (plerumque), not sin."[14] This inclination to sin is inherent in the nature that all humans have inherited. "Therefore because of this he said: 'I am a human being,' so as to indicate by naming the common nature that the inclination to evil belongs to the common nature."[15] Theodore affirms this even more clearly when he states, "For even if we make a good effort at being virtuous, it is not possible for us to be altogether without sinning many times. For without willing these, we are forced to fall because of [our] natural weakness."[16] In other words, as long as humans are not in a permanent state, their freedom can be used in both sinful and virtuous ways.

This propensity to failure will endure until one becomes sinless in the future heavenly state of immortality and immutability.[17] In the meantime, as long as humans freely continue to sin, death remains our universal fate, and we are all caught in a hopeless circle. But when a sinless Christ dies

12. The Latin reads: "mortales cum simus secundum presentem vitam, sequitur quodammodo mortalitatem facilitas peccandi."

13. *TEP* 1:147.

14. Ibid., 1:31.

15. *THC*, 546/547; *CH* 16:8. This same viewpoint is expressed in Theodore's commentary on Eph. 1:7: "because it is not possible that a mortal being can be seen at any time (aliquando) without fault" (*TEP* 1:126); and also "So it is more fitting to have you who are perfect call back with the gentlest words those who have sinned and at the same time reckon that you are also human, also like that one [the sinner mentioned in the passage], (you) who can experience considerable mutability because of the weakness of [your] nature" (*TEP* 1:103).

16. Ibid.; *THC*, 314/315; *CH* 11:15. See also *TJA*, 167–68/119–20: "For also the Apostle, when speaking in regard to our soul and our body in his Epistle to the Romans and teaching us how the soul can tend to virtue, then also said how by a motion of its nature the body is inclined to sin on account of its mortality."

17. For a contemporary view of original sin, see Daryl P. Doming, "Evolution, Evil and Original Sin," *America* (Nov. 12, 2001): 14–21.

unjustly, he vanquishes not only sin but also death, opening the way for his human nature and that of other creatures to enter into an immortal and sinless life with God. "It happened that the sin that was the cause of death was first of all lifted away and, after this, death was abolished with it. For if sin is not removed, we continue by necessity in mortality. In our mutability we sin. And when we sin, we are again subject to blame, with the clasp of death again holding on by necessity. . . . For after sin is abolished, there will no longer be an entry for death" (*CH* 5:10–11). The reason for this is that after Christ *qua* man has conquered Satan by living a sinless life and has achieved an immortal existence with God, he has also totally vanquished the power of death for all others as well as for himself. This does not mean that humans will not die in this earthly life. But they are assured that they will live forever in the next life, as Christ's humanity lives forever in his unity with the Word.

A Period of Educational Testing

Theodore perceives two advantages flowing from Adam's sin. The first is its educational value. Being mortal, humans can appreciate what it means to be immortal by experiencing its opposite. By sinning, Adam put humanity in a position where its mutable and changeable nature arouses inordinate human passions and appetites and thereby strongly encourages sin. But it also challenges one to learn how to respond in the correct way: "He gave us, however, this present mortal life, as I said, for the exercise of virtues and the learning of what is fitting for us to do. He has also given us various laws for assistance and morals" (*CH* 1:26). According to Theodore, God desires that humans not merely acquire knowledge of what is the right way to live but actually do what is really right. For this reason, God allows human beings to sin in order "to reveal that more than [being faithful to] religious and orthodox doctrine, it is also necessary to take care that our life be in accord with the divine commandments" (*CH* 11:1). In other words, Theodore believes the present life is a time of testing in which each human must choose freely to commit oneself to God or to evil. This means that God desires humans to have a major role in attaining their salvation: "For he (Paul) would not have said that the just who will rise are like angels, unless the voluntary manner of their life and their labors were also worthy."[18]

While Theodore insists upon a necessary role for human freedom in salvation, he is equally insistent that in this whole process God is the One who initiates salvation. "Since we can in no way [act otherwise] on account of the weakness present in us through mortality, and since we would not suffice [on our own] to advance in a direct way to perfect virtue, why, therefore, did God do this? He created us a second time, giving us that second immortal life. . . . God raised us up together with Christ, so that we can attain salvation beyond [this life] by means of [his] grace."[19] Our present existence would be a bleak state except that God has promised us the grace needed to overcome sin: "For it is wholly impossible that a living human being not sin. (The overcoming of sin) is acquired here through grace alone."[20] In fact, divine grace is so necessary that no one can accomplish any good without it: "For we know we cannot accomplish anything without the aid of God" (CH 11:13). Grace is continually needed throughout a person's journey in life until immortality has been attained in heaven. "For once we have been made immortal in the future age, we are no longer able to sin."[21] We will discuss the dispensing of grace when we treat of the Spirit's role in Christ's human life.

The Salvific Role of Christ's Humanity

Since "Adam is a type of the one to come,"[22] Theodore sees this typology as providing an insight into God's plan for the pivotal role that Christ's humanity is to play in salvation history. For there are similarities between Adam and Christ as human. Both are heads of the two classes of human existence, and their free actions have profound repercussions for the rest of humanity. Christ's human actions not only reverse the disastrous effect of Adam's sin for creation but also fulfill Adam's initial role in a perfect man-

---

18. *TFS*, fol. 26a/12.

19. *TEP* 1:147. The same idea is also expressed in 2:198: "The power of God is in him who has saved and called us to sanctification and the incorruption that we are expecting."

20. *TEP* 1:77.   21. Ibid., 1:173.

22. Rom. 5:14.

ner. Adam's sin kept all created beings in a mortal state, but Christ's human sinlessness initiated entry into a future immortal life. He images and fulfills Adam's role in that he is the principle of a wholly new life for those forming one "body" with him: "For each one of us is seen to have a role to play as a member of a common humanity. So also in regard to the future immortal life [that will be ours] after the resurrection, its principle [resides] in Christ. All of us, moreover, who share with him both in the resurrection and in that immortality [to be bestowed] after the resurrection, are made as one with him, while each one of us is likewise seen to hold the role of a common member in relation to him. Then there will be, therefore, 'neither male nor female.' . . . For all variety of things will then be ended."[23]

Salvation, therefore, is to be attained through, with, and in Christ. But before examining how humans can participate sacramentally in Christ's victory, we must first address the kind of life that Theodore believed a person shares as a member of Christ's body. The answer to this lies at the heart of why Wilhelm de Vries argues that Theodore's concept of the sacraments of baptism and the Eucharist is deficient. A distinction must first be made: is one united to God in the sense that he or she is joined to his divine nature in a substantial or an accidental way, or in the sense that one participates in God's immortal, immutable, and incorruptible life? In the fourth and the fifth centuries, many fathers thought that to share in God's eternal life meant that one has become divinized.[24] Relying, it appears, on Neoplatonic thought, which taught that a person can be united with the One while still maintaining an individual identity, many fathers interpreted

23. *TEP* 57. As Swete observes (xxxvii), Theodore uses words such as *videor* and *possum* in a periphrastic way. Unless the context indicates the contrary, I have omitted translating "seem to" in this and other works edited by Swete when the sense clearly permits it.

24. See Kelly, *Early Christian Doctrines*, 294–95, 444–45, and 450; and Jules Gross, *La divinisation du chrétien d'après les pères grecs* (Paris: Gabalda, 1938). It is difficult to accept Gross's contention (262, 270) that the main elements of divinization are found implicitly in Theodore. Much of course depends on what one means by "divinization," whether it signifies that one is becoming divine in a proper or improper sense, or how one understands "a sharing in God's divine life." Theodore looks upon it as a sharing in the immortal and immutable life that Christ's humanity now possesses and in the graces that flow from the divine *plerôma*.

John's Gospel and traditional liturgical expressions as revealing how Jesus can be one with the Word and his Father and how a believer can also be united to them through and in Christ. This perspective offered insight into how the Eucharist enables a believer to receive the nourishment one needs to grow in Christ's life. For if the recipient is receiving the body of Christ who is the Word, then such a one is participating in the divine life of the Word. In this sense, a baptized person can be said to be divinized. This possibility of being united directly with God also provides a basis for justifying those mystics who claim that they have experienced an immediate bonding with God.

Theodore was opposed to the concept of "divinization" in any strict or formal sense, for he was sensitive to how difficult it is to understand and to speak of the Word's and the Spirit's indwelling within Christ's humanity (and *a fortiori* with all other humans). "It is difficult for our tongue to discuss matters about created natures. . . . But those that surpass our nature—these are, in fact, the matters about which we want to speak—how does this [talk about the divine] not surpass all human thoughts?" (*CH* 1:1). Yet because he was utterly convinced that a transcendent Word and Spirit cannot be joined substantially in any sort of natural union with a creature, he opposed the view that Christ's human nature could be divinized: "Because there is a great separation between the Eternal One and the one who has received a beginning to his existence, there is such a distance between them there the two of them cannot be found together. . . . For one cannot limit and say how far that One who is eternal is distant from that one who has come into being" (*CH* 4:6). For this would mean in his framework that Christ's human nature has been assimilated into the Word's. He believed that the Word's and the Spirit's possession of the same divine nature precludes any possibility that a creature can be united to them on the level of nature and thus be said to be divinized.[25] For this reason Theodore postulates that human nature—even Christ's—must be joined to the Word and

25. For a further treatment of the topic of grace and divinization, see Joanne McWilliam Dewart, *The Theology of Grace of Theodore of Mopsuestia*, Catholic University of America Studies in Christian Antiquity 16 (Washington, D.C.: The Catholic University of America Press, 1971), 147–51.

his Spirit solely on the level of grace. In the case of Christ's humanity, grace is what empowers his human nature to be joined in a unique, "exact" union with the Word. This point will be elaborated in Chapter 7, where we shall see how Theodore justifies his belief that the divine and the human nature can function together as a true unity. Here I want only to set the stage for an understanding of what Theodore means when he says that baptism and the Eucharist empower one to participate in Christ's death and resurrection, not only in the future but in the present moment. We are not concerned about the graces the sacraments provide for living a good life but with the spiritual effects they have on their recipients' natures. We shall approach this question by first examining what Theodore intends when he speaks of the sacraments as types.

The Sacraments as Types

While the present life of mortality is a time of testing, it is not without divine assistance. For Theodore, all humans can now share in a participatory way in the immortal life that Christ's humanity enjoys. While personal prayer and good works can elicit the Spirit's graces, Theodore proclaims in his *Catechetical Homilies*[26] and his commentaries on the Pauline epistles that receiving baptism and the Eucharist are the principal ways we share in the victory of Christ's humanity. Theodore maintains that the reception of these sacraments assures us not only that Christ's humanity has triumphed over death but that one can truly share in his immortal life and union with God even here on earth. For a true sacramental type is guaranteed that its fulfillment will be achieved.

---

26. Theodore's *Catechetical Homilies* were delivered to catechumens before their baptism at Easter time. These homilies reveal his understanding of the Nicene Creed (considered to be early Nicene), the Our Father, baptism, and the Eucharist. I have used Tonneau's translation rather than Alphonse Mingana's English translation, as Tonneau's is closer to the Syriac and has the Syriac and French on opposite pages. We also now have two recent German translations: Peter Bruns's *Theodor von Mopsuestia Katechetische Homilien* and Simon Gerber's translation, *Theodor von Mopsuestia und das Nicänum: Studien zu den katechetischen Homilien*. These two works have introductions that treat in a summary but expanded way the secondary literature on Theodore.

Baptism

Theodore wrote at a time when the importance of receiving baptism was a controversial issue. As highlighted by the lives of Constantine the Great (emperor 306–337) and Augustine (354–430) (Augustine being an almost exact contemporary of Theodore), a large number of Christians were postponing their baptism, with the result that the Eucharist was considered primarily for the virtuous. We see this in the homilies of Gregory of Nyssa (ca. 335–94), Cyril of Jerusalem (ca. 315–87), Ambrose (ca. 337–97), and John Chrysostom (ca. 350–407)[27] against this practice. Their disapproval reveals a widespread lack of appreciation of baptism's fundamental importance in a Christian's spiritual life.[28] Like these fathers, Theodore wrote his catechetical homilies on baptism and the Eucharist to make his catechumens aware of the importance of the sacraments for one's life on the eve of their baptism.

Theodore looks upon baptism as an exceptional God-given means for helping humans achieve salvation. The question arises, however, as to what baptism meant to him and how effective he believed it was in bringing its recipients to an immortal and immutable state of union with God. Like his contemporaries, Theodore sees the sacrament of baptism as a type, symbol, and sign. As noted in the previous chapter, Theodore's criteria are that the type and the antitype must be historically real, that the type must image and not merely foreshadow its archetype, that the relationship bonding the two poles be real, not simply conceptual, and be dynamic, not static, and that the New Testament approve of the relationship. Theodore saw too that explanatory words are needed to illustrate the meaning and

27. Gregory of Nyssa, "Against those who deferred baptism," PG 46:415–32; Cyril of Jerusalem, "Oration on Holy Baptism," *NPNF,* 2d ser., 7:360–77; Ambrose, On the Decease of Satyrus," *NPNF,* 2d ser., 10:169n2 (it must be noted that the fathers condemn nothing more severely than postponing baptism in order to continue to sin); John Chrysostom, *Homily 23 on "The Acts of the Apostles," NPNF,* 1st ser., 11:153–55.

28. For a fuller treatment of the historical setting in which Theodore wrote, see Karl Baus, "The Development of the Church of the Empire within the Framework of the Imperial Religious Policy," in *The Early Church: An Abridgement of the History of the Church,* ed. Hubert Jedin, trans. John Dolan, abr. D. Larrimore Holland (New York: Crossroad, 1993), 170.

power of baptism: "For every sacrament is an indication in signs and mysteries of invisible and ineffable things. A revelation and an explanation for these things are required, if the one coming forward to receive is to know the power of the mysteries" (*CH* 12:2). For the sacramental rite of baptism, signifying as it does invisible and ineffable things, is not obvious. It needs to be explained, so that its symbolic power and spiritual fulfillment can be perceived. This need also explains why Theodore demands scriptural approval for a type to be truly sacramental, for God has revealed its meaning and power.

For Theodore, the sacrament of baptism enables one to participate in the death and resurrection of Christ's humanity and ultimately to achieve immortal life. As a type, it looks to a past time when Christ vanquished Satan by being raised from the dead. It not only images his death and resurrection to a new life but also provides assurance to those who sacramentally die and rise together with Christ in baptism: "For what we have in a mysterious way through faith in the matter of types and signs assures us that we will pass from one to the other" (*CH* 14:28).[29] It is also an assurance of future life: "[It is] through this mystery which you are about to receive that from now on you will share without doubt in these future goods" (*CH* 14:2).

The Dispute

To enter more deeply into the question of how Theodore understood the salvific benefits of the sacraments, it is helpful to look at his arguments against the backdrop of a controversy over the spiritual effects Theodore attributed to baptism and the Eucharist.[30] The specific question became, how does a believer now share in the future life? Wilhelm de Vries holds that Theodore looked upon the sacraments as purely symbolic anticipations of heavenly fulfillment, albeit ones that provided grace for living a good life and achieving forgiveness of sins. He sees this as a logical outgrowth of Theodore's Nestorian Christological thought. Baptism and the

29. See also *CH* 1:4. For a discussion of this point, compare Theodore, *Theodor und das Nicänum*, 79.

30. For a longer summary treatment of this dispute, see McLeod, "Christological Ramifications."

Eucharist are simply a foreshadowing of a future life, like Jewish rituals. For if salvation is a sharing in immortal life and not a divinized one, how can a baptized person be both mortal and immortal in the present life? De Vries regards Theodore's view of the sacraments also as eschatological in the sense that Theodore believed salvation is to be attained in a future life, not incarnational in the sense of being achievable here and now.

De Vries argues that Theodore's inability to accept a present divinization forced him to conceive of salvation as a future event that one can merely hope to attain. He sees Theodore's failure here as the result of two weaknesses. First, according to de Vries, Theodore was wholly unable to understand how a transcendent God can enter into a personal relationship with human beings by raising their natures through an elevating sanctifying grace. Second, Theodore's Nestorianism prevented him from fathoming how the Eucharist provides a supernatural participation in the body and blood of Christ, not as a man but as the Word of God. As a result, the Eucharist for Theodore provides its recipients only with graces helpful in leading a virtuous life in what is presently an intermediate stage between mortality and immortality.[31] Theodore himself seems to have asserted this: "He calls this church the body of Christ because in this world she receives at [one's] second birth of baptism communion with him in a typical way but [this will happen] truly in fact in the world to come when the body of humility will be changed" (CH 10:17).[32] Theodore affirms the same idea when he states that there will no longer be symbols, types, or signs in heaven: "When we become immortal in our body and immutable in our soul, the use of symbols and types will by necessity cease. Since by sharing in the realities themselves, we will no longer have needs of signs which evoke a testimonial of what is going to take place" (CH 15:3). Theodore also seems to hold that the recipients of the sacraments merely trust that the future life will come to pass. "Since we presently have not yet [gained] these heavenly goods, it is by trust that we now continue on until we ascend to heaven and advance to our Lord" (CH 15:18).[33]

31. On this point, see Theodore, *Theodor und das Nicänum,* 233.
32. See also Theodore's commentary on Col. 1:18 in *TEP* 1:273.
33. The same idea is expressed in the following statement: "These powerful

Ignatio Oñatibia was the first to oppose de Vries, in arguing that de Vries did not fully understand the fundamental kind of relationship that Theodore postulated between a type and its archetype.[34] He points out that they are two poles bound to one another in a way that reveals the unity of God's unchanging plan for salvation. He cites comparable parallels between the Hebrew Scriptures and the Church, between the Church and a future heaven, between the sacraments and their fulfillment in the next life, and between Jesus' baptism and that of others (103–9). These indicate, he believes, a real basis for the hope of attaining fulfillment in the future. He argues that the Spirit bestows immortality in a sacramental, embryonic way but in a real way that is an inchoate participation in an immortal life (107). For instance, because the Spirit seals a person at baptism, making a person a true child of God and a true member of the body of Christ, a real transformation has taken place (119).

Luise Abramowski expands on Oñatibia's position.[35] She begins by arguing at length that a newly discovered excerpt of Theodore reveals that he held for two kinds of *prosôpon:* one that is ontologically related to a *hypostasis* and another to the object of worship and honor. She believes that the latter liturgical sense ought to be understood as the primary usage in Theodore, and that the metaphysical understanding is secondary. She then lists almost every passage in which the term "participation" (or its equivalent) is found in Theodore's works. She points out that whenever Theodore wanted to express a real sharing, he had recourse to some equivalent of this term.[36] She also observes that Cyril objected to Nestorius because of his understanding of the Eucharist. While it is true that Theodore—like Nestorius—maintains that those receiving the Eucharist are participating in

mysteries have been fulfilled for us when we approach in symbolic and typical ways the future hope and without hesitating we have faith in these goods that are to come by persevering in a way of life conformed to the new world" (*CH* 1:4).

34. I. Oñatibia, "La vida christiana, tipo de las realidad celestes. Un concepto basico de la teologia de Teodore de Mopsuestia," *Scriptorum Victoriense* 1 (1954): 100–133, hereafter cited parenthetically in the text.

35. Luise Abramowski, "Zur Theologia Theodors von Mopsuestia," *Zeitschrift für Kirchengeschichte* 72 (1961): 263–93.

36. Ibid., 280–81, notes in passing that Cyril rejected the term "participation" for the Trinity but used it to express the relationship between the Eucharist and the Word.

Christ's body and blood, Cyril has detected a close parallel in their under-standing of how Christ's human nature is connected to the Word's divine nature and how the bread and wine are both united with Christ's flesh. Cyril believed that the Antiochenes, at least Nestorius and Theodore, held that the eucharistic bread and wine were transformed into the body and blood of Christ *qua* man. But Abramowski points out that Cyril failed to take into consideration that both Nestorius and Theodore always under-stood Christ *qua* man to be united in what he considered a true unity with the Word. For Theodore, a person receives in the Eucharist not the body of a man but Christ's "body" in its inseparable union with the Word.

Abramowski uses this last point to insist that de Vries relied on the Scholastic teaching that supernatural grace enables one to become di-vinized and able to share in God's divine life. To use this as the standard by which to judge Theodore is questionable, in her view.[37] Like Oñatibia, she holds that Theodore considered the first fruits of the Spirit much more than the reception of preternatural gifts, as de Vries maintains. Finally, she points out that if de Vries is right that Theodore believed there is no real content to the sacraments, then his Syriac translators would have em-ployed such phrases as "in the name of" and "under the appearance of" rather than such terms as "sharing" and "participating" to express what Theodore was affirming about baptism and the Eucharist.[38] But what role does "participation" play in the relationship between a type and its arche-type within baptism?

Theodore's Understanding of Baptismal Participation

Theodore concedes that the union baptism establishes with Christ's hu-manity is not easily explained. "But we look to the resurrection because we are bound by a spiritual rebirth to Christ in a way that defies description."[39] Yet he does offer a number of insights into the purpose of baptism by elab-orating upon the typology that he discerns in Paul. For, besides being fully committed to his literal interpretation of Scripture, he also belongs to a

37. For a similar view, see Theodore, *Theodor und das Nicänum*, 256.
38. Abramowski, "Zur Theologia Theodors," 293.
39. *TEP* 1:187.

sacramental tradition that characterized baptism only in terms of types, symbols, and signs.[40] For instance, he insists that the baptized have acquired new life as members of Christ's body, but in a typical sense: "Since we believe that we have been generated in these matters in a typical way through baptism, Paul states that we have become a member of Christ's body because of our communion [with him] by means of his resurrection, whose types we believe are being brought to fulfillment in baptism."[41] Christ *qua* man is the first one to achieve immortality. As such, he is the leader who enables those joined to his "body" to share in his immortal life and union with God, but in a typical way: the Church "regards that one in whom all things have been created as the head for the common good of those who have been made his body through a spiritual regeneration. This serves as a type [for us] of the future resurrection in which we have been baptized in the hope of sharing and participating with him in his immortality that is the fulfillment of the type whereby he is a leader for us."[42] In other words, the resurrection of Christ's body from the dead should be construed as a promise, at the very least, that a like kind of resurrection is now possible for all other humans. For Christ's humanity has achieved this for the common good of all those who are members of his "body."

As pointed out in the previous chapter, Theodore requires four criteria for a true type: (1) both the type and the archetype must be historical realities; (2) the type must "image" its archetype by possessing likenesses that in some potential ways resemble its fulfillment; (3) a real bond must exist between the two poles; and (4) because God has guaranteed in Scripture the type's inevitable fulfillment, there must be a dynamic element in the relationship that moves a type toward its actualization. There is no need to verify the first two of these criteria. For Theodore, the reception of baptism and the Eucharist and their heavenly fulfillment are or will be historical events. Their meanings and their relationships to each other are also ex-

40. For a treatment of this kind of sacramental outlook, see K. J. Woolcombe, "Le sens de 'type' chez les Pères," *Supplément de la Vie Spirituelle* 4 (1951): 84–100.

41. Theodore of Mopsuestia, *Pauluskommentare,* 124. He is commenting here on Rom. 7:4.

42. *TEP* 1:273.

plicitly acknowledged in Scripture, especially by Paul. We now want to establish, first, in what sense Theodore holds that a recipient of baptism participates in the spiritual realities that they image and, second, what relationship exists between them.

Theodore often speaks of baptism as more than an empty ritual offering only hope for the future. He insists that the first fruits bestowed by the Spirit at the moment of baptism are not merely a promise but a true, though initial, sharing in the future life. "[W]hen we also receive 'the firstfruits of the Holy Spirit' by [our] sharing in the mysteries, we believe that we already exist in these realities."[43] He expresses the same idea when he says, "you are born again to a new life as you have been steered by these signs and come to share in [their] reality" (CH 14:6). Central to this idea of a present typical sharing is Theodore's emphasis on how a person becomes a true member of Christ's body by means of his or her baptism and shares in this new life through the Eucharist. "For just as we all have become the one body of Christ by means of [our] new birth and by the Holy Spirit, so do we all become [one] by [our] one sharing in Christ our Lord whenever [we receive] the one nourishment present in these sacred mysteries, by whose means the grace of the Holy Spirit now nourishes us. For we are also baptized by the one Spirit into [Christ's] one body" (CH 16:24). A person is reborn to a new life in the Spirit and shares in the blessings of this new life by remaining a member united to Christ's "body." This is possible because by being joined to Christ's humanity, one participates also in Christ's union not only with the Word but also with his Father: "Therefore God the Word was united to His Father according to nature. So too through his union with (the Word), the assumed man also receives a union with the Father. And we in a similar way with the natural union that we have with Christ in the flesh, receive, insofar as it can be done, a spiritual participation with him and become his body, [with] each one us truly a member. So we hope to rise at the end [of time] as he has, and to be regenerated into eternal life. So by going through him to God, we possess necessarily a family relationship with the Father."[44]

43. THC, 582/583; CH 16:30.
44. TJA, 315–16/225–26. The same thought is expressed in CH 6:10–11 (THC,

While the members of Christ's body participate in Christ's present immortal life only in a typical way, their bodily union with him enables each to be a son or daughter in God's family. "For he gave them something exceedingly elevated that made them equal, insofar as it could [be done], with him in honor and enabled them to delight in the power of his sonship. They were not born again in a natural way according to a [regular] bodily generation but they received this birth by means of the power of God because of [their] likeness to and union with him."[45] So by having become living members of Christ's body, the baptized become God's children but adopted ones: 'Insofar as You (the Word) have united me to God [Your] Father by the power of the Spirit, you have also made me worthy of sonship, so that I can call You my Father. So after You have given me the grace of the Spirit, make them also sons [and daughters], so that, just as I have become [Your Son], they also may become one and have the same union with You in order to call You with confidence Father'" (315–16/225–26).[46]

Because the baptized come into union with God by being united as members of Christ's body and children in God's family, Christ serves as the true and only mediator, being both divine and human. Because of his humanity's union with the Word, he unites others to God their Father and bestows his graces and spiritual benefits upon them. Theodore, therefore, regards salvation primarily as a communal (in the sense of corporate) encounter with God. Yet he insists that one does share in an individual relationship with God as a member of his family. "For the divine nature is in him in whom we first believe and then through [our] rebirth we receive a

---

150/151): "because of the sharing we have with him in this world, we also receive with him a sharing in these future goods." See also *TEP* 1:34: "When truly passing from the present life, I think that I am living already in that life according to which Christ also lives in me. Being joined to him through his resurrection, I have been made a member with him (Christ), being worthy to be bonded to his body." See also *TEP* 1:56, 58.

45. *TJA*, 32/22. The next two citations are from *TJA*.

46. See also *CH* 10:21, where Theodore voices the thoughts of a person who is about to be baptized: "It is not because of small things but of great marvels and heavenly goods [that] I am going to be baptized. For I myself also expect to become from [my] baptism one of the church's children, which is the assembly of those believers who through their baptism have been deemed worthy to be called the body of Christ our Lord and who have received an ineffable holiness and a hope of immortality and future immutability."

natural household relationship with the *homo assumptus* and thence also an ineffable union with God the Word" (81/58). Moreover, this kind of union is also with the divine nature: "Just as I myself have an exact and ineffable union with You (Father), so also these who have become one in us by their faith . . . they possess a union with me by which they are elevated to the honor of [being in] a relationship with the divine nature" (*CH* 10:18).

What assures a baptized person, therefore, that he or she will attain a future immortal life with God is the fact that one is a living member of Christ's body. Just as a student who has attended class and received A's on all his exams and papers may expect to graduate, the baptized person possesses a surety guaranteeing him that he will achieve his promised immortal life, just as Christ's baptism assured him his future immortal life. But, in the meantime, a member of Christ's body must live the kind of life that is now anticipated: "(Paul) says that by (your) birth at baptism you have arrived at a new life and have become a part of the body of Christ our Lord. We expect to share with him. He now turns us away from the life of this world and we die to this world" (*CH* 6:13).[47]

Theodore explains what he means by the "body" of Christ in different ways. Following Scripture, he calls it the household of God. To grasp its full significance, one must remember that in ancient times not only the blood members but all those living in a household were considered part of a family.[48] An indication of how Theodore understood this "family body" is seen in his analogy of the union of the baptized with Christ's humanity with the natural affinity between Eve and Adam. This union results not merely from their mutual human nature but also from Eve's being physically made from Adam's body: "For just as Adam's wife was a portion taken from his bones and his flesh, so also are we members of the Lord's body, made so from his flesh and his bones because we have accepted grace from that Spirit who

47. See also *CH* 14.21: "From this (operation of the Spirit at baptism) we become children of God and the one body of Christ our Lord whom we judge to be our head as he is from our nature and is the first to have risen from the dead. For we receive participation in these goods by means of him."

48. McKenzie, *Dictionary of the Bible*, 273.

[entered] into him, so that we may attain to a resurrection and an immortality like his own."[49] Theodore also likens the two unions to the relationship between a type and its archetype: "Adam was created the first of all human beings, and afterwards God took a small [part] of him and formed the woman whom he united to himself in perfect love through conjugal intercourse, as it has been said: 'both are one flesh.' From this, the whole human race took the beginning of its existence. . . . God then took a portion from this grace and gave it in this way to others in order that they too might share in this. He made everyone a sharer in the Spirit whereby we are reborn in a spiritual way. And as we possess a natural union with him by a similar birth, so we receive by his means a household relationship with God the Word. It was not one of conjugal intercourse but one of faith and perfect love that unites all the believers to Christ our Lord."[50]

In noting that the union is not consummated by intercourse, Theodore is not denying that it is some sort of a "corporeal" union. He wants to avoid the impression that it is merely physical. For to be part of Christ's body, one must freely commit one's self in loving faith and remain committed to virtuous living. One can fail to live up to all that this truly entails, of course: "So also in your regard, consider me to be like a vine to you, as I am the first [who] has received the Spirit's entire grace. For you are like branches to me in that by your spiritual birth you have received a union with me. So therefore as long as the branches are in the vine, they provide fruit. But if they are cut off from there, they are found to be useless. For as soon as they are pruned away, they are reduced to aridity and sterility. So also you, as long as you are in my love, you bear of necessity the richest fruit of virtue. Then after the rest of the believers who were born anew by the power of the Spirit and have become the body of Christ by their thus receiving a union with him, he exploited the example of the vine to teach them in a spiritual way by this to maintain love toward him. For where [he says] 'the vine when implanted in the earth possesses its own individual life which it once received from the earth,' so too the branches which it produces bear fruit as long as they are [remaining] in it" (281/201).

49. *TEP* 1:186.
50. *TJA*, 80–81/57.

The Spirit's Role in Baptism

As the last quotation indicates, Theodore considers the members of the Church as a "living body." As its head, Christ is esteemed not only for his leadership role but also because he is the source of vitality for all the rest of the "body": "For he calls the 'church' the congregation of the faithful. He designates (Christ), however, to be our 'head.' . . . Therefore just as we think the more esteemed part in one's body to be the head from which all vital power flows to the rest of the body, so in the present life 'we (human beings) are all one body' because we are also of one nature."[51] However, it is the Holy Spirit who bestows on Christ's humanity the fullness of all the grace that the members of Christ's body require for life. While the Spirit's mediation will be discussed in Chapter 7, I want to highlight at this point the Spirit's role in promoting the body of Christ. Theodore derives his present thought on the role of the Spirit in baptism from the New Testament, especially from Romans 8:15, 23; Galatians 4:5; and Ephesians 1:5. Christ's mediating role in dispensing the grace of the Spirit is possible because of his human nature's intimate union with the Word: "'Of his fullness we have all received'; that is, the grace of the Spirit that we have received from the riches (Christ) is pleased [to bestow]. For here he is speaking of his human nature [in which] all grace is present. This [fact] makes known the greatness of the [divine] nature present in him."[52]

The Spirit is also the One who enables the baptized to become sons and daughters of God through the sonship Christ now possesses. "Through the Spirit's mediation, You have also made me worthy of sonship so that I might call You my Father. So also after the grace of the Spirit has been conferred, make them to be [Your] sons [and daughters], in order that, as I am one, they also may be one and have the same union with You and may confidently call You Father" (316/226). The role of the Spirit in baptism is primarily to bestow filial adoption upon those who are baptized and have become members of the body of Christ and of the family of God: "For the

51. *TEP* 1:139–40.
52. *TJA*, 37–38/26.

Holy Spirit grants us filial adoption at baptism, in whom we all believe are baptized and become one body according to what the Holy Spirit accomplishes in us at baptism. By this, we have now become children of God and the one body of Christ our Lord whom we designate as our head, as he is of our own nature and is the first one raised from the dead, so that we participate through him in these goods" (*CH* 14:21). Theodore, however, insists that the sonship that the Spirit has accorded Christ's humanity differs notably from that of the baptized. Whereas Christ is the true Son of God by grace, the baptized are adopted children because of their "bodily" union through baptism. "For by his union with God the Word, [effected] through the Spirit's mediation, he has been joined in a true sonship. We have ourselves received a portion of the Spirit's grace [present] in him, and by means of this we have been made participants with him in a filial adoption, even though we are far distant from this greatness."[53] To be called an adopted child of God, therefore, one has to be united in a vital way to the body of Christ. One cannot call God "Father" simply because one has been created: "But if He is called the Father of human beings it is not because He fashioned them that He is called Father but because they are kin to Him as His family members. Because of this, He is not called Father by everyone but by those who belong to His household" (*CH* 2:13). Therefore, when one becomes a child of God at baptism, the presence of the Spirit within the body of Christ assures believers that their hope for the future will be fulfilled: "Therefore he states that we who have believed and have received a share of the Spirit have become sharers in the assurance that Christ has received and that we have received because of [our] natural union with him."[54]

Before turning to a discussion of how sacramental types are related to their realities and how Christ relates as head to his "body," we need first to present Theodore's teaching about the Eucharist as a true sacramental type. While baptism signifies the beginning of one's union with Christ, the Eucharist looks to a kind of nourishment that a member of Christ's body

53. *CH* 14:21.
54. Theodore, *Pauluskommentare*, 205.

needs to feed upon and be thereby strengthened in this new life. Its significance lies in the real transformation that takes place when the Spirit changes the eucharistic bread and wine into the body and blood of Christ.

The Eucharist as a Sacramental Type

Like many other fourth-century fathers, Theodore employs the terms "type," "archetype," and "symbol" to express how Christ is really present under the appearances of bread and wine. It was a time, too, when theologians began to refer to the Eucharist in realistic terms rather than as a type, doubtless owing to the emerging crisis over how Christ's natures are united to one another. When one asserts that the eucharistic bread and wine are transformed into the body and blood of Christ, the question emerges, who is this Jesus Christ? Cyril for one identified Christ with the Word of God and concluded that when a baptized person receives the Eucharist, he or she participates in his divine life. Theodore, by contrast, understands the "body" of Christ as referring primarily to his humanity but in its essential relationship to the Word. The difference in these two outlooks has had major repercussions for understanding what occurs whenever the Eucharist is received.

When Theodore comments upon Jesus' words, "This is my body, and this is my blood," he pointedly observes the literal meaning of Jesus' own words: "It is well, then, that when giving the bread, [our Lord] did not say: 'This is a type of my body,' but 'This is my body'; and likewise with the chalice (of wine), (he did) not (say) that: 'This is a type of my blood,' but: 'This is my blood.' For after the (bread and wine) have received the grace and the coming of the Holy Spirit, he has wanted that we too not regard their nature (as being bread and wine) but take them as being the body and blood of our Lord" (*CH* 15:10).[55] True to his commitment to the text, Theodore admits that there occurs a real transformation of the bread and wine into the body of Christ, not as the Word but as Christ's humanity in

55. Theodore also affirms in *CH* 16:28 how the reception of the Eucharist nourishes one's life in Christ's Body: "When, therefore, all of us are nourished by the same body of our Lord, we participate in him through this nourishment. All of us become the one body of Christ and we receive thereby a participation in and union with him as our head."

its union with the Word. So when a person receives the Eucharist, he or she is truly partaking of Christ's body in a "physical" sense: "Then it is well [that] the priest, following the priestly ordinance, must present the petition and supplication to God in order that the coming of the Holy Spirit may take place and [His] grace come upon the bread and wine presented there, so that there is perceived that it is truly the body and blood of our Lord who . . . became immortal and the leader of immortality for others" (*CH* 15:10). One may still see the bread and wine with one's eyes, but one must believe that the Spirit has truly transformed these both into the body and blood of Christ. "When presenting [the host], the priest then says: 'the body of Christ.' He is thereby informing you by this that you not look at what is visible but imagine in your mind what the presented [host] has come to be, namely, that by the coming of the Holy Spirit it is the body of Christ" (*CH* 16:28). One must judge the reality of the Eucharist not merely by how it appears to the senses but according to its underlying reality. This thought will be developed more fully in our treatment of Christ's humanity as the visible "image of the invisible God."

Theodore also regards the priest's act of intermingling the bread with the wine at the Mysteries as indicating that the body and blood of Christ are not properly two elements but one. "(The priest) joins (the bread and the wine) and brings them together into one, so as to manifest to all by this (action) that even if these are two, nevertheless they are one in power and are the memorial of the death and passion that the body of our Lord [experienced], when his blood was spilled on the cross for us. . . . For it is one entire human body together with his entire blood that is intermingled there" (*CH* 16:15). Like baptism, the reception of the Eucharist equally expresses and effects a continuance of one's own natural union with Christ: "And (John) said: 'Who eats my flesh and drinks my blood,' [meaning that] this one will then have, as it were, communion with me through the work of the Spirit's grace and will possess, as it were, a natural union with me, perpetually enjoying eternal life."[56] Yet though the Eucharist is a type, the eucharistic bread and wine are to be regarded as truly the body and blood

56. *TJA*, 49–50/106–7.

of Christ's humanity when they are transformed by the Spirit: "It is also necessary for us who have received the grace of the Holy Spirit in sacramental types that we no longer regard what is presented as being bread and a chalice but [consider] that they are Christ's body and blood into which the Holy Spirit's graced descent has transformed them" (*CH* 15:11).[57]

Theodore, however, refers in other places to the Eucharist as a type: "For the bread which has been given by our Lord to his disciples is a type of the bodily food which we place upon the altar up to this day."[58] This statement does not contradict his earlier assertion of a real spiritual transformation when the priest changes the bread and wine into the body and blood of Christ. The Eucharist is really the body of Christ from the moment that the Spirit at the epiclesis has transformed the eucharistic bread and wine into Christ's body and blood. Theodore regards a type as possessing its reality. We can see how Theodore construes the Eucharist as a type in his analogy of a piece of coal that is transformed when superheated: "The carbon was first of all black and cold. But when this was plunged into the fire, the carbon becomes luminous and warm. The nourishment [provided here] by the sacred mystery also becomes something like [this]. For it is presented as bread and ordinary wine but by means of the coming of the Holy Spirit it is changed into [Christ's] body and blood" (*CH* 16:36).

As such, the Eucharist's transformed nature becomes true nourishment for our life below: "We have a vital need for a nourishment that belongs to this life here below—in a typical way that will nourish us with the grace of the Holy Spirit" (*CH* 14:3). It is meant to be a true kind of spiritual food that will nourish all those who constitute the body of Christ: "For the bread is one and the body of Christ our Lord into whom the bread placed [on the altar] has been changed is one—for it receives this entire change by the single coming of the Holy Spirit. And we all equally partake of it, because

57. The same idea is expressed earlier in *CH* 15:4: "When we have become immortal and attained a heavenly home, we will no longer need this nourishment [obtained] by the labor of (our) hands. The immortality which we will then have [will be supported] by a powerful grace that will serve as nourishment in our [new state of] existence."

58. *TJA*, 142/101. See also *CH* 16:15. "For this to be, we have necessarily a need for nourishment that is suitable for us in this life here below that gives us some [nourishment] by the grace of the Holy Spirit in a typical way."

we all are the one body of Christ our Lord and all of us are nourished by the same body and the same blood. For just as we all have come to be the one body of Christ by means of the new birth and by the Holy Spirit, so we all become by [our] one sharing in Christ our Lord the one nourishment present in the sacred mysteries by whose means the grace of the Holy Spirit nourishes us. For we are all also baptized by the one Spirit into one body" (*CH* 16:24).[59] The same emphasis on the need for continuing nourishment is expressed more clearly in the following passage, where Theodore likens it to what every animal's body requires from its nurturing mother: "For every animal who is born naturally from another animal and receives its nourishment from the body of that one who gave it birth. So also from the very beginning God has ordered this to transpire among created beings that every female animal engendering life has within herself the nourishment befitting those she has engendered. It is necessary then that we who have partaken of divine grace in a typical way also receive nourishment from above" (*CH* 15:5).

But in addition to providing nourishing grace for this life, the Eucharist foreshadows the benefits that the Spirit will supply in heaven: "It is not his own sacrifice that the priest offers there, as he is truly not the high priest. Rather he accomplishes the service of this ineffable sacrifice as in an iconic manner whereby he is [now] portraying for you an image of the ineffable heavenly things in imaginative ways" (*CH* 15:21). The main benefit for communicants is the true sharing in the present immortal union that Christ's human nature now fully enjoys with the Word of God: "When you see me become immortal . . . you yourselves because of your association with me also receive what has been accomplished within me by the divine nature dwelling in me" (*CH* 8:11). Apparently drawing on a passage from Hebrews, Theodore views those participating in the eucharistic celebration as also sharing in the eternal liturgy being solemnized everywhere and at

59. The same view is expressed in *CH* 16:30: "We need necessarily a nourishment which belongs to this life here below, which nourishes us with the grace of the Holy Spirit in a typical way. . . . For by [this] birth we receive these things [participation in immortality, unchangeableness, sinlessness], so that when we have been fed we are able to continue in this existence."

all times by the angels and the heavenly hosts: "But it is the same sacrifice that all the priests of the New Alliance offer in a continual way in every and all places and at every time. For this sacrifice is the one offered for all of us, that is, by Christ our Lord, who has accepted death for our sake and by means of this sacrificial oblation has achieved perfection for us" (*CH* 15:19).

The aim of the Eucharist, like that of baptism, also expresses the coming together of all the baptized into one body: "the grace of the Holy Spirit may come upon those who are assembled, so that, as they have been brought by the new birth into one body, they may also now be affirmed to be one body because of their communion in the body of our Lord and that by their unity and peace and effort to [do] what is right, they may come [together] and complete [their] oneness, in order that when all of us look at God with a peaceful heart, [this may] not be for our punishment. . . . We are, therefore, united by participating in the holy mysteries and will be united by this to our head, Christ our Lord, whose body we believe we are and by whom we now share in the divine nature" (*CH* 16:13). If one understands this kind of participation in the divine nature as a form of divinization, then Theodore's existential view may actually not be that far from the Scholastic theoretical explanation of divinization as a supernatural union whereby a person is joined to God's life and nature in an accidental sense.

The Sacraments and Their Realities

From what we have seen, Theodore looks upon the sacraments as acquiring their salvific power from this, that they integrate their recipients into the body of the risen Christ. "Therefore they will no longer be thought to be part of Adam but of Christ; and they will no longer name Adam their head but Christ, who is the one renewing them" (*CH* 1:4). Baptism and the Eucharist may not confer upon their recipients an immortal and immutable life such as Christ's human nature now enjoys; but they do transform one's life by enabling one to participate—in a limited way—in the fullness of the benefits that Christ's body now possesses. By their being joined to Christ's body at baptism as living members to their head and feeding upon this body by means of the Eucharist, they are guaranteed future immortality in the heavenly Kingdom, provided they remain faithful to this new "bodily" life: "without hesitation, we have faith in [the attainment of] those future goods, persevering in a conduct conformed to the new world and, as much as possible, ordering our life in this world" (*CH* 1:4).

Theodore insists that the saving power that flows through the body of Christ comes from Christ's human union with the Word and the work of the Holy Spirit. "For also the body of our Lord does not possess by its own nature immortality and (the power of) bestowing immortality. Rather it has come to him through the Holy Spirit. [For it was] at his resurrection from the dead [that] he received [full] union with the divine nature and became immortal and the principle of immortality for others" (*CH* 15:10).[60] We grant that it is the Spirit who operates in full collaboration with the human nature of Christ (in its union with the Word) and who likewise transforms the life of the baptized from a state of mortality to potential immortality, but what is the relationship between the present and future states of the baptized who are now members of Christ's body?

Theodore sees the relationship in scriptural terms. For instance, the sacrament of baptism seals a person in a way similar to how sheep and soldiers are branded to indicate their master: "But this seal with which you are now signed signifies how you have been marked from this point on as a sheep who belongs to Christ and as a soldier under the King of heaven" (*CH* 13:17). Besides permanently marking a person as a Christian, the seal provides a firmness that comes from the grace received that is a surety or guarantee of what is to come in the future. This grace may be slight at the present moment but it presages the full grace in the future: "'You have received confirmation by the Spirit's participation.' For (Paul) says: 'You have been sealed.' A firmness, however, was acquired for them through the grace of the Spirit. . . . Well, however, did he speak of the Spirit [as one] of promise, since all the good things expected in the future age are expected to be there for believers because of the participation of the Spirit . . . they

60. The literal view of the consecration is also affirmed in *CH* 16:12. Theodore's remark about Christ's humanity being fully united to the Word simply refers to the fact that Christ's human nature has now reached its final state of immortality.

regard the first fruits [to be] the small amount of grace [bestowed] in the present life as a confirmation of the things to come."[61] The baptized can share in Christ's immortal state because they now share in Christ's human nature as those united to his body: "(The assumed man) mounted to heaven in order that henceforth we might have a surety of a possessed participation because of [our] sharing in [his] nature" (CH 12:6).

Theodore believes too that the baptized receive a new birth that transforms their nature into a superior one: "the one who descends into the water is reformed by the grace of the Holy Spirit and is born again to another superior human nature. . . . you are again gladdened and formed so as to be changed to a superior nature. You set aside the former mortality and take on a nature wholly immortal and incorruptible" (CH 14:10–11). This new superior nature is, therefore, in some sense an immortal one. While one cannot be mortal and immortal at the same time, Theodore is referring, I believe, to the way that the baptized have become members of Christ's body and share in an inchoate way in his immortal nature. One's life as a member of Christ's body can be said to be a sharing in this superior life: "It is the grace of the Spirit who forms the one baptized in a second birth and makes him totally other. . . . but when he has been baptized and has received the divine and spiritual grace, he has become totally other in an absolute sense" (CH 14:9). Those who now possess this superior nature are assured of their future immortality: "We also ourselves expect to enjoy these [benefits] that are superior to our nature" (CH 12:10).

Theodore spells out through examples how the baptized share even now, in a potential way, in the new state that is evolving toward its promised fulfillment. In three remarkable analogies, Theodore illustrates how he conceives of the first fruits of this "superior" immortal nature and its future union with God. These analogies exemplify the criterion that Theodore laid down for the dynamic way in which a type is related to its archetype. The first example conveys how the fire of baptism has permanently remolded a person's nature: "But just as a vase made by a potter is fashioned and then molded anew in water, in such a way that its own nature remains as long as the clay is still soft and has not participated in the nature of fire, but

61. TEP 1:132–33.

when it has been plunged into the fire, there is no way for it to be refashioned and molded into another. So now also in our case because we are in a mortal nature, we must duly receive this renewal through baptism. But after we have been fashioned anew through baptism and received the grace of the Holy Spirit who strengthens us more than any fire does, we will no longer receive an additional renewal nor also will we any longer expect another baptism" (CH 14:13).

The next two examples provide a clearer insight into how Theodore understands the relationship between the renewal at baptism and its fulfillment in heaven. He likens it to how a fertilized egg grows within a pregnant woman and to the potential powers that a newborn child has for speaking and walking. The passage is a lengthy one:

> He shows that just as the womb of a mother receives [her husband's] seed in this carnal birth [and] the divine hand then forms it in accordance with [God's] decree at the beginning [of its fashioning], so also in baptism the water becomes a womb for the one being born. However, it is the grace of the Spirit who is forming the one baptized for a second birth and renders this one totally other. Thus in the same way that a seed enters into a mother's womb, [having] neither life nor soul nor sensation but, having been formed by the divine hand to issue into a living human being endowed with a soul, he has a nature that can experience sensation and every [kind of] human operation. Here also in a similar way to the womb, the one being baptized descends into the water like the seed without any sign that an immortal nature will come forth. But when this one is baptized and has received the divine spiritual grace, he becomes in every way wholly other. He is formed into an immortal nature from a mortal one, into an incorruptible one from a corruptible one, from a changing one to an immutable one and wholly other by the power of the One who formed it. Just as one born of a woman possesses the power to speak, hear, walk, and work with his hands but is completely undeveloped for all these (actions), but afterwards with time he will receive these according to the divine decree. So likewise now the one born at baptism possesses in himself all the power of an immortal and incorruptible nature and possesses all these, although he is now incapable of operating them and making them function and manifesting them until the moment that God has determined for us. (CH 14:9–10)[62]

62. See also CH 14:28.

The relationship, therefore, between the initial transformation and its later fulfillment in heaven, like that between a type and its archetype, is not a simple likeness or an empty, meaningless kind of participation. It is one where a potential power has been bestowed that will achieve its future realization, provided that nothing blocks its process. The typical relationships between Adam and Christ's humanity, between the two Testaments, and between Christ and his Church, on one side, and a husband and his wife, on the other, have been definitively established. Yet the situation is very different between a baptized person and his or her yet to be attained immortal life. The goal is guaranteed, but because of human freedom one can turn away from one's union with the body of Christ. So, for Theodore, the final fulfillment of sacramental types is always assured, but with the proviso that a baptized person has to remain corporally at one with Christ as a vital member of his body. One must also rely, of course, upon the spiritual nourishment that the Eucharist provides a person for living a loving and virtuous life.

Is the Church as the Body of Christ a Mere Metaphor?

Because Christ's humanity is united in a true "exact" union with the Word of God, those joined to him, as a bodily member to its head, will attain an immortal existence in heaven, just as a living body shares in the honors that its head has achieved. We need now to explore the kind of "body" about which Theodore is speaking. He often refers to the union of Christ and his Church in Pauline terms as one between a head and its body: "What I have said is: 'because I am in my Father' [it is] because of an equality of nature and inseparable union. . . . And 'I am in you,' [in the sense that] this union is the result of what happens when you have been born anew by the power of the Spirit and become my body, and I will become your head as it has been said."[63] When commenting on Ephesians

---

63. *TJA*, 274–75/196. See also *CH* 13:9: "Because you have called upon Christ and been inscribed in the church of God and expect to become the body and member of Christ through the birth of holy baptism, you also have communion with Christ our Lord as you are united to his head and distant from all those who dare to depart from the faith and profession of the church."

4:26, Theodore notes that, strictly speaking, we are not his body but rather members of his body: "So (Paul) did not say 'we are the body' but a 'member.' For we are greatly concerned for those members who belong to us, considering all these to be in a similar way communal parts of the [same] body."[64]

The question arises as to whether the phrase the "body of Christ" is to be interpreted as a simple metaphor or as something more. Ulrich Wickert believes that Theodore regards the body of Christ more as a metaphor, understanding the Church to be an assembled sum of its members and thus not signifying an organic relationship between Christ and his Body: "in essence the sum of the members clearly ordered to one another in a σύστημα without having any reference to an 'organic' kind of body."[65] The Church, for Wickert, is not an external structure but an interior one, made up of those who come together in devout faith as individuals who share a common belief. Theodore expresses such a view: "For this edifice built by [human] hands is not what (Paul) calls the church, even though it came to be so named because of the assembly of the believers within it. Rather he named the church to be the whole assembly of the believers who fear God in the right way, those who since the coming of Christ have in every place believed in him until . . . the coming of our Savior whom we expect from heavens" (CH 10:15).[66] For Wickert, the Church, as described in 1 Timothy 3:15, is the house of the living God that is the pillar and ground of truth. As such, it is not independent of human free choice, though it does require the assistance of the Holy Spirit to acquire holiness. For Wickert, such a view of the one body of the Church preserves the ability of believers to be in direct communication with God.[67]

---

64. TEP 1:174.

65. Ulrich Wickert, Studien zu den Pauluskommentaren Theodores von Mopsuesti: Als Beitrag zum Verstännis der Antiochenischen Theologie (Berlin: Töpelmann, 1962), 150. See 147–56 for the context.

66. See also CH 10:18 and 15:43–44.

67. See Wickert, Studien zu den Pauluskommentaren, 150.

Paul's Understanding of the Body of Christ

Since Theodore is committed to a literal interpretation of Scripture, it helps to consider how Paul regarded the body of Christ, as Paul is undoubtedly the source of Theodore's view on this question. Many scriptural scholars favor an interpretation much stronger than that of a metaphor, such as John L. McKenzie, who, in his *Dictionary of the Bible,* maintains that "The physical realism of these [Pauline] passages [about the body of Christ] is remarkable and should not be diluted to mere metaphor. The identity of Christians with the physical body of Christ is unique in Paul's presentation and is much more than the union of members of a society with the governing authority and with each other."[68] The Pauline passage that best bears this out is Ephesians 4:15–16: "But by speaking the truth in love, we will grow up in every way into him who is the head, into Christ, from whom the whole body, fitted together and knit together by every band with which it is equipped, as each part is working according to its measure, promotes the body's growth in building itself up in love."[69] In commenting on this passage, Theodore shows his dependence on Paul's way of conceiving the Body of Christ: "Since he called him the head, he showed that also those things belonging to the head are present to him; so that by these very things he reveals that a union of this sort with him is necessary for us . . . since just as all vital power is borne to the rest of the body from our head, from which each of the members both lives and is moved and is fitted together to the rest of the body, so also there comes to us as from Christ the head the spiritual grace of regeneration whereby we have received a union with Christ; so as to say that 'Christ acts thus for the purpose of building up of his own body by that love which he has toward us.' He shows by this that he is imposing a difference of graces, not a necessity of division, not only because Christ is one and bestows these things upon us as being one, but also because we all have been made his one body by a spiritual regeneration."[70]

68. McKenzie, *Dictionary of the Bible,* 101.
69. Paul expresses the same thought in Col. 2:18–19: "Do not be cheated by those. . . . who do not hold fast to the head from whom the whole body, having been supplied and joined by joints and muscles, will grow [with] the growth of God."
70. *TEP* 1:169–70.

There are other passages in the New Testament that at least insinuate a corporate union closer to an organic than a metaphorical one, such as those where Adam and Christ are said to be the heads of two different kinds of existence and whose free acts affect all those united to them by nature. Just as Adam's sin had a "physical" impact upon every one of his descendants, keeping them mortal, Christ's sinlessness also affected in a "bodily" way all those united with him as their sole head: "For insofar as Adam is called a 'human being' and each one of us and all of us participate in this name, so also those who are the body of Christ through spiritual generation are aptly denoted by this word 'body.'"[71] Theodore also asserts that other humans share in Christ's benefits by being united to him in a bodily way. "Since he called him the head, he showed that also those [benefits] belonging to the head are present to him; so that by these very things he shows that a union of this sort with him is necessary for us."[72]

We see the same outlook in many other biblical passages. In Luke's Gospel, for instance, Christ is identified in a "bodily" way with those in need: "those who hear you, hear me, and those who reject you, reject me. Whatever you do to the least of my brethren, you do to me." Paul portrays the Church, too, as a living organism whose life is quickened by the Spirit, and he argues in 1 Corinthians 6:15–16 that a believer involved with a prostitute forms one body with her, contrary to his role as a true member of Christ's body: "Know you not that your bodies are the members of Christ? Shall I then take the members of Christ, and make them members of a harlot? God forbid. What? Know you not that one who is joined to a harlot is one body?" All this suggests a corporate, organic sense of "body," where the whole suffers and rejoices in the actions of other members.

This kind of corporate concept is foreign to Western cultures that emphasize individualism whereby a son suffers for his own sins, not for those of his father. It is, as it were, a tribal view, which sees an individual as part of a family, race, and nation in which all strive for the common good, even to the point of sacrificing one's own personal good. It is an outlook that runs through the Hebrew Testament and is still prevalent among those

71. *TJA*, 319–20/229.
72. *TEP* 1:169.

Jews of other nations who are loyal to and fiercely supportive of Israel.

Pierre Benoit is another Scripture scholar who views the Church as an organic, "physical" body united to Christ as its head.[73] Benoit maintains that Paul conceived the union between the Christian and Christ as a physical (sacramental) union of the body of the Christian to the individual body of Christ. Contrary to others, Benoit is convinced that Paul did not derive his outlook from Gnosticism or any sort of sociological theory but from the Semitic recognition that the soul and its body are one and that an individual can represent a whole class in a manner of a corporate personality. For example, the sins of a ruler can affect the whole nation. Moreover, Paul compares and contrasts the union of Christ's body with a sexual union, where two bodies become one single flesh. Benoit concludes that Paul thought of the union as a "physical" one.

Admittedly, analogies are imperfect. To say that the union between Christ as the head and the Church as members of his body is strictly organic raises obvious problems. But there are other kinds of organic unions that are more than metaphorical. It is important to determine how much of this dispute is merely semantic. Like the word "cancer," "organic" is not a univocal term but one that can be applied in different ways. The ninth edition of Webster's New Collegiate Dictionary defines "organism" in one sense as "a complex structure of interdependent and subordinate elements whose relations and properties are largely determined by the function of the whole; an individual constituted to carry on the activities of life by means of organs separate in function but mutually dependent; a living being." The question therefore becomes, is the body of Christ a corporate, "physical-like" kind of reality whose members all contribute to and share in the well-being of the whole body, with an inward living vitality that actively grows and dies? Or, perhaps better, is the body of Christ to be understood as "one" in the way that the Hebrews regard the soul and its body as an organic whole rather than two separate realities?

As we have seen, Theodore considers the body of Christ a living

---

73. Pierre Benoit, "Corps. Tête et Plérôme dans les Épîtres de la Captivité," *Revue Biblique* 63 (1956): 6. See also 16.

"whole" whose collective existence is organized and unified around the goal of living only and wholly for Christ: "This good is common for all of us who believe. Why? Because all of us who believe are his body. . . . For what was bestowed upon him was received under the form of chrism. 'The Spirit of the Lord,' he said, 'is upon me on account of which he anointed me.' Also by our sharing in the Spirit at [our] rebirth, we perceive the sharing that he [already] has. . . . in whose form we now believe we have been already constituted, thinking that all those who believe are his body."[74] The members are attached to Christ, their head, by an indissoluble bond that the Spirit has bestowed at baptism and now nourishes through the Eucharist. In commenting on Colossians 2:18–19, Theodore urges his readers, as members of the body of Christ, to enable the whole body to grow by living in accord with the graces they have received as members: "Since it befits you to follow those things that are Christ's, in relationship to whom the common body is connected in accordance with that grace supplied them, you can make that increase to be in accord with God."[75] This is clearly stated in the passage cited earlier: "(Paul) designated him as our head . . . therefore we think the head to be the more privileged part of the entire body, from which all vital power flows to the rest of the body."[76]

Theodore regards the vital power that flows from Christ as the head of the body as the Spirit's graces handed on to Christ's human nature. I shall discuss Theodore's view of the *plerôma* in the next chapter, but suffice it to say here that Christ in his human nature distributes these to others, each in his or her own way:

For just as there is borne from our head to the rest of the body all vital power from which each one of the members both lives and is moved and is fitted to the rest of the body, so also spiritual grace comes to us as from Christ [our own] head through whose regenerating grace we receive communion with him in one body, showing the difference between the members by the different graces [bestowed]. For he maintains that the new body of the church is bound and contained by Christ as [its] head in such a way that there functions in each one of us [that] spiritual operation which each

74. *TEP* 1:139.   75. Ibid., 1:295.
76. Ibid., 1:140.

one of us in undertaking our ministry does so in an ineffable manner for the common good. . . . Not only because Christ is one does he as the one bestow these very things to us, but also all are made his own one body by a spiritual rebirth. And since the necessity of all is common, with each conferring what can be [a benefit] for the common good, so the one who is seen to have a meager grace is not thought to be of inferior [worth] for the common fulfillment, since there is one nature for the bodily members. Moreover we also have a common concern for all the members, thinking to perform everything likewise to secure the common body.[77]

Theodore describes the priest in the "body" of Christ as the one speaking out on behalf of the whole organism: "For although [the priest] holds this oblation up as an offering, nevertheless he offers it as the tongue does for the whole body. Likewise the oblation is offered for all of us as a community as being also a community benefit whose reception is reckoned as being for all of us equally."[78] Following Paul's lead, Theodore urges those who are members of Christ's body to act as a united body that is at peace with itself and feels for all its members: "By this [act of exchanging a gesture of peace in the Eucharist] we profess that it is necessary for all of us who have become the one body of Christ our Lord to be at peace with each member, that we love each other equally, that we sustain and aid each other, that we regard each other's affairs to be that of the community and that we sympathize with each other's sadness and rejoice in the blessings of each other" (CH 15:39). Theodore provides another organic analogy when he emphasizes the importance of all members', including priests', being spiritually healthy: "Just as these have need of their attached bodily members in order to fulfill their functions and require them to be healthy with their constitution in good order, if they expect to fulfill their functions without a failure, so also the priest as being part of the body of the church needs to be healthy in his rank" (CH 15:36). All this realistic language is more meaningful and convincing if Theodore indeed intends the members of Christ's body to be understood as corporately linked to each other.

The body of Christ also embraces those who are physically separated

77. Ibid., 1:170–71.
78. CH 15.41.

from those who are gathered for the eucharistic mysteries, indicating that the body of Christ is to be understood as a larger kind of organic body. The priest celebrates the Eucharist also for those who are absent but who are members of the Church: "A community sacrifice is immolated and a community oblation offered for all of them. This is not only for those assisting but also for those absent insofar as they share in [the same] faith whereby they are numbered among the Church of God and will spend their lives" (*CH* 15:44). Following Paul, Theodore rejects within the body of Christ the relevance of race, nationality, gender, and economic status. For all are one "being" in Christ: "Therefore what distinction is to be recognized between the Jews and the Arameans and between slavery and freedom among those who have become immortal and incorruptible in nature like the form of Christ" (*CH* 1:3). As we have seen, Theodore affirms that those regenerated by the Spirit become, literally, "one thing" (neuter): "Just as you have been given birth from the one Spirit so as to become 'one thing' by your birth, so it is fitting for you that you become bound and united one to another. . . . the one body of Christ . . . (with) the assumed man as its head by whom we have family relationship with this divine nature, so that we expect in the world to come to share with him" (*CH* 9:17).

Theodore also asserts a family relationship between Abraham and all the living members of Christ's body in that they have become, in Paul's words, the seed of Abraham: "Christ is the seed of Abraham. Being his body, you are also (Abraham's) seed of which he is also. Otherwise it is impossible to be one in a corporeal sense and to reckon that he is the head of one [body] and the rest [of us] belonging to another body."[79] While this does not mean that the members of Christ's body are blood descendants of Abraham, it suggests that they are related more than metaphorically. They are actually offspring who participate in the benefits that Yahweh promised to Abraham. The same idea is also expressed, in an expanded way, in the relationship between Christ *qua* man and the members of his body that renders null all gender and other kinds of distinctions: "So also in regard to the future immortal life which is [to come] after the resurrection, its princi-

79. *TEP* 1:59.

ple [resides] in Christ. All of us, moreover, who share with him in the immortality [to be granted] after the resurrection, are made one with him, while each one of us is likewise seen to maintain the role of a common membership in relation to him. Then, therefore, there will be 'neither male nor female.' . . . For all things will then be ended."[80]

Theodore does admit, as Paul does, that there exist in the body of Christ differing kinds of charisms and ministries but that all are one in Christ: "For 'above all' [in reference to the clause in Ephesians 4:6: 'who is above all and through all and in all of us'] means the one who surpasses all. 'And through all things' shows us his providence. And he is believed both to be and to dwell also 'in all of us.' And whereas he manifests by all this that there needs to be a harmony among them, there is, nevertheless, a difference that is present among them because of a variety of graces. For if each one of us has his or her own spiritual grace, the difference, indeed, occurs according to the gift that Christ the Lord has thought worthy for each one of us."[81] Theodore is using here an organic-like model to explain how there can be different functions within the Church but with all the members considered one "being," for whom all work for the benefit of the whole body.

Theodore also likens the oneness between Christ's humanity and the members of his body with what exists between Christ's humanity and the Word: "Hence just as (Christ) is one, we also are all named 'one being,' since each one of us has a membership role in relationship to the whole. In the same way those who are born in Christ are called his body and each one of them is his member with Christ being the head of all of us. But if these things have been said in another place in the evangelist's commentary, in no way do we think that they are superfluous. . . . God the Word, therefore, is conjoined naturally to the Father. But through his union with Him, the *homo assumptus* also receives a union with the Father. So likewise we also receive, insofar as we can, a spiritual sharing with the Father

80. Ibid., 57. As Swete observes (*TEP* xxxvii), Theodore uses words such as *videor* and *possum* in a periphrastic way. I have omitted translating "seem to" in the present text.

81. Ibid., 1:165.

because of the natural union that we have with Christ in the flesh. And we have become his body, and each of us a member. On that account we also hope to rise later like him and be born into an eternal life. When, therefore, we approach in the same way through him to God the Word, we necessarily receive a family kind of relationship with the Father."[82] Theodore's point seems to be that if the union between Christ as head and the baptized as the body is understood as constituting one reality, then the union between the Word and Christ's humanity ought to be interpreted in a similar way. We shall see in Chapter 7 how Theodore likens this union to that between the spiritual soul and its material body in an quasi-organic unity.

The material contained in this chapter shows how Theodore approaches the role of Christ's humanity in salvation from a literal, rational analysis of the New Testament, especially from what he discerned to be the significance of the typological relationship between Adam and Christ's humanity as heads of their respective "bodies," as well as between the sacraments of baptism and the Eucharist and their later heavenly fulfillment. Theodore sought to explain these roles in light of the answers that he found contained in the Scriptures, for he believed that these were inspired by God. From his examination of how Adam and Christ *qua* man are presented as the heads of two kinds of existence, he saw how humanity belongs to two "bodies" with different heads, Adam over the mortal state of creation and Christ's humanity over an immortal state. His view of how a type is related to its archetype enabled him to discern how the two states are bonded to each other in God's plan as a seed is to its later flowering. The two heads are similar to each other, but Adam's role is far inferior to that of Christ *qua* man. Both "heads" have a quasi-causal effect upon all those who constitute the members of their bodies. Adam's sin affects all humanity and all creation, just as Christ's victory over Satan and death enables all those who are united to him in a bodily way to achieve not merely the possibility but truly, in an anticipatory way, the reality of an immortal existence and an unending union with God.

We have seen that those who are united to Adam and Christ as mem-

82. *TJA*, 315–16/225–26.

bers of a body to their head personally share in Adam's failure and Christ's human victory. Because of the real relationship God has established between a type and its fulfillment, then, the type is truly programmed, as it were, to achieve its goal. Theodore acknowledges this when, following Paul, he looks upon baptism and the Eucharist as the main ways—in addition to the sharing in a common human nature—to achieve union with Christ and thereby one's own salvation. Both sacraments are types revealing and effecting in anticipatory ways the future realities that God has established for all who belong to Christ's body. The present and future states are like each other, but the final state brings the fulfillment of what the sacraments promise. The future immortal union with God is guaranteed because God has determined their relationship and outcome within salvation history. As long as an individual remains sacramentally a living member of Christ's body, such a one will certainly attain an immortal existence in a heavenly state—provided one lives a faithful and virtuous life.

At baptism the Spirit is the agent of rebirth for the baptized. The baptized are endowed with a new superior nature that has the potential to become immortal in a future heavenly life. As members of his body, the baptized participate even now in the victory of Christ's humanity over Satan and death, just as bodily members share in what their head has attained. But since they still exist in an intermediate state, a middle ground between two worlds, living in the present mortal existence yet belonging to the future, they are still liable to sin and death. They may be potentially sinless and immortal, but they can stray in their freedom as members of Christ's body. To assist them in this in-between time, the Spirit provides them with the eucharistic nourishment they need to live within a mortal state until they can finally partake of the heavenly graces in an immortal state and union with the Word of God. "For as members of Christ, their union with God is realized by their union with the assumed man."[83]

While Theodore offers no unassailable statement in his extant works that the union of the members within the body of Christ is strictly organic, he certainly reflects Paul's statements about the dynamic activity and

83. *TEP* 142n10.

growth that occur within the body of Christ: "Since it befits you to follow those things which are Christ's, in relationship to whom the common body is joined together in accord with that grace supplied them, you can make that increase to be in accord with God."[84] I shall expand upon this in the following chapters. Let us now turn to the question of how Theodore understands the role of Christ's body in the salvation of nonhumans.

84. Ibid., 1:295.

4. CHRIST'S SALVIFIC ROLE AS THE BOND OF THE UNIVERSE

AS WE SAW IN THE LAST CHAPTER, Theodore sees the pivotal role of Christ's humanity in the divine plan of human salvation as his mediating role as the head of his body, the Church. Those who are united to him share in the benefits that flow to his human nature because of its "exact" union with the Word of God in one "person." The question then naturally arises, how does the rest of the created universe participate in the salvation that Christ has brought to humankind? Theodore addresses this in his commentaries on Colossians, Ephesians, and Genesis—works apparently written in the first two decades of the fifth century. While his other works may not lend themselves to this specific theme, it appears that his thinking on this question evolved during this period, especially his view of how Adam is a type of Christ *qua* man and how Christ's human nature, in which the divine *plerôma* dwells, recapitulates the spiritual and material worlds "in a bodily way."

My intent here is to discuss in detail the salvific role Theodore assigns to Christ's human nature as the way for the created nonhuman spiritual and material worlds to become united with God in a future immortal existence. This chapter will be developed in light of Theodore's typology as it applies to Adam and Christ's humanity as the bonds of the universe. I shall begin with passages that indicate God's will for the salvation of all created beings and then discuss Theodore's view of Adam's human nature as the bond uniting the angelic and the material worlds as one "body" within the universe. I shall also discuss the other roles that Theodore associates with Adam as the bond uniting the cosmos as one "body," such as providing others access to God and the means whereby both the spiritual and the material worlds give God glory by caring for the needs of humankind. I shall then examine Theodore's thinking on humans as the bond of the universe as it relates to the effect of Adam's sin on the harmonious and peaceful unity of all creation.

I shall then consider Christ's role as the one who recapitulates the universe in his human nature and in whose humanity the whole divine *plerôma* dwells. I shall spend time in establishing Theodore's unique interpretation of what Paul means by the term *plerôma* and its implications for Christ's humanity's union with the Word. In response to the question Ulrich Wickert has raised, I shall look at the source and purpose of Theodore's view of Adam and Christ as the two bonds of the universe and then how the cosmos forms one "body."

God's Universal Intent

Theodore first indicates that God wants all of humanity to be saved through the true mediation of Christ: "For no one can contradict that God wants these [salvation and knowledge of the truth] for all humans. For it is evident that He wants all to be saved in that He also cares for all. It is therefore necessary that we also imitate his care for all, if we are completely eager to be wise[1] in ways similar to God. . . . The man Jesus Christ is the

---

1. The Latin text is: "Si tamen ad plenum adceleramus similia sapere Deo." Literally it means: "if nevertheless we completely hasten to taste similar things to God." The sense seems to be that we must strive to know and act as God does. The text is found in *TEP* 2:87.

one mediator for God and human beings. . . . But he is also the one mediator who strives to bind human beings to God, and hence he exists as a human being by [his] nature."[2] Theodore then argues that the central role of Christ's humanity as the mediator between God and humankind extends to all creation: "He aptly called him 'a human being,' above all especially in this place, in order to show the participation of [his] nature in his [act of] self-giving, with all necessarily confessing that by having a nature common to all, he is able, as a part of the universe *[universitatis pars],* to accomplish this self-giving [of himself for all] because of [his] likeness [to all] in nature. . . . For he also 'gave himself for all.' For he was not content to submit to death [only] for some. Rather because he wants to confer his benefit to all in common, he deigned to undergo his passion at that time [set] for his suffering."[3] Since Theodore is focused here upon how there is "one God and also one mediator between God and humans, the man Christ Jesus," his remark that a human being is "a part of the universe" may simply mean that humans are creatures. But, as we shall see, Theodore regards a human being as the bond uniting the spiritual powers and the material world in one "body." He suggests that he would not restrict God's universal salvific intent to humans alone and, if pressed, would grant that his *universitatis pars* includes nonhumans as well. Let us examine how Theodore explains that the universe shares in salvation and the role of Christ's humanity in this salvation.

Adam as the Bond of the Universe

Theodore holds the traditional view that, in making Adam and Eve in his "image," God intended humans as his crowning achievement and the keystone of the cosmos. He does this by binding the spiritual and material world to the spiritual and material components of human nature. "For (God) made (Adam) a being composed of an invisible, rational, immortal soul and a visible mortal body. The former has a likeness to the invisible

2. Theodore does not enter into the question of whether God intends absolutely all to be saved. But as he is commenting on 1 Tim. 2:4 in this section, he is probably looking upon God as offering all the opportunity to achieve salvation.
3. *TEP* 2:88–89.

natures, but the latter is akin to the visible beings. For since God willed to gather all creation into one 'reality,' so that though constituted from different natures, creation might be gathered into [this] one bond, He created this living creature who is related by his nature to all creation."[4]

This union of the spiritual and corporeal worlds is analogous to the way in which the human soul and body form one organic whole. God first fashioned Adam's body from the earth and then breathed a soul into his body, joining the two natures into "one being": "For because God wanted to collect the whole of creation into one being . . . contained by one bond, He created this living one who is akin to the whole of creation by its nature. He thus made Adam, creating two natures not simultaneously but by first forming a visible body and then breathing an invisible soul after [the creation of] the body" (*TFS*, fol. 22a/5). Theodore regards this harmonious bonding of the spiritual and the corporeal in Adam's nature and with the universe as an extraordinary sign of God's friendship:

> God made the whole creation one "body." Hence the cosmos is also said [to include] all beings, whether visible or invisible, as (Paul) says in his letter to the Corinthians that "we have become a spectacle to the cosmos and to both angels and material beings." Since, moreover, there is some difference among those who are visible and invisible, God in His desire to synthesize all into one has made the human being to be constituted from a visible body and akin to the visible creation—for he is fabricated from earth and air and water and fire—and from an invisible soul related as a kindred member to the invisible beings. And God made Adam to be a kind of pledge for the harmony of the universe.[5]

Besides being the bond of the universe and the pledge of God's friendship, Adam plays another significant role within creation. God wants all creation to come to him through Adam: "(God) made known the reason

---

4. *TFS*, 7–8 (fol. 22a) in the Syriac, 5 in the Latin text. In the initial citation, I have cited first the Syriac text and Sachau's Latin translation on the right side of the slash. When the following references immediately pertain to Sachau or to another author, they are cited parenthetically in the text.

5. Theodore of Mopsuestia, *Pauluskommentare*, 137. Theodore is commenting here on Rom. 8:19. One can interpret Theodore's remark on Adam being the pledge of harmony in two ways: as the pledge already established in Christ or as the bond that his own person forms. Either way, such a bond is only fully found in Christ.

why after [having created] all others He made the human being the outstanding living being and then completed the whole of creation in accordance with His will, when He fashioned this one in whom the whole of
creation was going to be bound. For [all] creation approaches its Creator
through this one and through those things that have been accomplished on
his behalf."[6] Because of this mediating role that Adam plays within God's
plan, the rest of creation must supply the material needs of humans and
strive for their salvation: "What he wants to say is this: the God of the universe made all creation, as it were, one 'body,' composed of many members, rational as well as sensible orders. . . . All sensible beings, however,
function for the benefit of human needs. The rational powers also struggle
to provide for the necessity of those of us who are visible. In addition, they
also minister on behalf of our salvation."[7]

Besides revealing God to the rest of creation and being the ones on
whose behalf the rest of creation must work, human beings also provide
the concrete way for all other created beings to give glory and worship to
God. They do so by caring for human needs: "For the human being was
fashioned from the beginning as a certain 'living being'[8] united to all [oth-
ers] by a kindred kind of relationship. . . . Indeed, the one universal bonding was seen to be made from this because of that kindred relationship
which all beings have to the human being, with all coming together so that
with their solicitous care they might render with one consent the cult due
to God" (*TEP* 1:lxxx). As H. B. Swete puts it, "Man, made of elements belonging to both sides of creation, was designed to be a bond of union internal to the κόσμος knitting together in a single nature its opposite factors
(Rom. viii. 19; Eph. i. 10; Col. i. 16), to the intent that the universe might
with sone accord serve its Creator and obey His laws."[9]

The Dissolution of the Bond

As noted in the previous chapter, Theodore seems to have allowed for
the possibility that Adam and all the rest of creation could have achieved
immortality had he obeyed God's command. But Adam sinned, with tragic

6. *TFS*, fol. 29a/18.

7. *TEP* 1:128–29.

8. The Latin word in the text is *animal.*

9. *TEP* 1:lxxx.

personal, communal, and cosmic effects upon all of creation. As the head of mortal existence, his action had consequences for all who are bound to his "body." Adam's sin condemned his descendants to continue to live in a mortal, mutable, and corruptible state. It also had a cataclysmic effect upon all of creation. Not only did it transform the human bond to God into a rebellious one, but the resulting splitting apart of the human soul from its body at death shattered the unity and harmony of creation. The "bond" uniting earthly creatures to one another and to God was now severed by death. Adam's role as the way to the knowledge and glory of God lost its meaning. "But death was introduced for those of us sinning. Henceforth there was brought about a separation of both the soul from its body, and the body when separated underwent a complete dissolution. Because of this, the bonding of creation was dissolved" (*TEP* 1:129–30).[10]

The angels responded to Adam's disobedience with shock and wanted to terminate their service to humankind. But God persuaded them not to do so by promising that he would restore harmony to the universe in the future: "For on account of human malice, all creation, as I have said, was seen to have been torn apart. The angels and all the [other] invisible powers turned away from us on account of the wickedness we committed against God. Moreover we ourselves are also separated by death when it comes to pass for our soul to be released from our body. Indeed the interconnection of all creation was also henceforth dissolved. . . . with our binding kinship [to the rest of creation] being dissolved from this time on, so that the invisible powers did not think that they would in the future be in communion with us [and having to be] concerned about our body. . . . and they were no longer willing to fulfill these [tasks], if they had not been satisfied by God's promise that all the harsh [punishments] would be removed [and that] death and corruption will also cease, with all reintegrated into a harmonious whole [in the future]" (*TEP* 1:268).[11]

10. The same thought is expressed in the following: "Moreover, we ourselves are also dissolved by death, whereby it befalls the soul to be separated from the body. The union of creation was also truly split apart from that time on. For the human being was fashioned from the beginning as a certain 'living being' united to all by a family relationship" (*TEP* 1:268).

11. The citations from *TEP* 1:253 to 1:287 are Theodore's comments on Colossians.

In brief, Theodore looks upon Adam as playing a central mediating role within creation. Composed of a spiritual soul and a material body, Adam initially united the spiritual and material worlds in a harmonious whole. God chose Adam to reveal himself to the rest of creation. He wanted other creatures to worship and glorify him by fulfilling the material and the spiritual needs of humankind. This union of the cosmos under Adam, however, was fragile and depended on Adam's freely obeying God's commandments. In his sin of disobedience, his role as the symbolic bond between God and his creation collapsed, and the bond uniting the human soul to its body was severed. This breach meant, further, the destruction of the harmonious union between human beings and the rest of creation. But God foresaw all this and prepared for it by sending the sinless Christ to be the perfect archetypal bond, the one who will recapitulate the universe within his humanity and serve as humans' divinely appointed mediator through his union with God the Word.

Christ as the Recapitulator of the Universe

Theodore develops the role of Christ's humanity as the universal savior primarily on the basis of Paul's letters to the Colossians and Ephesians. These can be summed up under two headings: Christ serves (1) as the one who recapitulates the universe, as a head does for its body, and (2) as the one in whom the whole divine *plerôma* dwells. First, Christ fulfills his role as the one who recapitulates the universe by recreating, reintegrating, and perfectly binding all of creation within his human nature and uniting nonhumans to God because of his "exact" union with the Word's divine nature. "Therefore in our renovation when the interconnection of all creation is reintegrated, our first fruits are Christ according to the flesh in whom the perfect and, as I have said, the comprehensive re-creation of all creatures will be accomplished. . . . Well, therefore, did he state: 'in him are created all beings,' not only because we have obtained through his accomplishments the promise of future blessings, but also since the perfect binding together of all beings will be preserved in him because of the divine nature that is dwelling [within him], so that nothing can cut us off from what is common to us" (*TEP* 1:269).

Theodore maintains here that the Son who recapitulates the universe is Christ in the flesh. To justify this interpretation, he explains that the reference to the Son as the first born of creation must be understood in its own context. Since Christ in the flesh is the "visible image of God," "first born" does not refer to the Word's eternal generation from his Father. Rather it is Christ in the flesh who is the "first one honored" with immortality: "He is not [temporally] prior to all creation. Rather he has accepted that he would be so in the final times. We do not understand 'first born' only in a temporal sense but also often in the sense of being first honored in that the first born is truly said of those born after this one" (*TEP* 1:264). In other words, Christ *qua* man is the first one honored with immortality.

Since Adam's sin dissolved the integrity of human nature, Theodore saw that Christ in his human nature had the role of restoring and perfecting the harmony of creation in an archetypal way. Nothing less would suffice than a reconstitution of heaven and earth in a permanent, that is, in an immortal, binding union with God. Since all creation is bound in one way or another in Christ's human nature, as it was in Adam's, it follows that when Christ's humanity becomes immortal, those united to him, as bodily members to their head, can share in the same destiny. Theodore probably found his inspiration for this in Ephesians 1:9–10: "He has made known to us the mystery of his will, according to His good pleasure that in regard to [His] plan for the fullness of the ages God recapitulated all things in Christ, those that are in the heavens and those on the earth [being united] in him," and in Colossians 1:16–17: "For in him were created all things in the heavens and on the earth, the visible and the invisible, whether thrones or lordships or rulers or authorities; all things have been created through him and for him. He himself is before all things, and in him all things are bound together."

Theodore could move from the Pauline understanding of how all things are in Christ to a realization of how Adam also recapitulates the universe in a way similar but inferior to Christ's role: "'Recapitulation' is clearly used as a brief summing up of many meanings. What he wants to say is this: the God of the universe made all creation, as it were, one body, composed of many members, rational as well as sensible orders. He fashioned, however, one living being who would claim a relationship also to the invisible natures by his soul and would be joined to [all] visible natures by [his] body. . . . He made the human being to be [His] pledge of friendship for the whole creation. For all have been united together in him" (*TEP* 1:128–29).[12] Theodore considers both Adam and Christ heads of the "body" that the universe forms: "For everything is joined together as a body because of their kinship to him." Swete describes this role well: "To restore man and through man the harmony of creation, nothing less was necessary than a reconstitution of the κόσμος; a gathering together anew of all things under a new Head, who must be at once a sinless and immortal man, and indissolubly united to God (Eph. i. 10; Col. i. 16)" (*TEP* 1:lxxxi).

Christ as the Plerôma

Theodore's thinking about the role of Christ's humanity in the salvation of the universe can also be seen in his unique interpretation of Paul's writings on the divine *plerôma*. Almost all Christian exegetes translate Ephesians 1:22 thus: "the church is his body, the *plerôma* of him who fills all in all." While the original Greek verb here for "fills" can be translated as a deponent verb with an active sense, Theodore, uniquely, translates it in the passive voice: "The church is the body 'and the fullness of that one who is filled up in all respects in all.' He did not say 'he fills all,' but that he himself 'is filled up in all'—that is, 'he is fully in all.' For he is wholly in each one because his nature is not circumscribed, and he is not divided according to any parts. Moreover, the addition whereby he said 'all in all' is necessary, showing that when he is in all, he exists wholly in each one, howsoever anyone would want to think, whether by essence or operation or virtue or power or also in any other way, because he is not circumscribed by all things and so he is seen within all things to be wholly in each one" (*TEP* 1:140–41).

Swete observes in a note that Theodore's interpretation of *plerôma* is singular among all the Fathers: "Th. here prefers the wider interpretation of

12. Theodore's remarks on "recapitulation" are drawn from his interpretation of Eph. 1:10.

πλήρωμα—'all nature as restored and reunited to God through the *homo susceptus.*' I cannot find this view in connection with the present text advanced or even alluded to by any other ancient commentator. . . . Th.'s explanation of σωματικῶς is similar . . . but extended, as his view of πλήρωμα requires, to the creation at large" (*TEP* 1:286n3). But Swete believes that the one who is said to be fully in all things is the Word, "who by virtue of His omnipresence is in all things with the fullness of His indivisible Deity" (*TEP* 1:141n2). But, as the immediate context indicates, the "he" being referred to is Christ in his human as well as his divine nature. This is the way Theodore understood it: "For it is evident that these things [God's bestowal of the divine *plerôma* and universal domination upon Christ *qua* man] pertain to the human nature which receives domination over all things by [its] union with God the Word."[13] For Theodore, it is not only the humanity of Christ that is fully in all things but also all things are *in* him because of his unique "exact" union with the Word and because all creatures are bound to his human nature. In this sense, all reality is contained in him, truly forming one "body" with and in him: "God created all creatures which came to be in diverse ways. He made all creation one body; that is, the heaven above and the earth and all the rest of the visible and the invisible beings. Therefore all these created beings are [united] among themselves and the visible ones are moved by the invisible" (*TJA*, 27/18).

Pierre Benoit agrees with Theodore's rendering of the Colossian passage.[14] After carefully examining the context, Benoit insists that not only is Theodore's interpretation plausible but that it also makes the most sense of what Paul is attempting to affirm in the overall context. After demonstrating that the *plerôma* that dwells in Christ does not reside solely in the Church or in the cosmos, Benoit asks, "What then?" He concludes: "I find there the plenitude of being, not only the plenitude of the divinity according to an interpretation which we have refuted, but also that of the cosmos, and not only the plenitude of the cosmos, as perhaps the exegesis of Theodore of Mopsuestia can be understood, but also that of the divinity. All this

13. *TJA*, 83/59.
14. Benoit, "Tête et Plérôme," 5–44. The English translations from the French are my own.

is found combined in Christ. He is God and, by his redemptive work, he assumes in himself as a new creature not only the regenerated humanity that is his body but also the entire new world that constitutes the core of this body."[15] In other words, Benoit believes that the correct way to interpret the divine *plerôma* as Paul uses the term is to see it as flowing through Christ into those belonging to the ecclesial body of Christ and the universal "body" of the cosmos.

Christ's double role as the one whose *plerôma* is present in the members of his Church and the rest of creation indicates how Theodore conceives of the union of Christ's two natures. Christ's humanity in its union with the Word serves as the true mediating bond between God and creation because his human nature is simultaneously united with all created beings and with the Word's divine nature. I discuss the Christological significance of all this in a later chapter; my principal concern here is the relationship between Christ and the created universe. For Theodore, as we have seen, all creation is bound to Christ as the members of a body to its head; the divine *plerôma* embraces "the whole creation that (Christ) has filled . . . that all creation dwells within him, i.e., is conjoined to him and is in itself a particular body [whose members are] fitted together by being bound to him."[16]

Theodore, therefore, believes that the divine *plerôma* is present in the Church and in all things: "(Paul) also calls 'the *plerôma* of God' the church and indeed also wholly [the repository of] everything, as it were, because (Christ) is both in all things and fulfills all things. This is clearly to be learned from what he appears to have said when he wrote to the Colos-

15. Ibid., 35, 37, 36. The original text is as follows: "J'y vois la Plénitude de l'être, non seulement la Plénitude de la divinité selon une interprétation que nous avons réfutée, mais encore celle du Cosmos; et non pas seulement la plenitude du Cosmos, comme le donne peut-être à entendre l'exégèse de Théodore de Mopsueste, mais aussi celle de la Divinité. C'est tout cela qui se trouve rassemblé dans le Christ. Il est Dieu et, par son oeuvre rédemptrice, il assume en lui comme Nouvelle Créature, non seulement l'Humanité regénérée qui est son Corps, mais encore tout le monde nouveau qui constitue le cadre de ce Corps."
16. *TEP* 1:286. The Latin text reads "universam creaturam repletam ab eo . . . quoniam omnis creatura in eo inhabitat, hoc est, ipsi conjuncta est, et quasi quoddam corpus in se retinet aptatum."

sians: 'He gave him to be the head over the whole church which is his body, the *plerôma* of that one who fills *(adimplet)* all things in all.' (Paul), therefore, says that it pleased God that the entire *plerôma* dwell in him, i.e., in Christ, in order to say that He approved conjoining to him all creation which has been filled up by him. . . . He reconciled all things by his death and united both those on the earth and those above in the heavens by his dying and rising. By his rising he has, in fact, shown that the promised resurrection and immortality are common to all. Everything from now on is joined for harmony, as we have just said above, and looks to him as clearly the author of this harmony. For he says 'in him.' Well did he speak thus. For he joined together all things by his death and constituted [them] in peace through that binding [of everything] to himself" (1:275–76).[17] This passage may seem to contradict in one respect what was just affirmed above about Theodore's insistence, in his commentary on Ephesians 1:23, that *"adimpletur"* is to be translated in a passive sense. However, I believe that Swete is correct when he notes that in Ephesians "L.c. *adimpletur* not only stands in the text, but is defended in the comm. (p. 142, l. 1, sq.); so that the reading of the MS. in this place must be an error, due either to the translator or to the scribes, probably to the latter" (*TEP* 1:275n14).

For Theodore, the Pauline phrase "in Christ" is meant, in addition, to indicate not merely Christ's mediating role in salvation but also his role as the *plerôma* because he is fully present in all things and all things are present in his humanity. As the head of the body that is his Church and of the "body" that is the universe, Christ recapitulates in himself all those who belong to the Church and the cosmos: "(Blessed Paul) adds: 'since all things are created in him.' He did not say 'through him' but 'in him.' For he is speaking not of the first creation but of that restoration of creation which has been accomplished in him whereby everything that had been dissolved up to then has been brought back into one gathering, just as he states in another place: 'to recapitulate everything in heaven and on earth in Christ.' . . . For the human being was fashioned from the very beginning as some living being joined by a kinship to all. . . . Therefore in our renovation

17. Theodore is commenting here on Col. 1:19–20.

whereby the interconnection of all creation is again integrated, Christ according to the flesh is our first fruits in whom the best and, as I have said, the comprehensive re-creation of all creatures will be effected. . . . Well, therefore, did he say: 'in him are created all beings,' not only because we have obtained through his accomplishments the promise of future blessings, but also since the perfect binding together of all will be preserved in him because of the divine nature dwelling [within him], so that nothing can cut us off from those things common to us" (*TEP* 1:267–69).

By "taking up" all things in himself, Christ in his humanity can be proclaimed the "head" of the universe because of the divine *plerôma* dwelling in him. He reunites the universe in a higher peaceful harmony than that under Adam: "(Paul) again says in this place 'the whole *plerôma* of the deity' [to reveal] that the entire creation was filled by him. He means by this—what was seen posited above—that all of creation dwells in him, i.e., is conjoined to him and forms, as it were, a certain well-fitted body because creation is bound to him. How unbecoming is it, therefore, to hearken to one who teaches other than what (Paul) taught about the one to whom all things are fitted and bound" (*TEP* 1:286). But, as we saw in our treatment of the Spirit's fullness of grace that Christ's humanity bestows on the members of his Church, the same can be asserted of Christ's vivifying role as the divine *plerôma* within all creation. His *plerôma* is in all and leading all in a dynamic way to their fulfillment in a new immortal heavenly existence.

If we have correctly understood Theodore's thought as elaborated above, then we can assign a deeper meaning to how Theodore would interpret the adverb "bodily" in Colossians 2:9: "all the *plerôma* of the divinity dwells bodily in him." He would understand "body" in a far broader sense than merely Christ's physical body. For him, the term would also include all those who are members of Christ's "body," embracing not only his body that is the Church but also the "body" that is the universe. Because of his union with Christ's humanity, the Word has made it possible for the whole plenitude of the divinity to dwell there. Then, because all who are bound to Christ's humanity as members of his body can share what their head has received, the divine *plerôma* can be truly found in all of creation insofar as all creation belongs to the body of Christ, each participating in the divine *plerôma* in its own measure.

Ulrich Wickert's Critique

The bonding whereby all creation is united to Adam and Christ's human nature so as to form one "body" raises two pointed questions as to ˋTheodore's source for such a viewpoint and as for what kind of "body" he means. Swete believes that the "κόσμος which Theodore identifies with Creation (Rom. viii. 19; 1 Cor. ii. 12), is regarded as an organic body, whose members are partly rational and invisible, partly visible and objects of sense. Originally (Rom. viii. 19; Eph. 1. 10), this body, notwithstanding the diversity of its component parts, was at peace with itself" (*TEP* 1:lxxx). This view is repeated in the unsigned (but doubtless Swete's) article on Theodore in *A Dictionary of Christian Biography, Literature, Sects and Doctrines:* "The Universe (ο κόσμος = η σύμπασα κτίσις) is an organic whole (ἐν σῶμα), consisting of elements partly visible and material, partly invisible and spiritual. Of this organism Man is the predestined bond."[18] Ulrich Wickert takes exception to these statements, arguing that whenever Theodore speaks about the cosmos forming one "body," he is primarily adapting to his soteriology Stoic viewpoints about the "body" of the universe and human beings as its "bond."[19]

Wickert contends that one must prove that Theodore actually regarded creation as a true organic unity. He believes that Theodore betrays no interest at all in the idea of the universe as a living organism acting according to its own inner dynamism. If true, this view would make the union too close to the Stoic world soul—something that Theodore would radically oppose because it would mean the world soul determined absolutely everything. In support of this contention Wickert points to the writings of Nemesius, an early contemporary of Theodore, on the organic unity within creation (11). Nemesius shows how the lowest elements within creation evolve to the highest, ending up in an organic whole in which all the low-

18. [Swete], "Theodorus," 943.
19. Wickert, *Studien zu den Pauluskommentaren,* 10, hereafter cited parenthetically in the text.

er members live and work in harmony for the good of all. Wickert contrasts this with Theodore's silence on such an evolution or dynamic, for he thinks that Theodore realized that these views would have no application within his synthesis.

Wickert believes that the world as a "body" means nothing other than that the universe in its entirety is a "structure" ordered in itself (13). He holds that its unity is due to a command of God and that Theodore has combined the Greek understanding of the universe with the Jewish belief in the intervention of a transcendent Creator at creation (14, 24). Theodore was seeking, as the saying goes, a wedding of Athens with Jerusalem. His universe is to be understood in the Greek sense only as a "body" that comprises and bridges two opposites, the spiritual and material worlds (27–28). It is simply the sum total of all its members that is to be taken as detached from its relationship to a creating transcendent God. Theodore resorted to this Greek understanding because of the unbridgeable chasm he perceived between God and all creation—as well as between all spiritual and material beings (13–14, 22–23). In justification Wickert quotes Theodore's statement that "(Paul) called this (body), therefore, the 'capitulation' [a gathering under one head] of all because all things are collected into one and they look to some one 'thing.'"[20]

Thus when Theodore speaks of the cosmos as one "body," Wickert is convinced that humans and nonhumans are not united by any immanent force that binds them together, as would be true if the cosmos were a living organic "being" (10–14). Rather they ought to be regarded as one "body" in a merely extrinsic sense, because God has willed that this is how the universe can function in its own created order. For Wickert, such a viewpoint enriches both the Greek and the Jewish understandings of the cosmos by melding together what is best in both frameworks. It allows each tradition to be consistent and meaningful in its own right. These worldviews are, in fact, complementary, the Jewish dealing with how God

---

20. *TEP* 130. Theodore is commenting here on Eph. 2:10: "For having been created in Christ Jesus for good works, we are his work (poiēma)." The same idea is expressed in Eph. 1:14, "For he is the one who has made both one." For Wickert's comment, see *Studien zu den Pauluskommentaren*, 16.

speaks directly to creation and the Greek with how creation can have a value in itself. Wickert also believes that Theodore has employed the Greek concept of humans as the bond of creation to further his own synthetic approach to salvation (20). He sees that Theodore has appropriated the Greek word *sundesmos* (a bond) because it fits in very well with his Christological purpose of reconciling the Jewish idea of an intervening divine Creator with the reality of all created things (18–20, 24–27). Wickert sees that this term provides Theodore with an insightful way to connect the Fall and Christ's role in redemption (25).

Another Perspective

Wickert offers a number of astute observations on Theodore's view of salvation and raises valid questions about what Theodore means when he refers to humans as the "bond" of the universe, in light of how this was understood in Stoic thought and Nemesius. I think, however, that it is unnecessary to appeal to a direct Stoic influence to understand how Theodore views the union of all creation as united in one bond and forming one "body." For one thing, Theodore is truly dedicated to the Scriptures as the source for providing God's revelation about his divine plan for salvation. While exposed to and doubtless influenced by Greek philosophical thought, Theodore would use this only as a tool to understand the Scriptures.[21]

Theodore appears to have arrived at his position regarding salvation of the universe from a literal, rational interpretation of what he thought Paul was affirming in Colossians 1:15–20. He stresses Paul's statements about Christ as the visible "image of God" in whom the heavens and the earth are bound, recapitulated and filled by the Word's divine *plerôma*. This expresses God's plan of how the heavens and the earth are to share in the future immortal state and union with God. By being recapitulated in the risen Christ's human nature, they can share in the immortality that Christ's human nature has now attained. This view appears to have awakened Theo-

21. Dewart, *Theology of Grace of Theodore*, strikes me as right on target when she states: "Theodore did not consciously use philosophy as a theological tool because he had neither the training, nor, more basically, the inclination to do so" (3).

dore to the realization that he could apply this role to Adam because of the typological relationship that Paul reveals between Adam and Christ. For if Christ is the one in whom heaven and earth are bound, then it stands to reason that Adam, as a type of Christ's human nature, must resemble Christ in this regard as a bond recapitulating the entire universe. This is confirmed by the roles that Theodore discerns Adam mirroring—in an inferior way—as the visible way whereby all other creatures can come to know and worship God. Why else would Theodore attribute these latter roles to Adam as the bond of the universe, unless he was comparing and contrasting these to the role of Christ's humanity in salvation as the mediating bond uniting creation to God?

In other words, one may argue that Paul or his disciple was influenced in his writing of Colossians and Ephesians by Stoic thought, but it is doubtful that Theodore drew directly upon Greek thought, especially given his negative attitude toward Greek philosophy. As we have observed in our treatment of his exegesis, his very caustic language berating Origen for turning to a Stoic allegorical method strongly discourages the view that he would resort to a Stoic view of how humans are the bond of the universe and how the cosmos constitutes one "body." This is especially true given that Theodore was doubtless familiar with Diodore's works (now lost) against the Greek philosophical understanding of nature. It seems unlikely, too, that Theodore would appeal to the Stoic worldview given his contempt for Greek philosophy, as we see in his statement that "(Paul) asserts that 'philosophy' is a wordy pompous teaching which is customarily made by (our) adversaries with some pretense to seduce its hearers, indicating thereby that philosophy was not true but that [their] seductive words are contrived and invented for the deception of its hearers."[22] He is also rigorous in his own judgment: "We ought to consider angels of Satan all those humans who are engaged in profane wisdom and introduce the error of paganism into the world. . . . Angels of Satan are those who in the name of philosophy present pernicious doctrines to the pagans and have corrupted the multitude to the point they do not adhere to the word of God's reli-

22. *TEP* 1:285.

gion."[23] While other fathers may have incorporated Stoic ideas and terms into their theological works, the Antiochenes, if one may judge from their angry rejection of Origen's allegorical method, seem to have stoutly resisted this trend. They were all committed to seeking theological answers primarily from the Scriptures.

What Kind of Universal "Body"?

When Theodore speaks of the whole universe as constituting "one body," does he speak metaphorically? If so, then Wickert would seem to be correct that the spiritual and the material worlds are one "body" in the sense that they constitute the universe in an extrinsic way.[24] Since Theodore could not accept that Christ and the cosmos were related to each other in a substantial organic way, which would entail pantheism or that they were joined to each other by a moral bond, he had no choice but to understand the cosmos as being one "body" in a metaphorical sense. This argument recalls that of the preceding chapter, in which we saw that Wickert maintains that Theodore understood the Church as a gathering of believers in Christ. But Theodore's vivid language about Christ's "body" in both instances does strongly imply that he was thinking of some sort of a real, "physical" unity, along the lines of an organic model. Again, much depends here on how one interprets the term "organic." Does one restrict the term to a living human being or widen it to include those members of an organization who function in an interdependent and subordinate way as a whole "body" striving for the good of its members? The latter sense can be employed in an analogous way to how a biological organism operates. This seems to be Theodore's meaning when he speaks of the kinship between the angels and the human soul and between material beings and the human body. One can argue that, just as the human soul and its body make up one organic being, so too the union of the spiritual and material worlds

---

23. *THC*, 380/381; *CH* 13.8. Another condemnation is found in *TFS*, fol. 22b/6: "It seems to me to be superfluous to bring into our midst the pagan histories, since what they teach is unprofitable. For they are in various and complicated [kinds of] error with no fundament and no true substance."

24. Wickert, *Studien zu den Pauluskommentaren*, 13.

make up one organic being, at least paradigmatically. As we noted in our discussion of Theodore's understanding of the word "as," Theodore does expect that an analogy ought not to be interpreted according to every detail but in respect to the point being emphasized. If so, his term "body" is to be taken not in the sense of a nature formed by the union of a soul with its body, or as a mere "community" that God has arbitrarily formed. It is not a community in the sense that today's social scientists envisage a "body," but in the biblical, Semitic sense whereby the members of the Jewish people consider themselves intimately committed not only to one another in a familiar, tribal, and national union, but also as bound in a covenantal relationship to Yahweh. The members of this kind of union are so connected to each other that the sin of a leader can have physical as well as spiritual repercussions for all.

Whether this kind of "organic" model was Theodore's own or one that he found in Paul is incidental. The point is that just as, existentially speaking, one can regard the soul and its body, which are two distinct realities, as one "reality," so too something similar can be said of Christ's bodily relationship to the cosmos. This is a continuation of the relationship we argued for in the previous chapter between Christ's humanity and those who are united to him as members of his body, the Church. For Theodore, the bottom line is that Scripture reveals that Christ recapitulates the spiritual and material worlds that are bound together within his human nature. Moreover, since he possesses the divine *plerôma* that enables him to be fully in all and all in him, his humanity can be said to be in all. Theodore does not develop this idea but one can carry out the analogy of the soul/body relationship by asserting that Christ's divine fullness is fully in and empowering all the members as the soul does its body.[25] Furthermore, this kind of "organic" unity helps to explain why both Adam's sin and

---

25. In his *Early Christian Doctrines*, J.N.D. Kelly discusses how Athanasius professed a similar view: "Christ's human nature was, as it were, a part of the vast body of the cosmos, and there was no incongruity in the Logos, Who animates the whole, animating this special portion of it. The paradox was rather that, while present in the body of the Incarnate, animating and moving it, He was simultaneously present everywhere else in the universe, vivifying and directing it with His life-giving power" (285).

Christ's sinless life affected the members bound to them. It is, in addition, ideal for expressing the harmony and peace that will be achieved perfectly when all creation is united in Christ and shares together with him in the immortal life that his humanity now possesses in heaven.

Wickert rejects the view that the universe is a living organic "body" on the grounds that it lacks an inner dynamism. While Theodore does not explicitly elaborate on this point, one can respond that since the spiritual and material worlds are said to be bound to human beings, they too ought to share in the vital life and growth that the Spirit bestows on the members of the body of Christ. This growth that the Spirit imparts would seem to be the dynamic element that enables the universe to expand until it reaches its fullness in Christ's immortal human nature. In his exegetical study of Colossians, Benoit addresses this point, noting that Christ is being "filled" by the world to the degree that the Church and the world grow over time progressively more and more complete. This growth cannot be static. For Christ not only commands but also nourishes, reconciles, and unifies the whole universe so that all emerge as one *plerôma*.[26]

Christ, therefore, is indeed vitally present in all things as he nourishes all, assures cohesion for all, and draws all toward a peaceful harmony in heaven. This would be due to the activity of the divine *plerôma* that is dynamically seeking, under the Spirit's impetus, to return all creation to God under the headship of Christ's humanity:

Therefore, (God) "restored" or rather "recapitulated" in Christ everything that is in heaven and on earth, making, as it were, a complete renovation and reintegration of all created beings through him. For by making the body incorrupt and impassible by means of his resurrection and returning it to its immortal soul, so that it could not from now on be separated into a corrupted state, he was seen to have restored the bond [vinculum] of friendship for the immortal [state] of the universal creation—[a bond] that is much more fully accomplished in him, with all creation looking to us for this [restoration] because God the Word dwells [within him], while the divine nature [present] in him is thought by all to be visible through this nature. Therefore he called this a "capitulation of all" because all are collect-

26. Benoit, "Tête et Plérôme," 43, 44.

ed into one and look to this one by being in harmony among themselves. For in the past the Maker had this intention and fashioned everything from the beginning for this purpose that He now fulfills with much ease in these matters regarding Christ. This, however, will take place in the future age when the rest of humans and rational powers will look to him, as divine law demands, and obtain harmony and a firm peace among themselves.[27]

Theodore acknowledges that God's mysterious plan for the salvation of all creation is to be accomplished through and in Christ's human nature. He develops the Pauline idea that both Adam and Christ are the heads of two kinds of existence, Adam being the head of a mortal existence that all of creation share because all are bonded in his nature, and Christ the first born to immortal existence because, though sinless, he died unjustly for others and has enabled all created beings to share his newly acquired immortal human nature. All who are bound by the same nature also share in the effects of Adam's and Christ's free human actions, as do all the members of a body as a result of what their heads do. All humans and those other spiritual and material creatures united to them through their soul and body remain mortal because of Adam's sin, while those humans who are bound to Christ as members of his body through baptism, and all others who are recapitulated as members of Christ's universal "body," possess, at least in a typical potential way, immortality. This latter state will be fulfilled in heaven, when all things in heaven and on earth will become fully and harmoniously one "body" under the human headship of Christ's humanity who unites all, so that they can share in his "exact" union with the Word.

Besides being the source for acquiring immortal life, Christ's humanity possesses the divine *plerôma* and enables those who constitute one "body" with his humanity to both share and grow in the spiritual benefits that the Spirit distributes through Christ in his humanity. When this unity is attained in heaven, there will also be a perfect organic harmony and peace, where all creation will be truly one. As such, both on earth and in heaven Christ's humanity becomes the consummate mediating partner for all cre-

27. *TEP* 1:130–31.

ation. Because Christ is both truly divine and truly human, existing in one common *prosôpon*, he serves as the true mediator between God and all creation. For Theodore, this is the archetypal state that Adam anticipated in a typical way when he served at the beginning of creation as the head and bond of the universe. In brief, what we have just sketched is the integrated synthetic way Theodore has skillfully woven his typical/archetypical outlook into his theological understanding of God's plan for the salvation of all created beings. We turn now to consider how Christ, in addition to being the mediating bond for all those bound to his body, also serves in his humanity as the visible "image of the invisible God" to all creation.

5. CHRIST'S SALVIFIC ROLE AS GOD'S PERFECT IMAGE

U P TO THIS POINT we have examined how Theodore considers Christ's humanity's twin roles in
salvation as the head of the body that is his
Church and as the mediating bond who recapitulates and reunites all creation with his Father. Both roles exemplify how
the baptized and the whole universe are related to Christ's
humanity in some sort of a bodily, quasi-organic union. We
turn now to consider how Theodore views Christ's role as the
perfect, visible "image of God."[1] This role sums up some major points we have already treated, especially in the way the

---

1. Five studies are noteworthy for their treatment of this issue. They
are August Dorner, *The History of the Development of the Doctrine of the
Person of Christ*, 5 vols. (Edinburgh: Clark, 1863–66); Devreese, *Essai sur
Théodore de Mopsueste*, 13; Norris, *Manhood and Christ*, 140–48; Nabil
el-Khoury, "Der Mensch als Gleichnis Gottes: Eine Untersuchung zur Anthropologie des Theodor von Mopsuestia," *Oriens Christianus* 74 (1990):
62–71; and McLeod, *Image of God*.

idea of "image" is present in the relationship between a type and its archetype and in the way that Christ's humanity serves as the bond of the universe. It highlights, moreover, how Theodore differs in significant ways from his fellow Antiochenes over what "image" means and whether it applies to women as well as to men.

I begin with a consideration of what Theodore says about "image" in general, then about Adam and Eve as the "image of God" and the Fall's effect upon Adam's role as "image." I then inquire into how Theodore considers Christ *qua* man to be the "perfect image." His interpretation differs notably from that embraced by Diodore, John Chrysostom, and Theodoret, which shows how the Antiochenes can apply the same exegetical principles to reach varying conclusions. To further explicate his meaning, I provide passages from Narsai, a fifth-century Syrian theologian, who saw Theodore as the preeminent interpreter for the East Syrian Church. I also point out the parallels in the ways Adam and Christ in the flesh each function as God's "image." This will exemplify once again how Theodore understands type and archetype. Then, since Theodore speaks of "image" in one of his *Catechetical Homilies* as the ways humans can be said to *imitate* God's spiritual manner of acting, we need to reconcile this with the explanation of how "image" exemplifies Christ's functional roles in salvation. I conclude with a consideration of whether Theodore maintains that women are also God's "images." All these points about Theodore's understanding of the "image of God" will assist us in grasping what he means when he speaks about the union of Christ's two natures in one *prosôpon*.

The Meaning of "Image" in General

One of the most enigmatic passages in Scripture concerns the meaning of how Adam and Christ in the flesh are to be interpreted as the "image of God." Most fathers follow a tradition (with at least Neoplatonist undertones) that situates this "image" as residing in the human *nous*, or highest rational part of the soul. According to this way of conceiving "image," humans can image God only in spiritual ways because of God's transcendent nature. The concept is based on the idea that the *logos* of the rational soul is similar to God's *Logos*. In such a framework, the Father is viewed as the archetype, the Son as his image, and human beings as created "according to the Son's or the Word's image." Then, following the Neoplatonic belief that humans can share in the nature of the One while still maintaining their own identity, some fathers took the term "image" to be the dynamic component within the human person that enables one to grow in one's spiritual relationship to God. "Image," therefore, not only signifies how a human being can be declared to be like God but also indicates the divinizing process whereby a person can grow spiritually in God's divine life. The problem with this approach is that it implies that the human soul images only the Word as Son and not God as Triune. In addition, Diodore, John Chrysostom, and Theodoret all reject this view, agreeing with Theodore that "image" must refer to the whole human being. They differ with Theodore, however, by understanding "image" as the authority that God has granted men to rule over the material creation and women.[2]

While it may seem logical to conclude that a human being can truly image God only in a purely spiritual way, Theodore, like all the Antiochenes, insisted that an "image" by its nature must be visible and must be applied to the whole human person. He cites passages in Scripture where "image" pertains to human beings: "I am dumbfounded, however, by those who attribute this (image) to the divine nature and do not see that Blessed Moses also says of a human being that 'God made this one to His image,' and likewise blessed Paul that 'man ought not to cover his head, being the image and the visible glory of God.' For this would never have been said of human beings, if it were properly [said only] of the divine nature. Moreover, these [who hold image to be spiritual] have not seen that every image, as long as it is seen, shows what is not seen. It is impossible, therefore, that an image be so fashioned that is not seen. For it is clear that images are ordinarily made for this [purpose] by their makers: either for honor or affection, so that they may be a [source of] remembrance of those not seen for those nevertheless able to see."[3]

2. See McLeod, *Image of God*, 58–61, 78–80.
3. *TEP* 1:262–63.

Adam and Eve as God's Image

When God created the various elements of creation, he uttered the simple command "Let it be." But God acted uniquely when he created Adam and Eve, exclaiming, "Let us make humans in our image." Theodore assumes that this is a divine hint from God that he is more than one—a hint whose full meaning about the Trinity became known only with Christ: "For I say with assurance that the rational and invisible natures also acquired knowledge of this [the Trinity] at the beginning by means of the words that God spoke aloud. A [more] accurate understanding, however, came to them at that time when Christ our Lord conveyed this [full knowledge about the Trinity] to the Apostles. . . . The reason why He uttered the phrase 'according to' in His declaration is that 'according to' [points] to one Maker. One can assert this from a close reckoning [of the context]. He also then attached [to this the phrase] 'according to our image.' He did not say 'to my image' but 'to our image,' additionally to confirm the hint present in this [phrase] 'let us make.' 'He said' indicates one nature and 'let us make' the three Persons in which the divine Nature is known."[4] Thus Adam's creation in God's "image" reveals one of his main roles, namely, imaging who God is as triune.

Besides revealing his triune nature in the Genesis passage, God is emphatic that other creatures must respect his "image" as being at the center of creation and the "means" whereby they can know and honor him as their Creator (as we saw in the last chapter) by their caring duties for human beings. Theodore brings this out when he compares God's creation of the universe to a powerful king's foundation of a new city: "If some king, after having constructed a mighty city and adorned it with numerous and varied works, ordered upon the completion of everything that his image, having been fashioned the greatest and most remarkable, be set up in the middle of the entire city as proof of his founding of the city, the image of the king who built the city would necessarily be venerated, with all in the city confessing their gratitude to their city's founder for having given them

4. *TFS*, fol. 27a/13–14.

such a [fine] place to live. So also the Artisan of creation has made the whole cosmos, embellishing it with diverse and varied works and at the end established a human being to serve as the image for his household, so that all creation would render their honor due to God by their care for and veneration toward him."[5] As the final clause points out, Theodore grasped how humans, as God's image, have unparalleled prominence within all of creation and serve as the medium whereby other creatures can glorify God by fulfilling human needs.

Theodore also connects the honor that humans enjoy as God's image to the role they play as the bond *(sundesmos)* of the universe: "He made known why He fashioned the human being after everything else to be the outstanding living being and then completed all creation according to his will by forming this one in whom all of creation shall be bound and have access to their Creator through this man by the actions done on his behalf."[6] The reference to the "one in whom all creation shall be bound" is, as we saw in the last chapter, initially Adam: "He also made the human being at the end of [His] creating all beings, fashioning him as His image and uniting all creation in him" (*TFS*, fol. 29b/19). In fact, a human being's importance in creation is centered in the fact that it is through Adam as God's "image" that all other creatures have access to God: "He shows by repeating his statement that the human being is the most important being in that he is [created] in God's image. . . . So he wrote here 'God made him in His image' to indicate that this one is most important because of his constitution wherein all beings are collected, in order that they might have access to God through him as the image of God, when they fulfill the laws decreed here regarding their service to him. They are reconciled to the Legislator by [their] care for this one. For since God needs nothing and is invisible, they offer the honor due Him by [being] useful to him who is in need and visible to all" (fol. 28a/15). Theodore, therefore, combines the roles of "image" and "bond" of the universe together, not in the sense that they are identical but that they overlap and elide functionally within one being.

5. Theodore of Mopsuestia, "L'homme créé 'à l'image de Dieu': quelques fragments grecs unédits de Théodore de Mopsueste," ed. and trans. Francoise Petit, *Le Muséon* 100 (1987): 276.

6. *TFS*, fol. 29a/18.

We see the same outlook expressed in Narsai, who promoted Theodore's thought among the East Syrians in the fifth century. First, he agrees that "image" applies to the whole human being: "The Creator willed to call the (soul) and the body His image."[7] Like Theodore, Narsai envisages image as connected with Adam's role as the bond of the universe: "(The Creator) fashioned and skillfully made a double vessel. A visible body and a hidden soul—one human being. He depicted the power of His creatorship in him as in an image: mute beings in his body and rational beings in the structure of his soul."[8] For Narsai, Adam's image is also the conduit through whom other creatures can manifest their love for God by caring for humankind: "(The Creator) has exalted His image with the name of image, in order to bind all (creatures) in him, so that they might [thus] come to love [Him] by knowing Him through having knowledge of His image."[9] Finally Narsai brings out even more clearly than the extant texts of Theodore the relationship between Christ and Adam, namely, that Adam is an "image" in a secondary sense and Christ the true "image": "(The Creator) called (Adam) an image of His majesty in a secondary sense. For everything created is vastly inferior to the divine essence."[10] And, in a more specific way: "(The Creator) called the first Adam by the name of image in a secondary sense. The image is in reality is the Messiah, the second Adam. Thus 'Come, let us make a human being in our image' was fulfilled when the Creator took His image and made it a dwelling place for his honor. The promises to Adam came to pass in reality in the Messiah."[11]

7. Narsia, *Narsai doctoris syri homiliae et carmina*, ed. A. Mingana, 2 vols. (Mosul, 1905), 2:251.

8. Narsai, *Narsai's Metrical Homilies on the Nativity, Epiphany, Passion, Resurrection and Ascension*, ed. and trans. Frederick McLeod, Patrologia Orientalis 40, fasc. 1 (Turnhout: Brepols, 1979), 38/39. The same idea is expressed in Narsai, *Homélies de Narsaï sur la creation*, ed. and trans. P. Gignoux, Patrologia Orientalis 34/3–4 (Turnhout: Brepols, 1968), 534/535. "Come, let us make a reasonable human being in our image, and let us bind all to the kinship of his soul and his body. Let him be akin to the heavenly beings by the life of his soul [and] also a neighbor to bodily beings by [his] bodily structure." See also 588/89.

9. Narsai, *Narsai doctoris syri homiliae*, 2:239.

10. Narsai, *Narsai's Metrical Homilies*, 38/39.

11. Narsai, *Homélies sur la creation*, 602/03.

Robert Devreese's Interpretation

Robert Devreese presents a notably different understanding of "image" in Theodore from that outlined above. He depends upon one section from Theodore's *Catechetical Homilies* in which humans are said to "imitate" God but in very inferior ways: "Because we have come to be in the image of God, we consider, when reflecting on what is proper to us as an image, that what is said of God is more sublime."[12] The reason for this is, of course, the transcendence of God. This means that God needs a visible image in order to reveal to others the cause and purpose of their creation. "Because we have then come to be in the image of God, we agree with that is affirmed about God is on reflection more than what is peculiarly ours as image. . . . it is possible to conceive of God from what is properly ours. For since it is thereby clear that there exists a great difference between us and God, it is necessary to consider carefully the divine nature and the works [done] by Him."[13]

Theodore offers examples of how humans image God's activity. Devreese sums up these similar activities under four categories: (1) human beings share in a limited way in the power of creation, possessing a *mimesis* of the divine creativity; (2) humans, like God, can conceive from one end of the world to the other, while still remaining in one place, reflecting the indivisible, immanent presence of God to his entire creation; (3) the human prerogatives both to rule and pass judgment relfect those of the divine; (4) human life and reason in their relation to the soul supply a reflection of the Trinity in that the soul has two powers, life and reason, in virtue of which it lives and vivifies the body.[14] Richard Norris Jr. makes the same point in a more general philosophical way: "To say of man that he is in the image of God is to say, essentially, that in a human being's nature and in his activities one may discover various clues or aspects of the reality of the Divine Nature itself. . . . The relationship is one of *representation* founded on *resemblance;* the resemblance in question is defined externally, without reference to the themes of participation or natural affiliation."[15]

12. *THC,* 48/49; *CH* 2:16.   13. Ibid.
14. Devreese, *Essai sur Théodore de Mopsueste,* 14–15.
15. Norris, *Manhood and Christ,* 142.

Can Devreese's presentation of "image" be reconciled with what I have argued above are the roles of God's image in salvation, namely, to reveal in a visible way the existence of God, to be the bond uniting creatures to God and among themselves, and to serve as the way that creatures can offer glory to God by caring for humans? If the latter interpretation is defensible, why is there no allusion to it in the *Catechetical Homilies?* Perhaps the answer is simply that the homilies belong, as Gerber suggests, to a period around 392, that is, prior to his commentaries on Genesis and the Pauline letters, especially Colossians and Ephesians.[16] Theodore may have recognized at this later period how Adam as God's image is able to typify Christ's roles in salvation as highlighted in these later epistles. For, as I have pointed out, a type is similar to—in this sense it imitates—its archetype. Whether this is true or not, Theodore's main concern in remarks on "image" as an "imitation" is to show how humans can be said to act like God but in completely inferior ways that do provide some analogical knowledge of God's transcendent nature.

One of Theodore's surviving fragments may supply the answer to the different meanings of image: "Rightly then has (Moses) also added the [term] 'likeness' to [the phrase] 'according to the image.' When indeed God bestowed on a human being the function of image, [it is,] as I have said, for such a reason that He has also rightly given him [ways] to imitate divine attributes but [in a manner] far inferior to [His] substance and to the extent that [every] image is inferior to its archetype's image and yet bearing imitations and reflections of that One's majesty."[17] The last part of the quotation bears out what I have asserted above about the way a type can image its archetype. But what is noteworthy here is that Theodore links the concept of "image" to that of "likeness." "Likeness" seems to refer to the ways human beings imitate God's way of acting, for example, "We reflect and imitate in a certain way this power of critical discernment of (human) acts, insofar as we function as [God's] image, which is in fact far inferior to its archetype. But it suffices in a certain imitative way to lead us to perceive the grandeur of God's attributes in relation to this."[18] In other words,

16. Theodore of Mopsuestia, *Theodor und das Nicänum,* 266.
17. Theodore, "L'homme créé," 276.   18. Ibid., 287.

Theodore appears to understand "image" as a type or symbol and "likeness" as providing some limited knowledge of the *imitative* ways that humans are like God in an inferior, analogous way. But it is because humans are made in God's "image" that they can be said to be like God in similar but secondary ways. "Likeness," therefore, is one aspect of the typological roles that Adam as God's "image" plays within creation.

Sin's Distortion of the Image

Granted that Theodore looks upon Adam as playing a critical and central role in creation and salvation, what happens then when Adam sins? Does he relinquish his image? This seems to be suggested in catechetical homily 12: "Our Lord God made a human being in His image from the earth and honored him in many other ways. He then conferred especially on this one (Adam) the honor of being named His image whereby a human being alone is called God and a son of God. If he were discerning, he would have remained with the One who was responsible for all the benefits that he truly possessed. But he accepted and completed the image of the accuser who had risen as a rebel against God and wanted to usurp the honor that belongs to Him."[19] Thus, while Adam seems here to take on an "image" of the devil, he does not lose his "image of God." For Christ in his humanity is the true archetypal image who truly reveals God and unites creation to God. Adam may tarnish his typical image, but he cannot destroy it, because the roles assigned to him are fulfilled in Christ. "Image" belongs to human nature as such because it is Christ's humanity that is united to the Word such that his humanity uniquely makes visible the divinity of the Word, binds all creation within his humanity and then to God, and can receive the worship due God.

Adam, however, becomes a total contradiction when he sins and remains mortal. He no longer serves as an image of faithfulness to God but as an image of the rebel Satan. Nor can he act as a permanent bond uniting creation in harmony with God. For death has begun now to separate the body from its soul, with the result that humanity is no longer a sign of

19. *THC*, 332–34/333–35; *CH* 12:8.

peace and harmony with God but one of disintegration and disharmony. When the bond between soul and body is broken, so too are sundered the soul's bonds with the spiritual and material worlds. The rest of creation no longer possesses a living visible pledge of God's friendship. Sin, therefore, has not only a personal consequence but also a communal and a cosmic one. To reverse this human failure, Theodore believed it was necessary that Jesus also had to be tempted and had to prove himself totally faithful to God's will (with the Spirit's special graces). His sinlessness made him worthy to be God's perfect image and, because God foreknew this to be so, suitable to be united to the Word and to become the true mediator uniting all of creation to God. Moreover, he exemplifies to all others how everyone ought to use his or her freedom in order to achieve an immortal union with God in a heavenly life like unto what his human nature now possesses: "We were from the beginning [made] in God's image. Yet we lost this honor by our failure, but we have received the honor of a [restored] image by the gift of God, and because of this we have become immortal and we [will] dwell in heaven."[20]

Christ's Humanity as God's Image

From all appearances, Theodore derived his rather distinctive understanding of "image" from Colossians 1:13–20. Here the Son is said to be the visible "image of the invisible God" in whom all things visible and invisible have been created through him and for him, with all things being bound[21] in him who is the head of the body, the Church. As we saw in the previous chapter, Theodore argues that Paul is speaking here of Christ in the flesh. Having made peace through the blood of his cross, Christ *qua* man has reconciled and recapitulated all creatures in himself. In this passage, the writer of Colossians is highlighting the various roles Christ plays as God's visible image: "And because the divine nature is not seen in a visible way, (Paul) reveals it to human beings according to the ability of his

---

20. Ibid., 356/357; *CH* 12:21.

21. Literally, "And he is before all things and all things *sunestēkev* in him." The verb connotes such senses as "consist," "set together," "combine," "associate," "unite," "put together," "organize," "joined with," and "stand with."

viewers. But under what form then do we expect the divine nature will be revealed? (Paul) makes us know by adding 'the Savior Jesus Christ.' He points to this corporeal man and he clearly indicates that the divine nature reveals itself by his coming and his appearance."[22] Theodore also maintains that those who are seeking to be united to God must conform not directly to the Word as such but to his own visible image, Christ *qua* man: "And those who are conformed to him according to that likeness they have from God, they rightly recognize him to be the first born in relation to themselves inasmuch as he is super-eminent for this reason. For he did not say there that they are 'conformed to His Son' but to the 'image of His Son' by clearly speaking of the image of His Son as being a visible nature."[23] Theodore would be strongly opposed, therefore, to any view that implies that it is the Word to whom one must be conformed. Rather it is to the assumed man who is the visible image of the Word.

Theodore holds that the reason why Christ serves as the visible image of God is that the Word of God is united "exactly" with his humanity. This indwelling has enabled Christ's humanity to image the divine nature to others. "Well did he add 'invisible' [to the phrase 'who is the invisible image of God'], not because God is visible but for the manifestation of his majesty. However, if we see that [God's] invisible nature [is present] in (Christ's humanity) as His image, in that he is united to God the Word and will judge the whole world when he appears, as is right, according to his own nature. When he will come in great glory from heaven in the future age, he holds the title of 'image' for us because clearly we all infer that the divine nature, whose image he is, is to be assigned the magnitude of what is being accomplished. For we do not consider the authority for his judgment [as belonging] to the visible nature."[24] One can easily speculate here that the reason why Christ's humanity can be shown worship is on account of his role as image. If he is the visible eschatological judge because of his union with the Word, the same can be said of his mediating revelatory role as the perfect "image of the invisible Word." As such, one adores

---

22. *THC*, 184/185; *CH* 7:15.   23. *TEP* 1:264.
24. Ibid., 1:261–62.

the Word who is hidden within Christ's visible humanity. Just as the outward appearance of a person reveals his inner nature, the same can be said of Christ's visible appearance in relation to the hidden Word.

In the following passage, Theodore exemplifies how Christ in the flesh fulfills a cultic as well as a revelatory role as the visible "image of God" because of the way the divine and human natures are united as one in him:

> Christ fulfills the role of image in two ways. Those who love certain individuals often set up their images after death and deem this as providing them with solace for their death. By looking at their image, they think that they see, as it were, that one who is neither seen nor present, thereby appeasing the flame and force of their desire. Also those who have the emperor's images [set] within their cities seem to honor by cult and adoration those [emperors] who are not present, as if they were present and witnessing all this. Both of these [purposes] are fulfilled in the case of Christ. For all his followers, who pursue virtue and promptly fulfill what is due God, love him and greatly honor him. Even though the divine nature is unseen, they still manifest love to the one seen by all. For they all think of Him as being seen by means of him and being always present to him. They fully honor him as [God's] imperial image, seeing that the divine nature is, as it were, in him and is seen in him. For if the Son is indeed the One said to be dwelling within him, then the Father is also with him. For everyone believes that He is altogether inseparable from the Son. And the Spirit is not absent in that He came to him in the form of an anointing and is always with the assumed one.[25]

In other words, to look upon Christ's humanity is to see not only the Word but also the Father and his Spirit, and to worship Christ as God's visible image is to adore the triune God.

Narsai illuminates how Theodore must have thought about how and why divine worship can be shown to Christ as God's visible image: "Angels and human beings will be united together by the yoke of his love, and they will celebrate him as the image of the transcendent King. . . . They continually worship in the temple of his body that One who is hidden in him and they offer therein the pure sacrifices of their minds. In the haven of his body come to rest the impulses of their thoughts, as they become worn out

25. Theodore, "L'homme créé," 274–75. My translation.

in [their] search for the incomprehensible hidden One. For this reason, the Fashioner of the universe chose him from the universe, that by his visible body he might satisfy the need of the universe. A creature needs to search out what is hidden and discover the meaning and intent of what is secret. Because it is impossible that the nature of the hidden One appear in an open way, He limited their inquiries to His visible image."[26]

Though much of Theodore's writing on Christ's roles as God's primary image is cryptic and full of comments made in passing, it does reflect the roles that Theodore has assigned to Adam. In a passage that is corrupted, Theodore alludes to how Adam's role as image typifies Christ's. The text begins, "the new creation is much more important than the first state. And so we hold as true that the second creation is [more excellent] than the first. But if this is not [so]—and it is impious to think and speak otherwise—we are clearly convinced that in the past we were created in the name of that one in whom we receive restoration at the beginning—that one in whom it appears we first came to be in accordance with His power and His wisdom." As we seen above, Narsai is more explicit on this point: "(The Creator) called the first Adam by the name of image in a secondary sense. The image is in reality Christ, the Second Adam."[27]

26. Narsai, *Narsai's Metrical Homilies*, 176–77.

27. Narsai, *Homélies sur la creation*, 602/603. I have translated from the Syriac text. We see this same view also in Irenaeus, who regards Adam as imaging the incarnate Word and being made on the model of the Christ who was to come. For Irenaeus, the aim of the Incarnation was to unite God and humanity and bring them into communion. Irenaeus believes that it was only when the Word became flesh that the Word as God's invisible image became visible: "For in times long past, it was *said* that man was created after the image of God, but it was not [actually] *shown;* for the Word was yet invisible, after whose image man was created. Wherefore also he did not easily lose the similitude. When, however, the Word of God became flesh, He confirmed both of these: for He both showed forth the image truly, since He became Himself what was His image; and He reestablished the similitude after a sure manner, by assimilating man to the invisible Father through means of the visible Word." Irenaeus, "Adversus Haereses," ed. Alexander Roberts and James Donaldson, vol. 1 of *Ante-Nicene Fathers*, 5.16.2. One cannot assert that Theodore is dependent here upon Irenaeus, as Theodore differs with Irenaeus as to the meaning of the phrase "according to likeness." But they both understand "image" as referring to Christ as the human visible expression of the invisible Word. Both regard Christ's human nature in its union with the Word's divinity as acting as the perfect visible image that draws all creation to knowledge of God.

One may ask whether Theodore is projecting onto Paul his own views of the roles of Adam and Christ's humanity as God's image, or whether they are really present in the text. From what we have seen, Theodore has found a basis for these in Paul and has carried out his thought in a logical and deductive way. I believe that Greer is right when he remarks that "Theodore managed to avoid to a great extent reading his own assumptions into the text"[28] and, on the question of "image," that "There is a subtle shifting from man as the corporate image to man as an individual, and eventually to Christ, who embodies both the individual and corporate aspects."[29] In other words, Theodore grasped how Christ's human nature plays an individual as well as a corporate role as the visible "image of God." In addition to revealing God to others, Christ in his humanity also binds all creation in a harmonious union with God. He can mediate between God and the cosmos because as the Christ he is both divine and a creature.

In summary, Theodore understands the term "image" as not merely pointing to another reality which it resembles in an inferior way but also as serving as a true religious symbol, somewhat in the sense that Paul Tillich discusses, as pointing to another reality and participating in its power and dignity.[30] But Theodore understands Christ's humanity's role as a symbolic "image" as being unique. For the reality of the Word is not beyond and outside his humanity but dwells within it, as we shall see, as the soul resides within its body in such a way that they both form one true "person." For this reason, Christ *qua* man reveals the actual intent of God because of his functional role as God's visible "image" within creation. As such, he is able to receive worship as well as exercise full divine power over all those in heaven and the earth. We have noted the entrusting of similar roles, but in a lesser degree, to Adam at creation; the principal exception is that creatures are to give glory to God by fulfilling Adam's needs, whereas they worship God through Christ as God's true "image" in a true sacramental sense. When Theodore connects Christ's humanity's role as image with his image as the one who binds and recapitulates the cosmos within his hu-

---

28. Greer, *Theodore of Mopsuestia*, 20.
29. Ibid., 21.
30. See Paul Tillich, *The Dynamics of Faith* (New York: Harper, 1957), 42.

man nature, it reinforces the belief that Theodore has synthesized into one these two independent views. The source for this is, as I have argued, Colossians 1, where Christ is proclaimed the visible "image of God" in whom the divine *plerôma* dwells and who recapitulates the spiritual and the material worlds "in a bodily way," as a head is united to all the members of its body.

Women as God's Image

Many fathers have considered men *qua* males as the ones created as the "image of God." Diodore, John Chrysostom, and Theodoret upheld this view, believing that "image" refers to the authority that God bestowed upon Adam over material creation and Eve.[31] They were doubtless influenced by Paul's statement in 1 Corinthians 11:7 about man (*qua* male) being the "image of God" and woman the "glory of man"[32] and Genesis 3:16, where Adam is said to be Eve's master. They took both as clear revelations that God intended to appoint males as the sole heads of their families. This view was undoubtedly confirmed by the patriarchical attitude of their own day, which insisted that a woman's duty was to be submissive to her husband. Theodore's position on this point is clouded, however. For, on the one hand, he maintains: "(Paul) said that woman is the 'glory' [of man]. But he did not attribute 'image' to what is obscure since 'glory' refers to 'obedience' and 'image' to 'rule.'"[33] Theodore echoes this in another passage: "(Paul) spoke of a wife as [her husband's] glory. He did not add 'image' because it is not clear [how this could be], seeing that 'glory' looks to a [submissive] response and 'image' to [that one with] principal power."[34]

---

31. For a treatment of these views, see McLeod, *Image of God*, 43–85.

32. Paul seems to be arguing here from Gen. 1:27 and 2:22–23. Since Eve was formed from Adam's side to be his helper, she reflects his glory as the representative of God's majesty. In his commentary on "The First Letter to the Corinthians," *The Jerome Biblical Commentary* (Englewood Cliffs, N.J.: Prentice-Hall, 1968), Richard Kugelman raises the question whether "*exousia* (power) is used in 1 Cor. 10 because of a similarity between the Aram words for veil and power. The context seems to impose the meaning 'sign of authority' or 'submission to authority,' but the use of *exousia* with such a signification in unknown" (51:69).

33. Theodore of Mopsuestia, *Pauluskommentare,* 188.

34. Ibid.

He makes this distinction again when he explains why a woman ought to keep her head covered: "Whenever a male covers his head, he dishonors his head, as he is a head as Christ is. Whenever a woman prays with her head uncovered, she too dishonors her husband, her head, by secretly undercutting his own honor by aiming to be the principal head. In many official documents[35] there exists a prescription [requiring a woman] to wear a hat on her head, in order to signify thereby her subordination to her husband."[36] Such a viewpoint, equating "image" with "authority," seems similar to that of Diodore, John Chrysostom, and Theodoret, who interpreted "image" as signifying the authoritative role men exercise over material creation and women.

Theodore, however, is faced with an exegetical dilemma. Because he understands the term "image" as referring to the whole human nature, he must logically assert that a woman is also created in God's "image." Theodore explicitly affirms that when the author of Genesis spoke about God fashioning "man," he meant not a man *qua* male but a human being as such: "Thus also when pondering upon the word of God, (Moses) interpreted: 'He made the human being' in a general sense, namely that it refers in a generic sort of way to man and woman together. For after he said in the narrative account that 'God made a human being in the image of God,' he added that 'He made them male and female,' thereby [indicating] that the generic nature is being designated.' [He said this] not rashly but because they had not come to be masculine and feminine at the same time. Here he had to affirm that 'He made them male and female.' For they had come to be in a separate, not in the same, way. He is thus affirming that, even though their coming-to-be differs in accordance with the will of their Maker, the two of them are still one entity and one nature, despite the fact that they are male and female."[37]

Theodore is then faced with the perplexing problem of explaining in a

35. It is not clear from the text what Theodore means by the word *antigraphois*. It primarily denotes the copies of an edition or a certified official document. It may be alluding to what were accepted versions of Paul's letter to the Corinthians.

36. Theodore, *Pauluskommentare*, 187.

37. *TFS*, 28 a–b/16.

literal way Paul's statement from Corinthians. Since he is committed to a faithful interpretation of all Scripture as inspired, he must seek a rational explanation that makes sense. The answer may lie in the ways in which he contrasts Adam and Christ *qua* human as the heads of those united with them in mortality and immortality. He could not include Eve as the head of mortal existence, seeing that she was fashioned after Adam. This would also run counter to the balanced contrast that he saw existing between Adam and Christ *qua* man as the heads of mortality and immortality. Theodore nevertheless saw that Eve shares with Adam in the roles that belong to "image," as she shares the same human nature, though in a subordinate way, like the rest of creation, because she was fashioned after him. Only Adam and the assumed man are the heads; all others are members of their "bodies."

Further evidence of Theodore's position on the confusion he saw in Paul's statement appears in the writings of Išoʿdad of Merv,[38] a ninth-century Syriac exegete who is now acknowledged as a committed disciple of Theodore. To the question whether women were created as "images of God," he writes: "It is the male whom Scripture calls the image. [It is] not that a woman is not the image but Scripture attributes it to a male, since it is to him that the good things of nature have come, seeing that he was created first. As the Apostle says, 'A man must not cover his head because he is the image etc.' Yet just as a man and a woman are one body, a woman is equally included with him under this term."[39] This seems to be Theodore's position as well. It suggests, furthermore, that Theodore regarded the terms "image" and "head of the body" as overlapping with each other but not identical. Eve would be an "image of God" *qua* member of the "body" of which Adam was the head. Like all others, she serves in a subordinate role to Adam, whose actions affect the good of the whole body. This seems borne out by Theodore's statement that "This [verse from 1 Corinthians 11:3] wants to say that we advance from Christ to God from whom he is

38. Išoʿdad of Merv, *Commentaire d' Išoʿdad of Merv sur l'Ancien Testament*, I. Genèse, trans. C. Van den Eynde, Corpus Scriptorum Christianorum Orientalium 156/Syr. 75 (Louvain: Durbecq, 1955).

39. Ibid., 155.

and from the male to Christ. For it is from him [we have] a second existence according to whose resurrection we will also be all incorruptible on account of [our] sharing in the grace of the Spirit [dwelling] in him. For we who are liable to change hold Adam [to be] the head from whom we have taken [our] existence. But since we have become impassible we hold Christ as [our] head from whom we have [our] existence as impassible beings. Likewise [the verse] states that [there is] also [a difference] from a wife to her husband since she has her existence from him."[40]

Note that when Theodore explains why he thinks a woman ought to be quiet in church, he asserts that it is for the common good. This means that a woman as a member of the body of Christ has to be sensitive to and struggle for the benefit of the entire body: "Then to interpret more clearly his [last] statement, (Paul) adds: 'I do not, however, permit a woman to teach or to have authority over her husband. Rather [she is] to be silent.' It is evident that he is adding what was then being done for the common good—namely, that it was not fitting for women to teach in the church. Such a prescription, however, was necessary at that time, as women were divinely inspired prophetesses, [some] of whom seemed to have exhibited a great deal of confidence [in their right] to speak out regarding the common good. So it was that those who ought to be looking after what was advantageous for others in [their] households were of necessity being instructed not to abuse [their] spiritual gift by causing a disturbance at church. He says these things, therefore, as I have said, for what will enhance the common good. For in [this] part of the epistle, he was apparently speaking at length about what was most appropriate for the common good, by stressing at length that it is not proper within a general gathering for women to teach rather than to be silent."[41]

These statements suggest a kind of unity in which the members work in their own ways for the good of the communal body. The context seems to indicate that Theodore recognized the charism of women to speak out, but thought they ought to be silent for the common good so as not the

40. Theodore, *Pauluskommentare,* 187.
41. *TEP* 2:93–94.

threaten Church unity. A woman is thus subordinate to community leaders. But this does not mean that Theodore saw women as inferior to men by nature. For they possess the same nature and form one corporate body with no distinction between men and women. This idea is forcefully expressed in Galatians 3:27–28: "For all of you who are baptized in Christ have clothed yourself with Christ. There is neither Jew nor Greek, there is neither slave nor free person, there is not male and female; for you are all one in Christ Jesus." While all are one in Christ and work for the common good, this does not mean that if and when the situation changes, the common good always requires that women be silent.

Theodore's thought on the "image of God" is a rich teaching that seems to date from his later years. It seems quite likely that Theodore derived his understanding of the "image of God" from a literal and rational approach to Colossians 1 and applied this to Genesis. He discerned that the phrase "image of God" must refer to the way Christ's humanity visibly manifests the transcendent Word. Since Genesis applies "image of God" to Adam as well as to Christ in the flesh, Theodore looks upon Adam, as Paul affirms, to be a type of Christ *qua* man. As such, Adam must fulfill his criteria for a true type. He is, in Theodore's understanding of Genesis, as historical as Jesus Christ, whose relationship to him is sanctioned by Scripture. So too are they both similar to each other, but Christ is the archetype who is the perfect "image." In other words, Theodore took what he saw to be the roles that Paul attributed to Christ in Colossians and assigned them to Adam. Like Christ, Adam is the visible revelation of God, the bond uniting the spiritual and the material beings as one body and the way for angelic powers and material beings to offer glory to God. These roles are similar but inferior to Christ's roles. For Christ's humanity is the preeminent visible "image of God" who recapitulates the whole cosmos within himself and mediates their harmonious union with God because of his "exact" union with the Word. To show adoration to Christ *qua* man is, in fact, to show worship to God. Theodore believed that this is the mystery Paul asserts has been hidden for ages and has now been revealed through Christ's humanity. He was doubtless convinced that he was simply systematizing Paul's thought here.

What we see as unique in Theodore's view of "image" is the way in which he views the roles Christ is meant to play in God's plan of salvation. Because of his stress on God's transcendence, he detects the central revelatory, mediating, and cultic roles of Christ's humanity in the work of redemption. Christ's human nature has been divinely chosen to be the true medium of revelation and access for others to come into union with God. Adam shares in these roles but in a limited, typical way, whereas Christ's humanity possesses these characteristics in a consummate way. What is significant is how the assumed man is the bond uniting the members of his body, the Church, to the Word and the bond recapitulating the whole universe, uniting all in peace and harmony with God. This understanding of "image" highlights for us how Christ is not merely an individual as such but one whose humanity possesses essential relationships to the Word and others through his bodily existence. As we shall see in the following chapter, this essential "corporate" aspect of his existence as a "person" cannot be overlooked or minimized. Let us turn now to the relation between Theodore's view of Christ as the perfect visible "image of God" to his teaching about there being one common *prosôpon* in Christ.

6. THE SALVIFIC ROLE OF CHRIST'S "COMMON 'PROSÔPON'"

T HE PREVIOUS CHAPTERS have prepared us for our next inquiry: what does Theodore mean by the phrase he often uses to express the "person" of Christ, his common *prosôpon*? I have pointed out the quasi-organic union between Christ's humanity and those who are united to his "bodies," the members of the Church and the universe, as well as the quasi-organic union between his exterior "visible image" and the inward reality of God's Word. Because of Christ's human nature's "exact" union with the Word, he can serve as the true mediator between God and all of creation. I shall now address the question of how Christ's humanity as the head of the Church and the cosmos is "exactly" related to the Word. In other words, what are the kinds of union and unity that Theodore argues exist between Christ's divine and human natures in one "person"?

Theodore derives his understanding of the unity of

Christ's natures from the exegetical and dogmatic tradition that he inherited at Antioch and that shaped his literal, historical, and rational exegetical method. He was especially convinced of the need to preserve the integrity of Christ's two natures in a union where the Word's transcendence was not compromised. My purpose here is not to determine whether or not Theodore's common *prosôpon* truly expresses a substantial union. Rather it is to validate whether this study into the salvific roles Theodore sees Christ playing within the universe can help to determine how Theodore regards Christ as one "person." In other words, my approach is a functional, existential one. It wants to establish who Christ is as a "person" by a close consideration of his salvific activity. This is how the Synoptics have depicted Christ. Because he acts as one in human and divine ways, they presume that he is not only human and divine but also truly one person. This seems to be Theodore's outlook as well.

When pressed, Theodore expresses the union of Christ's divine and human natures in two different ways. The first sums up the union as occurring in one *"prosôpon."* The other describes the union as one wherein God "dwells according to His good pleasure as in His Son."[1] The present chapter treats what Theodore means first by *prosôpon* and then by a union in a common *prosôpon*. Chapter 7 examines what he intends when he asserts that the union is an "indwelling of good pleasure." Because the matter is so complex, if not confusingly dense, it is imperative that we proceed one step at a time.

This chapter begins with a long overview of how the Christological terms "substance," "nature," *hypostasis,* and *prosôpon* were understood within the cultural settings of the fourth and fifth centuries. I shall then look at how Theodore views these terms, especially a common *prosôpon.* To further clarify the kind of unity Theodore espouses between Christ's two natures, I shall then explore three major analogies that he presents to illumine his Christological union between two natures in one *prosôpon.*

1. As I shall discuss in Chapter 7, the phrase "as in His Son" can also be interpreted "as in a son." I shall show that the first rendition ought to be the preferred translation.

The General Meaning of the Basic Christological Terms

There was considerable fluidity in the late fourth and early fifth centuries regarding the use and understanding of the terms *ousia, physis, hypostasis,* and *prosôpon.* We see this fluidity in the struggles of the fathers to agree on how to express the existence of three Persons in one divine Nature and one Person in two natures in Christ.[2] Bitter controversies lasting almost a century forced the Church fathers to establish authoritatively an acceptable understanding of the two terms "nature" (*ousia* and *physis*) and "person" (*hypostasis* and *prosôpon*) and how they all relate to one another. In his *Theological Dictionary of the New Testament* Helmut Köster notes no consistent evolution in the meanings of these terms until the start of the fifth century: "One has rather to consider at every step the corresponding usage in the period concerned."[3]

Köster regards *ousia* as signifying the primal nature as such of a being. It is translated as "substance." Another term close in meaning but conceptually different is *hypostasis,* the root of which literally means "that which stands under" or is the "foundation" of something. The term has a number of connotations, depending on whether one situates its origin in the intransitive verb *hyphistēmi* or the transitive verb *hyphistamai.*[4] As an intransitive verb, its meanings range from "source," "being," "nature," "reality," to "substantive existence," "concrete entity," "individual," and "person," and as a transitive verb from "origination" to "sustenance" and "actualization," connoting that the substance of a being has entered into existence. The next term is *physis* (nature). It includes everything given to a being when it then came into existence, as well as everything that belongs peculiarly to its substance. Aristotle appears to be the first to have distinguished between an "abstract universal nature" and a "concrete nature," that is, a

2. Kelly, *Early Christian Doctrines,* 253.

3. Helmut Köster, *Theological Dictionary of the New Testament,* ed. Gerhard Friedrich, trans. Geoffrey W. Bromiley (Grand Rapids: Eerdmans, 1968), 8:589. I am also indebted in this section to G.W.H. Lampe, ed., *A Patristic Greek Lexicon* (Oxford: Clarendon Press, 1961).

4. Köster, *Theological Dictionary,* 8:573. Köster objects to those who propose different meanings for these two verbs.

specific individual. The final term *prosôpon* ("person") means primarily a "face" or an "individual's outward being." It connotes, however, that this outward appearance of an individual is real. It was also employed to signify a "mask" worn by an actor and extended to a person's "role" within a play or one's "position" within a community.[5]

The Christian Understanding of the Terms

In addition to being aware of the meaning these four terms had in the cultural setting of the late fourth and the early fifth centuries, Theodore was also probably influenced by the way these words were understood by Christian theologians, especially by the fathers at the Councils of Nicaea (325) and in the Synodical Letter written the year after the Council of Constantinople I (381). In the Creed of Nicaea (325), we read that the fathers looked upon *ousia* and *hypostasis* as interchangeable: "those who say . . . that (the Word of God) came to be from things that were not or from another *hypostasis* or *ousia* . . . these the catholic and apostolic church anathematizes."[6] This led some to view the Nicene fathers as crypto-Sabellians. Doubtless the fathers at Nicaea chose these terms as a way to explain their intent, namely, that the Word did not come from the "Person" of the Father but from his substance.[7] They wanted, in fact, to avoid a Sabellian interpretation on the one hand and an Arian on the other. However, it was not until about forty years later, when the *Tomus ad Antiochenos* (362) and the Cappadocians were able to help forge a consensus as to there being one divine *ousia* and three divine *hypostaseis* (Persons) in the Trinity, that there

5. For a discussion of how the ancient understanding of "nature" and "person" differ from contemporary usage, see Dermot A. Lane, *The Reality of Jesus: An Essay in Christology* (New York: Paulist Press, 1975), 111–14. Lane remarks, for instance, on the meaning of person: "This ontological concept of person exists in complete contrast to the modern understanding of person, which is informed primarily by psychology" (112). It signifies an individual reality. Lane is, of course, speaking of "person" in the sense of a *hypostasis*, not as a *prosôpon*.

6. Norman P. Tanner, ed., *Decrees of the Ecumenical Councils*, vol. 1: *Nicaea I to Lateran V.* (Washington, D.C.: Georgetown University Press, 1990), 5. For a theological understanding of the terms used in the Nicene Creed, see Grillmeier, *Christ in Christian Tradition*, 1:264–73.

7. See Kelly, *Early Christian Doctrines*, 242.

ceased to be a controversy about the choice of words regarding the Trinity.

In 382 most fathers who attended the Council of Constantinople I wrote a Synodal Letter that doubtless reflects the thought of the lost Tome of the Council. In this letter they profess their belief that the Father, Son, and Holy Spirit possess "a single Godhead and power and . . . three most perfect *hypostases* or three perfect *prosôpa,* so that there exists no place here for the disease of Sabellius wherein the *hypostases* are confused, with the result that their peculiar characteristics too are destroyed."[8] By distinguishing the Greek word *ousia* (substance and, in the context, the same as "nature") from both *hypostasis* and *prosôpon,* the fathers insisted on the necessity of making a distinction between "substance/nature" on the one hand and both *hypostasis* and *prosôpon* on the other. They affirm in fact that these latter two words are approximate in meaning (though *hypostasis* is said to be "most perfect" and *prosôpon* only "perfect").[9] The constant use of these last two terms as synonyms suggests continuing uncertainty among the fathers about which is the more appropriate term to describe the reality of a "Person" in the Trinity. But it also may indicate that each of these two terms signifies a "person" but that each has a special connotation, whereby *hypostasis* denotes the specific inner personal uniqueness of each existing divine Person in relationship to the other two divine Persons, while *prosôpon* brings out how one Person in the Trinity relates to the Others and can manifest itself outwardly to created beings.

In the late fourth century, therefore, the fathers understood the terms *ousia* (substance) and *physis* (nature) to be what is common to the Father, Son, and Spirit, and the terms *hypostasis* and *prosôpon* as that which are characteristic of each individual divine "Person" as a "person." They also commonly maintained that the "nature" of the Trinity is the source of its activity and the reference point for the divine attributes, except in those personal ways that the Father, Son, and Spirit uniquely differ as Persons.[10]

8. Tanner, *Decrees of the Ecumenical Councils,* 28. Sabellius held that the three divine Persons were but the manifestations of one God.

9. Dr. Kenneth Steinhauser of St. Louis University has suggested to me that the fathers used the phrase "most perfect" to bring out more clearly that the three divine Persons are equal to one another. No one is more perfect than the others.

10. Kelly, *Early Christian Doctrines,* 258.

Applying these distinctions to the Trinity, we can advance as probable that the term *prosôpon* denotes the external ways each divine Person reveals himself in a relational way as a real individual member of the Triune Godhead, even though united with the other two Persons in the same nature. The term *hypostasis,* on the other hand, denotes rather what characterizes each Divine Person inwardly as uniquely existing in a common divine nature.

Another fifth-century source for Theodore's terms is Nestorius's extended analogy on their meaning.[11] Because Theodore is proclaimed the father of Nestorianism, there is a very definite probability that Nestorius is reflecting Theodore's thought. Nestorius explains these terms in light of a king who dresses as a common soldier. The king's "substance" is the same as that of every other human. It is the fundament for all other terms. The word "nature" qualifies and delimits the king's "substance" to the particular human being the king is, just as a species does a genus. Both terms indicate that the king is a human being. The term *hypostasis* appears to add to "substance" and "nature" the notion that this complete specific, substantial nature now exists. In Nestorius's example, the term affirms that the king really exists as this particular king who is the bearer of his own individual properties and the guiding subject of his own freely willed actions.

Nestorius introduces another term, *schêma,* to the mix. Though used in Theodore's extant works, it is not found as such as a technical term.[12] But it is important if one is clearly and fully to understand Theodore's meaning of *prosôpon* and a common *prosôpon.* Nestorius understood *schêma* to designate the specific form or visible appearance under which something or someone is *now* recognized. Thus, although the king's *schêma* may change outwardly, his underlying concrete, substantial nature and his *hypostasis* are the same. For example, running water and ice are both water, though different forms of water. There is one *hypostasis* (that is, of water) but two different *schêmata* or concrete forms that it can assume. Thus the king

---

11. Nestorius, *The Bazaar of Heracleides,* ed. and trans. Godfrey L. Driver and Leonard Hodgson (Oxford: Clarendon Press, 1925), 20–23.

12. Theodore, of course, uses the term in the sense of a "form," "appearance," "manner," and often in a prepositional phrase, such as "in the pattern of."

who has assumed the *schêma* of a common soldier is still kingly in his nature, despite being dressed in an ordinary soldier's clothing.

The term *prosôpon*, like that of *schêma*, connotes a person's concrete, outward appearance but adds as an essential element the sense that one's external aspect is intimately related to who and what a person is inwardly. It expresses the relational bond between the "outer" and "inner" makeup of a person. Nestorius's explanation of how the two terms *schêma* and *prosôpon* differ is illuminating. A king may exchange his regal robes for an ordinary soldier's garb, but he is simply exchanging one *schêma* for another. *Prosôpon* by contrast means that he is the king outwardly as well as inwardly. When understood in this sense, *prosôpon* can be taken as a functional, not a strictly ontological, term. For the king is acting according to his nature. In fact, this is how many people today describe a person, not in a substantial metaphysical way but in the way that a person is known as such by his or her interior and outward activities.

Theodore's Understanding of the Christological Terms

When Theodore employs the different terms "substance," "nature," *hypostasis,* and *prosôpon,* he writes as if their meanings are self-evident, as we must assume they were in his own mind. We are fortunate to have several extant passages in which he addresses his understanding of these terms, though no specific passage where he spells out fully how these terms, especially *hypostasis* and *prosôpon,* differ from each other. In the clearest passage Theodore refers to *physis, hypostasis,* and *prosôpon* as they are present in the union of Christ's divine and human natures: "For when we distinguish the natures, we say the nature of God the Word is perfect and [his] *prosôpon* is perfect. For it is not [possible] to say that there exists a *hypostasis* without a *prosôpon.* And the human nature is perfect and likewise [its] *prosôpon.* . . . But when we look to the union, then we say one *prosôpon.*"[13] For Theodore, therefore, every perfect nature, if it is a truly existing being, has its own *hypostasis,* which is turn has its own *prosôpon.*

13. *TEP* 2:299. I have translated this passage from the Greek text contained in the Appendix.

How then can we make sense of Theodore's statement that the term *hypostasis* belongs to both nature and *prosôpon?* It signifies that whenever one encounters a *hypostasis* or a complete existing nature, both terms imply that they have at least the potential to manifest themselves in a real visible way. In other words, in its most elemental meaning *prosôpon* refers to the external ways that a hypostatic nature can reveal itself. It is the concrete, visible "person" whom we see and touch—the person who manifests in an outward way one's own inner subsisting nature. In other words, every nature that is a complete, hypostatic nature has at least the potential to reveal itself in a visible, external way as a *prosôpon.* Thus when Theodore speaks of there being but one *prosôpon* in Christ, he would mean, in light of our last chapter on "image," that God has chosen to reveal himself outwardly through and together with the visible prosôpic appearance of Christ's humanity. This is possible because there exists an "exact" union between Christ's human and divine natures. Since each nature can reveal in a prosôpic way, Christ's way of acting visibly as one in both divine and human ways reveals that he is inwardly both divine as well as human. This is the way the Synoptics portray Jesus.

As discussed in Chapter 2 on exegesis, *prosôpon* has an additional significance in Theodore's commentary on the psalms. *Prosôpon* does not refer here to a "person" in a metaphysical sense. Rather it is employed at times as signifying an individual and at other times as signifying a group that is considered as one. Christ's common *prosôpon* can be understood in two ways—first, as an individual subject who is speaking or a person about whom one is speaking or to whom something is being said, and, second, in a communal sense. The *prosôpon* of Christ *qua* man also implies the presence of all the members of his ecclesial and cosmic "body," while that of the Word would include the presence of the Father and the Spirit. Since Christ's human *prosôpon* must always be understood as in an inseparable relationship with the Word's, their common *prosôpon,* as I shall discuss more fully below, sums up and expresses how Christ is the true mediator, being both God and a creature. It is the basis and reason why the common *prosôpon* as God's image can be shown adoration. While this unity will be developed at greater length in the next chapter, Richard Norris Jr.

summarizes this point about Theodore's one *prosôpon nicely:* "When Theodore speaks of Christ as one *prosôpon,* he means that, because of the union between the Word and the assumed Man, the Lord presents himself to the world and to the believer as a single object of knowledge and faith and a single agent of reconciliation with God."[14]

Theodore's Understanding of Hypostasis

Theodore understands the term *hypostasis* in a way far different from Cyril of Alexandria, who regards it as signifying the subject to whom attributes and operations can be applied within a true substantial unity.[15] He takes it not in the psychological sense of a self-conscious individual but as a true existing individual. For Theodore, by contrast, it designates a real, complete, existing nature; and since Christ has two complete natures, it follows that he must possess two *hypostaseis.* To maintain, therefore, as Cyril does, that there is only one *hypostasis* in Christ, could only mean that there exists but one real nature in Christ, that of the Word, and that Christ's human nature has lost its own reality and been changed into the divine nature: "Therefore [the phrase] 'he became' is used in Scripture in many senses [as] it is also usually employed in many senses by us. . . . For it is affirmed sometimes in an active and then sometimes in a passive sense. . . . But it is also employed in the sense of becoming a *qnômâ* [the Syriac word for *hypostasis*]—correctly as many think. But as a *qnômâ,* it is used in two ways: either as an eternal coming to be [of the Word] at the beginning [of creation] or as a change of one thing into another."[16] In other words, when the Word is said to "become flesh," Theodore interprets this to mean that the Word must maintain the *hypostasis* that Christ has when eternally generated from the Father or, if not, that he must be changed into another nature. If the latter is true, then he has lost his nature as God. To corroborate his conviction that a person's *hypostasis* is insepa-

---

14. Norris, *Manhood and Christ,* 231.

15. For a lengthy statement of Cyril's thought, compare the English translation of Cyril's twelve anathemas with some commentary in Percival, *Seven Ecumenical Councils, NPNF,* 14:206–18.

16. *THC,* 120–22/121–23; *CH* 5:15–16. My translation.

rable from one's nature, Theodore adduces what he believes to be scriptural examples confirming that a *hypostasis* must always be associated in meaning with nature, as pointed out above, where he speaks of the three *hypostaseis* as being three "realities" in the one divine nature.

Another valuable passage for understanding *hypostasis* is one that has survived partially in Greek and wholly in Syriac. I have translated the last line of the Greek text first and then the Syriac: "When, however, we return to the union [of a soul with its body], then we announce one *prosôpon.*[17] Likewise, when we define a human nature, we say that the nature of the soul is one [and] that of its body is another, since we acknowledge that each one of these has a *qnômâ* [Syriac for *hypostasis*] and a nature and are convinced that the soul, whenever it is separated from its body, remains in its nature and its own *qnômâ.*"[18] Here Theodore refers to an existing human being composed of a real soul with its real body, each with its own (incomplete) nature and thus its own *hypostasis.* But when death occurs, the *hypostasis* of the soul will continue in its existence, indicating that the *hypostasis* of its body does not. This implies that Theodore regards the soul's *hypostasis* as a real, existing nature that is self-subsisting, whereas the body does not subsist on its own. The soul has been created immortal while the body in its earthly life is mortal and must perish whenever it is separated from its life-sustaining soul. As we shall see later, a critical distinction must be made in the application of this analogy likening the soul's separation from its own body at death to that between the Word and Christ's humanity. Theodore insists that the *hypostasis* of Christ's humanity is never separated from that of the Word, not even at Jesus' death on the cross.

The following passage affirms what was implied in the previous one: that the human body exists in the *hypostasis* (subsistence) of its soul during the union and ceases to exist when it is separated from its soul at death: "For the human soul differs from the souls of animals only in this that this latter's soul does not possess its subsistence as an element of its

17. From this point on, I have translated this section from the Syriac text that Sachau provides in *TFS.* It adds material not contained in Swete's Greek text.

18. *TEP* 2:299.

nature. An animal's existence does not subsist alone in its makeup; and after the death of the animal it is believed no longer to exist. . . . As regards the human (soul), it is not like this. The soul exists on its own (in its *qnômâ*) and is much more exalted than the body. It continues forever on its own (in its *qnômâ*) because it is immortal."[19] It is worthwhile to point out here that Theodore does not distinguish between a complete and an incomplete nature. Besides indicating here his lack of philosophical precision, his understanding of nature may reveal that Theodore is speaking not abstractly but concretely. He is referring here to a subsisting existential being whose human body has its own *hypostasis,* but one that is not self-subsisting, at least until it becomes immortal.

In the next passage, Theodore likens—with reservations—the Word's relation to his Father to an idea's relation to its soul: "(The Word) was with (the Father) from eternity, being similar to the word in the soul that always issues from it and with it. Because the word [proceeding] from the soul is seen to be something other even though it exists as [part of] the soul's self-subsistence *(qnômâ),* as the word does not have [its own] self-subsistence *(qnômâ),* it is viewed then [to be existing] in that of its soul. But lest in following out this comparison, we believe that the Son is also not an existing *qnômâ* or a stranger to the nature of the Father, the evangelist briefly adds that 'the Word was God.'"[20] In other words, Theodore uses this analogy to illustrate how the Word can be one with the Father. He recognizes its limitation, however, because he explicitly asserts that the Word is a subsisting divine Person (a *hypostasis*) who is at the same time not separated from his Father or existing apart from the divine nature.

The quotation above also highlights why Theodore is opposed to the statement that there is only one *hypostasis* in Christ. The analogy between the body in its relation to its existing soul and Christ's humanity in its union with the Word may appear consistent with the view that Christ's human nature subsists in the *hypostasis* of the Word's divine Person; but Theodore would reject such a conclusion. As we shall see in Chapter 7, he

19. *THC,* 120–22/121–23; *CH* 5:15–16.
20. Ibid., 74/75; *CH* 3:14. Because the Syriac text is illegible at the head of this citation, I have translated this section from the French.

grants that the Word empowers the humanity and completes its activity, but not to the point that the Word supplants the humanity's *hypostasis*. For this would mean there is only one *hypostasis* and therefore only one nature in Christ, that of the Word's divine nature. Moreover, Theodore would not have been able to conceive Christ's human nature as abstract, the Word using it as a *principium quo* or instrument of operation.[21] If he could, Theodore would interpret this to mean that the assumed man has no real existence and therefore no free activity. This would rob his humanity of the essential but secondary roles in salvation pointed out in earlier chapters. Rather, Theodore maintains that since Christ's humanity really exists, it must be concrete with its own *hypostasis*. As Norris puts it, "the human nature of Christ would be 'impersonal' in the sense that it has no ὑπόστασις of its own, but subsists in an attributive relation to the Person of the divine Son."[22]

Let us take one final example of the consistency of Theodore's understanding of *hypostasis* (*qnômâ* in Syriac) as an existing real nature. Theodore is speaking here of how the Word of God must be taken as an existing Being and not simply as a spoken or written word: "Why did he call this One the 'Word'? We say [in response] that in no [other] instance does the Scripture employ this term 'Word' in [the sense of] a self-subsisting being *(qnômâ)*. But here he names the Son to be the Word in [the sense of being] a self-subsisting reality (a *qnômâ*) when he names Him in a singular and absolute sense without [any] addition or definition."[23] Theodore could accept the meaning of *hypostasis* as an existing person for every person except Christ in the flesh. But in the case of Christ's humanity, one *hypostasis* means but one nature in Christ. In the case of the Trinity, the Person of the Word can never be separated from the divine nature that he shares with the Father and the Spirit. The problem regarding Christ is that Christ

---

21. As we shall see in Chapter 8, this is how Kevin McNamara views it. Kelly points out that Cyril of Alexandria also considered Christ's human as well as his divine nature to be concrete: "The humanity was as real as the divinity, and the modern allegation that he regarded it as a collection of purely abstract qualities conflicts with his express language" (*Early Christian Doctrines*, 319).

22. Norris, *Manhood and Christ*, 235.

23. *TJA*, 21/14.

has two different real natures, which means that both must have their own *hypostasis* that somehow function as one and constitute one individual.

The Difference between a 'Hypostasis and a Prosôpon'

In the following passage, Theodore indicates how a *hypostasis* differs from a *prosôpon*. He says that the Spirit's *hypostasis* (real existence within the divine nature) is not known until Christ reveals His *prosôpon:* "We have learned that the Father possesses His own *prosôpon,* and the Son His *prosôpon,* and the Holy Spirit His *prosôpon,* considering that each of them is equally [sharing] in the divine and eternal *ousia. . . .* The Old (Testament), as I said, did not know of the Holy Spirit [existing] in His own *prosôpon* and of His *hypostasis* as being separate from God.[24] It called the Holy Spirit [in various ways] the spirit of God or His grace or authority or care or disposition or something of this sort."[25] In other words, the Spirit really exists as a *hypostasis* in the Trinity but is not known as such until the Spirit's presence has been revealed in the New Testament. But even when Jesus affirms the real existence of the Spirit, it is difficult to recognize the Spirit's visible presence: "Therefore, you hear His voice; that is, you perceive the sound of His coming, but you do not know the place where His Person *(qnômâ)* is present, being aware [only] that His operation is active."[26] The Spirit's *hypostasis* and *prosôpon* are known to be present by his activity within the visible appearance of some other reality. As we shall see, the same will be said of the Word's *prosôpon* as actualized in his common *prosôpon.*

When Theodore speaks of the Persons of the Trinity, he does employ the term *hypostasis:* "the divine nature is known [as present] in the three *hypostaseis* of the Father and of the Son and of the Spirit."[27] He says the same thing later: "Each of these three *hypostaseis* is in truth God; and unique is the divine nature of the Father and the Son and the Holy Spirit"

24. Like many of the fathers, Theodore considers the term "God" as referring to the Father. See Kelly, *Early Christian Doctrines,* 100.
25. Theodore, "In Haggai," PG 66:485A.
26. *TJA,* 69/48.
27. *THC,* 32/33; CH 2:3.

(*CH* 2:3). This shows how Theodore understands the term *hypostasis* as being always associated with "nature." But when he uses this term, it is in the context of a revelation of a divine Person: "But by adding the *prosôpon* of the Father, (Paul) also reveals the Son" (*CH* 3:2). I believe that this is how the following is to be understood: "Those who speak of the one *prosôpon* of the Son as two teach us about the 'exact' union of the two natures" (*CH* 3:6).[28] In other words, Theodore's phrase "one *prosôpon*" reveals the presence of two natures within Christ. There is no conflict with the trinitarian language. Each of the divine *prosôpa* has one nature, while Christ's common *prosôpon* (that is, the union of Christ's human *prosôpon* with the Word's *prosôpon*) possesses two natures.

Rowan Greer offers a constructive insight into how the terms *prosôpon* and *hypostasis* in Theodore can be said to be distinguished from one another: "Theodore seems to use ὑπόστασις as a strictly ontological word to describe what the Godhead really is. . . . Contrariwise, πρόσωπον seems everywhere linked with the revelation and man's apprehension of it. . . . God exists in three ὑπόστασεις and is recognized in three πρόσωπα. The word πρόσωπα for Theodore as for Nestorius, refers to something definite. That is, a πρόσωπα is an existing thing or entity and not simply an abstraction; and πρόσωπα have this supra-ontological sense of recognition."[29] Greer, however, raises a prudent caveat: "However, too much must not be made of the particular words Theodore has used. Theodore was not really interested in fashioning a technical, philosophical vocabulary. Rather it is the tendency of his thought to fashion a theology built of Biblical, pictorial images."[30]

One last point must be made before we undertake a deeper examination of what Theodore means by one *prosôpon*. It is critical because it highlights a major difference between Theodore and Cyril of Alexandria. Cyril understands his term for "person" *(hypostasis)* as the subject of unity and attribution in Christ, whereas Theodore holds that the centers for divine

28. It is difficult to read some words here because they are smudged in the Syriac text. I have translated from the French text.
29. Greer, *Theodore of Mopsuestia,* 28–29.
30. Ibid.

and human activities are their existing natures—though always in relation to the ego of their common *prosôpon*. Theodore's adversaries point out that since he regards all existing natures as concrete, he could not have conceived of an "abstract" nature as really existing apart from the "person" of the Word. For Theodore, everything that exists is a particular existential nature, not an abstract reality. We can see this expressed in the following passage, in which Theodore refers to the phrase "divine nature" as interchangeable with the concrete title "Lord": "(the assumed man) is then connatural to David from whom he has descended. We maintain that He is also the Lord because of the union he has with the divine Nature that is the Cause and Lord of the universe."[31]

As Norris notes, this identity of concrete and abstract nature was common in Theodore's day: "errors in using this language [where one uses abstract and concrete natures interchangeably] were in fact the common habits of his time, which was quite accustomed to references to the 'Man' in Christ."[32] As Graham Warne points out, this usage was in fact quite common among the ancient Jews as well: "the Hebrews used one single term to express both a concrete, observable reality (to which they could readily relate), and a non-concrete, or figurative meaning. . . . That which was concrete and observable provided the means whereby the non-concrete could be perceived. The human person, therefore, was characterized by function, rather than by metaphysical abstraction."[33] In other words, the concrete, visible nature of reality illumines its inner nature. This seems to be the way Theodore has understood the term *prosôpon*.

The Problem Regarding the Terms of Unity

Before delving into what Theodore means by one *prosôpon*, we need to situate the problem of Christ's unity in the context of the fourth century. Two different Christological models, probably with lengthy traditions, predate the controversy between Apollinaris and Theodore. These are repre-

31. *THC*, 192/193; *CH* 8.4.
32. Norris, *Manhood and Christ*, 209.
33. Graham J. Warne, *Hebrew Perspectives on the Human Person in the Hellenistic Era: Philo and Paul* (Lewiston, N.Y.: Mellen, 1995), 59–60.

sented by Paul of Samosata and Malchion[34] (both were active at Antioch in the middle of the third century). Paul seems to have put forward what can be described as a "divisive" kind of Christology as he separated the Word and Jesus Christ into two individuals. Malchion, by contrast, spoke of the unity of the Word and the "flesh" in terms of the unity between the body and the soul in a human being. Malchion rejected what he believed to be Paul of Samosata's empty moral indwelling of the Word in the humanity. For Malchion, the Word does not dwell in Christ as it does in other humans but truly becomes a human being.

The Arian crisis brought this issue to a head. Arius argued logically that if the Word was the subject of Christ's human operations and truly suffered, the Word must be mutable and thus a creature. He consider the Word to be a *theos* but not true God.[35] The Alexandrians agreed with Arius's premise that the Word was the subject of Christ's human operations, but they distinguished two forms of predication. The first form can be described as a "natural" one and the other as an "economic" one; that is, the Word does not suffer in his divine nature but can be said to do so for the salvation of humanity. As we shall see when we examine Theodore's method of speaking about Christ, Theodore assigns attributes appropriate to a nature to its own nature. But he does allow those peculiar to each nature to be truly affirmed of the ego of the common *prosôpon*. This was also probably Diodore's basic position, which Theodore may also have adapted in light of objections raised against Diodore's statements about two Sons.

To counteract what he believed to be the divisive Christology that he saw in Paul of Samosata and Diodore, Apollinaris proposed the existence of a natural "organic" unity within Christ. He accomplished this by holding that the Word supplanted Christ's rational human soul. He argued that since two complete natures cannot be made into a substantial unity, the humanity of Christ must have been an incomplete nature.[36] By so doing, he

34. For a brief background, see Kelly, *Early Church Doctrines,* 158–60; and Grillmeier, *Christ in Christian Tradition,* 1:164–65.

35. For a fuller treatment of Arius's Christology, see Grillmeier, *Christ in Christian Tradition,* 1:245–48.

36. For a summary treatment of Apollinaris's position, see Kelly, *Early Christian Doctrines,* 291–96, esp. 293, and Grillmeier, *Christ in Christian Tradition,* 1:329–43.

was able to affirm that there is only one single person present in Christ, that of the Word of God. Theodore rejects this, thereby earning the lasting enmity of the Apollinarians. Such a position ran totally contrary to two of the Antiochene basic commitments: first, to preserve the Creator-creature distinction and Christ's full humanity within the union. By stressing the immutability of the Word and the full humanity of Christ, Theodore was forced in effect to make—what appears to many—a complete separation of Christ's human nature from the Word. This is exemplified in Theodore's attempt to prove Apollinaris wrong by appealing to human acts that Christ *qua* man performed, thus establishing that he had a rational soul. For instance, he argues: "If someone wants to contend that the soul of a human being can exist without reason, how did Jesus grow in wisdom?"[37] His more persuasive argument against Apollinaris is that the union Apollinaris proposes between the Word and Christ's bodily humanity is in fact of a hybrid nature: "For if the life of the body is governed by the soul wherein understanding resides and whereby we understand the divine nature to be the cause of every effect and the divine plan as governing all things that have been fashioned and will be—for all these acts are connected with a rationally endowed nature—why do the heretics say a third nature is needed which they have conceived and called 'rational'?"[38]

Kinds of Union

At this point, it will be helpful to know clearly what kinds of union were being broached in the fourth century. At that time, various terms were employed to describe the different kinds of union. First, Aristotle distinguishes a *krasis* (mixture) from a *sunthesis* (juxtaposition). In the first case, the "mixture" results in a tertium quid, and in the second no change takes place in the combining of the natures.[39] The Stoics also spoke of a union by "mixture" *(sunchusis)* where the elements are altered without any possibility of their being restored to their original state. They also pro-

37. *TFS,* fol. 4b/38.
38. Ibid., fol. 4a/37.
39. For a treatment of the different kinds of union, see Norris, *Manhood and Christ,* 68–78, 216–17.

posed a special kind of "mixture through all its parts" *(krasis di' olôn),* which connotes a total interpenetration of two substances. In this mixture, each nature retains its characteristic properties unaltered, with the result that in their union the two inhering natures remain distinct. When applied to a human being, this means that when a human soul is united to its body to form a new organic nature, each nature can interact reciprocally with the other while still maintaining its own properties, even though each has lost its own identity as a substance.

Theodore repudiates the language of the first two forms of mixture above as insufficient for explaining the union of Christ's natures. He sees the Apollinarian attempt to define the union as a composite as blasphemous: "They say, therefore, just as from two natures [i.e., from the soul and flesh] one human nature is composed, so from the deity and humanity there is then composed the one nature of Christ. . . . Of the incontrovertible simple divinity of Christ, one cannot assert without [committing] a monstrous blasphemy that the divinity can be composed into one nature along with the assumed human nature."[40] Theodore also signals his outspoken opposition to Apollinaris when he speaks of the union as an *asunchutos henôsis* (an unmixed unity) instead of as a mixture. As we shall see, he draws his evidence for the unity of Christ's natures from the New Testament, believing that it provides the only adequate language for describing, if not formulating, the unity present in the Incarnation.

Theodore frequently calls the unity of the two natures in Christ a *sunapheia akribēs,* that is, an "exact union" or an "accurate or perfect combination." He regards it as an indissoluble binding that will last forever: "For it is also necessary for us to preserve our knowledge of this indissoluble union. For never, even for an instant, can this form of a slave be separated from the divine nature which has possessed it."[41] Even though Theodore insists that the Word was not generated by Mary, he nevertheless insists that there is an "exact union" between the Word and Christ's humanity. He contends that his way of speaking about the union of the two different natures is what is found in Scripture: "(The Word) did not take

40. The citation is found in Facundus of Hermiane, PL 67:556D.
41. *THC,* 204/205; *CH* 8:13.

his beginning from Mary. But those who speak differently [as does Theodore] about the natures adhere to the Holy Books by teaching about one *prosôpon* because of the 'exact union' that has taken place."[42]

But is this "exact union" of Christ's two natures a true substantial kind of union? Cyril interpreted *sunapheia* in a Stoic sense as the combination of two independent subjects within a moral union.[43] In her customary painstakingly scholarly way, Luise Abramowski has carefully scrutinized how the terms *sunapheia* and *asunchutos henôsis* were used in the writings of the early fathers. She points out that both expressions were used to designate the trinitarian and Christological unity.[44] She notes, for instance, that Tertullian used the former term to affirm the indissoluble unity of Persons in the Trinity and of the natures in Christ. She also observes that Pope Leo's and the Chalcedonian conciliar wordings reveal a verbal agreement with Tertullian, as do Eusebius, Basil, Ambrose, and Gregory of Nazianzen. She believes that all of these examples lend credence to the view that *sunapheia akribēs*, when used to express the union both between God the Father and his Son and between Christ's two natures, affirms a union that is more than an accidental and moral one.[45] This is also substantiated by Theodore's own reliance on this same phrase to affirm the union between the Son and the Father in the Trinity: "so that by His union *(sunapheia)* with His Father, He is known to be the Only-Begotten."[46] The conclusion to be drawn from Abramowski's detailed study is clear: Theodore was employing an accepted Christian—not a Stoic—word to express the unmingled union of Christ's natures. This is affirmed in a passage where Theodore rejects a simple moral kind of union between the Word and a mere man: "For [my adversaries] do not consider [the fact] that they are dividing

---

42. Ibid., 134/135; *CH* 6:3.

43. See Theodore, *Theodore und das Nicänum*, 248n669.

44. Luise Abramowski, *Drei christologische Untersuchungen*, Beiheft zur Zeitschrift für die neutestamentliche Wissenschaft und die Kunde der älteren Kirche 45 (Berlin: de Gruyter, 1981). See esp. 70–103.

45. Ibid., 108.

46. *THC*, 62/63. Theodore uses the expression "natural binding" in *CH* 15:40 in order to affirm the fundamental relationship that all believers achieve among themselves at baptism as well as between God the Father and the Logos.

up the 'exact union' that the one assumed has with the assuming One. For if this union is abolished, the assumed one appears to be nothing more than a simple man like us."[47] Therefore, Theodore believed that his phrase for the union denoted more than a simple juxtaposition of two external natures, as Cyril would have it.[48]

As we shall see, Theodore's adversaries judged Theodore's "exact union" in light of what he could and could not affirm about the Word. I want at this point simply to underscore that Theodore assumed he was holding for a true unity. He was convinced that his own position was fully backed up by Scripture: "For just as we are taught about the differences of natures by such sayings from divine Scripture, so we also learn of [their] union[49] as being one, as it often brings together into one the properties of both of these natures and speaks [of them] as belonging to one being."[50] He cites as an example of this the universal domination that God has bestowed upon the humanity of Christ because of the union: "For it is clear that these [words from John 3:33–35] pertain to that human nature which, because of its union[51] to God the Word, received domination over all things."[52] While it is true that Christ's human nature possesses this power in a functional way, it flows from his unique "exact union" with the Word.

Theodore's Understanding of a Prosôpic Union

Theodore expresses the union of the two natures in Christ in two ways: as a union in a common *prosôpon* and as an "indwelling of good pleasure." I shall discuss the latter in the next chapter, preferring to first understand clearly what he means when he says: "But when (John) spoke of those two (natures) as one, he was signifying the unity of the person."[53] Theodore does not attempt to explain fully the meaning of a prosôpic union between

47. Ibid., 134/135; *CH* 6:3.
48. See Henry Chadwick, "Eucharist and Christology in the Nestorian Controversy," *Journal of Theological Studies*, n.s. 2 (1951): 155, esp. n. 4.
49. The Latin term is *adunationem.*
50. *TEP* 2:301.
51. The Syriac term is *naqîpûtâ.* It is the Syriac equivalent of the Greek *sunaphia.*
52. *TJA*, 83/59.
53. Ibid., 113/81.

Christ's humanity and his divinity. In his surviving works, he relies upon the phrase one *prosôpon* to formulate this. Francis Sullivan concluded from his close analysis of Theodore's use of *prosôpon* that it does not denote a "person" in the strict philosophical sense: "It seems, rather, simply to be a way of saying that the Word and the man together constitute one subject of whom one can say what pertains to either of them."[54] *Prosôpon*, of course, is to be understood in this passage as Christ's one *prosôpon*. Sullivan's point, however, is on the mark. But, as we saw in the previous chapters, Christ's human *prosôpon*, as distinct from his common *prosôpon*, can also be understood as a personification of all those who are "corporally" united to Christ's humanity as bodily members to their head. In this sense the term *prosôpon* connotes the harmonious union that God intends for all members of Christ's body, the Church, and all who constitute the body of the universe. Norris expresses this well, but in a broader way than he himself intends in regard to Christ's two natures: for Theodore the term *prosôpon* signifies "the outward manifestation by which one or more concrete 'natures' are recognized as an hypostatic, historical, functional, or generic 'unit.'"[55]

From where does Theodore derive this communal outlook on "person"? From what we know of Theodore, he would have sought his understanding from Scripture. Bruce Malina and Jerome Neyrey argue that the notion of "person" in Saint Paul primarily denotes a communal rather than an individual meaning: "For all of the 'independence' claimed for Paul by modern Western readers, he presents himself as utterly dependent on group expectations and the controlling hand of forces greater than the ancestors, groups, God. He was a typically group-oriented person."[56] Malina and Neyrey are certain, too, that the common cultural practice in Paul's day was to know a person from the way he or she acted: "The rhetorical documents of antiquity indicate that ancient Mediterraneans thought much and hard about how to approach another self, how to have an impact on other

54. Sullivan, *Christology of Theodore*, 263; see also 235.
55. Norris, *Manhood and Christ*, 230.
56. Bruce J. Malina and Jerome H. Neyrey, *Portraits of Paul: An Archeology of Ancient Personality* (Louisville: John Knox, 1996), 217.

selves, and in the process they gave more than enough indication of what they thought those other selves were like. From the documents that have come down to us, we can see that the ancients would quite readily agree that you can indeed tell a book by its cover. So too you can tell another person by the way he or she looks and moves. Thus any intelligent person can tell what any other person is like by his or her 'cover' as well."[57] This certainly appears to be how Theodore understands *prosôpon*.

Whether Malina and Neyrey's understanding is rightly applied to Theodore is beside the point here. The question is whether Theodore, in fact, reflects this outlook in Scripture. He does seem to do so in his explanation of John's statement that "the Word became flesh." Theodore replies: "And it is understood that it is the custom of Scripture to denote the whole human being by [the term] 'flesh'; e.g., 'All flesh will come to you.' As he also clearly states here 'He became flesh' for 'He came to be in man.' For he said: 'he became,' because it did not come to be [in the sense] that he was changed, but rather that he was believed to have been because of [his] visible appearance."[58] Theodore is not simply asserting, I believe, that the Word becomes human only in the sense that he appears to be human. Rather he is affirming that the Word is united to Christ's humanity in such a way that his humanity visibly images the Word's union with him. But the onlookers who judge a person solely on his appearance and activity did not recognize this. For, as Theodore affirms, this ability to recognize the presence of the Word within Christ's common *prosôpon* depends on the capacity of the viewer, doubtless meaning by "capacity" an individual's graced faith vision: "Because the divine nature is not seen in a visible way, He reveals Himself to humans according to the capacity of His viewers. Clearly he indicates that by Christ's coming [to be in his birth from Mary] and, by his visibility, He reveals [His] divine nature."[59]

57. Ibid., xiii.
58. *TJA*, 33–34/23.
59. *THC*, 184/185; *CH* 7.15.

The Relationship of an Individual 'Prosôpon' to the
Common 'Prosôpon' of Unity

When Theodore speaks of a *prosôpon* for each of the divine and human natures and one *prosôpon* for both, he appears to be talking in a confusing, nonsensical way. How can each nature possess its own *prosôpon* as well as one common to both? Some insight can be drawn from the distinction that Theodore sometimes makes between an "inner" and an "outer" person. All recognize an inseparable nexus between the two. The problem that Theodore faces is that for all human beings except Christ, one's own *prosôpon* is identical with one's own *hypostasis* in the sense that one's outward person is also one's inner person. Theodore cannot affirm that the common *prosôpon* is exactly the Word's own *prosôpon* or that of Christ's humanity. This would mean that for him there is only one *hypostasis;* that is, either the Word has been transformed into a human being or Christ's humanity has been fully absorbed into the divinity.

What, then, is this common *prosôpon?* As our general summary of the cultural connotation of *prosôpon* and our observation of how Malina and Neyrey understand the meaning of "person" in Paul have suggested, *prosôpon* connotes the external appearance or outward form that expresses what pertains or at least ought to pertain to one's own *hypostasis* and nature. Because Theodore is so careful to stress the reality and completeness of Christ's two natures, it follows logically that he must allow each of the two natures to possess a possible visible manifestation of itself. So when an individual encounters Christ during his earthly life, there is one visible appearance for the Word and Christ's humanity. But because this common *prosôpon* acts in divine and human ways, one can discern that this one common *prosôpon* has both a divine and a human *prosôpon* as well as a divine and a human *hypostasis.* As the gospel accounts reveal, Christ's outward acts point to an inner state where his two natures are inseparably interacting as one complete visible whole. So understood, Christ's common *prosôpon* can in no way be regarded as truly a new composite. Rather it indicates the unique relationship that the divine *hypostasis* of the Logos has entered into with Christ's human nature. As Paul Galtier puts it, "The [common] πρόσωπον of Christ is thus the ultimate expression of the close conjunction which exists between Christ's humanity and the *hypostasis* of the Logos."[60] While Leonard Hodgson believes Nestorius defined *prosôpon* as "the appearance of a thing . . . not as opposed to the thing's real reality, but considered as an objectively real element in its being,"[61] this explanation can also apply to what Theodore means by his one *prosôpon.*

Galtier believes that the common *prosôpon* is that of the Word. I think some nuance needs to be introduced here, so as to make the definition more precise. If I am right, the one *prosôpon* would have to be visible and therefore pertain more to the humanity but include the Word's *prosôpon.* For the Word's transcendence excludes any visible presentation of the Divinity as such other than what can be known through his activity. It would also be similar to the ways that the *prosôpon* of the Father has revealed itself in the burning bush, in the cloud in the desert, and in the ark, and in the way that the *prosôpon* of the Spirit revealed itself in the dove at Jesus' baptism. In other words, the Word has chosen to reveal himself together with Christ's humanity's *prosôpon* in such a way that both inner natures can be recognized as present but different. Since Jesus acts visibly in both human and divine ways, he must possess a divine as well as a human nature. As mentioned above, Christ's own common *prosôpon* can be thought of as practically equivalent to Christ's humanity's role as the perfect visible "image of the invisible God."

In his explication of the way Nestorius interpreted the second chapter of Philippians, Greer discusses Nestorius's explanation of how the form of God humbly assumes the *prosôpon* of the servant, and how that of the servant is exalted to become the *prosôpon* of God. Greer shows how Nestorius exegetes the passage in light of Genesis 1:26–27 and indicates how Nestorius has expressed, rather awkwardly, what he means by the prosopic union: "the nature of the humanity should become his eikon and his *prosôpon* in such wise that his *prosôpon* is also the *prosôpon* of the other. . . . The very image and *prosôpon* [are] the humanity of the divinity

60. Galtier, "Théodore de Mopsueste," 343.
61. Nestorius, *Bazaar of Heracleides,* 415.

and the divinity of the humanity."[62] While this makes sense if understood in the context of there being a common *prosôpon* in Christ, Greer brings out another important point regarding how *prosôpon* and "image" are related to each other in Nestorius. He concludes that Nestorius has returned to the strictly biblical foundation of the "image of God"—a viewpoint that "marks his position as being strikingly original."[63] But, as pointed out in Chapter 5, one can argue that this is also Theodore's own position. I think that Nestorius has either derived his view regarding the relationship between "image" and *prosôpon* from Theodore directly or has drawn out, as I have done, the implications of his thought.

All of the above indicates, in my opinion, that Theodore's prosôpic union ought to be taken in the sense that whoever sees Christ's visible humanity sees in the words and miracles of Jesus the presence of the Word (as well as that of his Father and his Spirit). As will be made clear in Chapter 7, Theodore can not only assign divine attributes to Christ because the Word and Christ's humanity share a common *prosôpon* that demonstrates an inner unity of natures but can also justify John's remark (14:9) that the one who sees Jesus sees the Father.

> There is no difference, because the one who sees me [Jesus as the Christ] sees the Father Himself. For the perfect likeness[64] of the two reveals that the Father is [present] in me [through my union with the Word]. . . . In all that has been said earlier [and] now in these statements, he clearly makes known that [Christ] is speaking about a likeness. For by applying what is said equally to himself and [his] Father, he has pointed out the exact likeness in nature [between the Word and His Father]; that is, he is in the Father and the Father in him, whereby the true likeness of both of them can be shown to be in each other. . . . [He says]: "the Father works," in order to show that [their] nature is common [and] also [their] words are common and moreover [their] works are common. Hence it is evident that I am not speaking of my own accord. I am not speaking about (my) deficiency [as a

---

62. Rowan A. Greer, "Image of God and the Prosôpic Union in Nestorius' *Bazaar of Heracleides*," in *Lux in Lumine: Essays for W. N. Pittenger*, ed. Richard A. Norris Jr. (New York: Seabury, 1966), 50–51.

63. Ibid., 51.

64. The Syriac term is *dmûtâ*, which means "likeness" but can be translated as "image."

human] but about my exact and inseparable union[65] [with the Word]. This is known especially from the context of what is said. Nevertheless it is not surprising that, when he was prepared for (his) Passion and when he was saying many things as a human, he passed from these to words that pertain to [his] divinity.[66]

This passage indicates that Christ, both as the Word and as man, is truly united to the Father, the Word being of the same nature as the Father and his human nature being united too to the Father because of his inseparable union with the Word. Thus when Christ as the assumed man speaks of being truly one with the Father, it is indirectly so because of his direct and immediate "exact" union with the Word. Because of the union, Christ can speak in a human way and then pass to a divine way of speaking because, as we shall see, divine and human attributes can be referred to their common *prosôpon.*

The phrase one *prosôpon,* therefore, indicates not merely the external appearance of Christ as both divine and human but also the perfect interior communion and sharing between these natures: "Also as regards me, know that you do not know me perfectly. For although you may know me a great deal in an exterior way, but you do not know me much in regard to [my] interior hidden appearance" (159/114). This sharing of the two natures' activities in human and divine ways is manifested in the visible way Christ's humanity exercises universal dominion: "For since the divine nature is invisible to all creatures, the judge ought to be visible for the sake of those who are to be judged. For this reason God the Word assumed in an appropriate way the man, completing in him the whole economy for our salvation and gave to him [the power] to judge, by judging through him in order that He who is judging and commanding may be made visible" (116/82). It is the Word who is judging through Christ's visible humanity, just as it is the Word who is adored when adoration is shown to Christ's humanity. Theodore expresses the same view when speaking about who is

65. The Syriac is *šâutâpûtâ,* the Greek equivalent of which is *metechô.*
66. *TJA,* 268–69/191–92. I believe that Sachau's Latin translation of the clause "dum in eo erat ut pateretur" in the last sentence is better rendered from the Syriac as "when he was prepared for [his] passion."

actually performing the miracles that the assumed man performs: "But how can these (miracles) show his likeness to the Father or that he is the Creator of heaven and earth and all that has come to be? Rather what he says is that he was affirming the likeness of his divine nature with the Father. For the assumed man cannot be like to God the Father. But the works performed by the man are seen to far surpass the [human] nature of the one doing these things. If, therefore, he says that all this power is given him, know Who it is Who is in him, seeing that in all this he is not like the One who does all that He wants and in the way He wants by His natural power" (270/193). This passage demonstrates clearly how Theodore sees Christ's human and divine natures functioning as one *prosôpon*.

Analogies of the Union

To clarify even further how Theodore conceives of the union of Christ's two natures in one *prosôpon,* we turn now to the three analogies he offers to elucidate this union where two different natures can be said to be one. First of all, it is important to note that each of the analogies, as we would expect, is taken from Scripture and should be interpreted in light of the context in which it is found. Our concern here is to determine what specific point is being made and whether the three analogies affirm or imply that a prosôpic union is greater than the presence of a moral and accidental union. The three are: that of God in his temple, that of a husband and a wife, and that of the soul with its body.[67] One should recall here what Theodore says about the meaning of "as" in a comparison: one should attend to the specific point that is being examined and not attempt to apply the analogy in every detail.

The Temple

The first analogy deals with how God is present within his holy temple. Theodore is clearly referring here to John 2:19–21. Here John has Jesus affirming that he will raise up the temple that is his body in three days. As he consistently does, Theodore uses this Johannine passage to demonstrate

---

67. For a treatment of these analogies, see Norris, *Manhood and Christ,* 59–61, and his chapter 6, "The Union of the Body and the Soul," 67–78.

that since the union of Christ's two natures is forever, the Word is still inseparably united with his humanity at death: "Through these words, he shows the difference between the Word and what was destroyed. For the latter is the temple and the former is the One who dwells there. . . . And God the Word is not in the temple for only a short time and does not dwell in him then from time to time. No! He has never been separated from this temple, which has an ineffable union with the One dwelling in him."[68] Theodore, in fact, insists that there is no union closer than the Word's indwelling within his temple, so much so that they have the same will and operation: "For by being conjoined to God the Word according to the mode of good pleasure, as we have stated, that temple that has been born of the Virgin's womb remained undivided, having the same will and same operation with him in all things, [a union] than which nothing can be more conjoined."[69]

The fathers at the Council of Constantinople II condemned Theodore on the grounds that this analogy indicates that he regarded Christ and the Word to be two separate beings. It is hard to take such a charge seriously as John the Evangelist employs it. As Facundus of Hermiane, who wrote a defense of Theodore in the sixth century, points out, other fathers have employed the same analogy, and even Cyril approved of it: "But (Theodore) confesses that the One dwelling in him also [does so] as in a temple. . . . because we arrive at knowledge of the Divinity through the humanity of Christ. His humanity is mentioned first with the Divinity dwelling in [His] temple. Paul of Emesa spoke thus: 'See John preaching two natures and one Son, one the tabernacle and the other in the tabernacle; one the temple and the other who dwells [there], God.' Therefore if the venerable Ibas is blamed because in his epistle he first spoke about the temple and the one indwelling [there], the blessed Cyril ought also to be blamed because he praised the sermon of the aforementioned Bishop Paul who spoke first about the tabernacle and the temple, and later about the One in the tabernacle and God who dwells in the temple."[70] This shows

68. *THC*, 196–197; *CH* 8:7.
69. Theodore, "Epistola ad Domnum," PG 66:1012C–13A.
70. Facundus of Hermiane, PL 67:703. Kelly, *Early Christian Doctrines*, 285, mentions how Athanasius also speaks of the Word dwelling as in a temple.

that it is not the reference to the temple that is objectionable but the way Theodore's adversaries interpreted it to mean that he regards Christ as a separate individual from the Word. Theodore's point is simply to emphasize the inseparable union between the Word and the assumed man that continued even when Christ in the flesh died on the cross. The same can be said of the charge that Theodore holds that Christ *qua* human is adored.

Husband and Wife

Theodore's second analogy likens the union of Christ's natures to that between a husband and his wife. The context for understanding its meaning are three Scriptural passages: Genesis 2:22–24, in which Eve is said to be taken from the side of Adam with the two becoming one flesh; Matthew 19:5–6, in which a man and his wife are said to be one flesh whose union should not be severed because God has joined them together; and Ephesian 5:31–32, in which Paul compares the mystery of Christ's union with his Church to the union of a husband and his wife. The point that Theodore is making in this analogy is that there can be two in a permanent unity that is more than a moral union. First, the analogy appears in general to suggest, granted Paul's view of marriage mirroring Christ's relationship to his Church, a union suggesting an apparent "physical" dimension that is also permanent and indissoluble, as a marriage is meant to be.

The analogy seems based on Genesis 2:22–23. If so, Theodore's point is not how a husband and wife are one flesh in sexual intercourse but how Adam and Eve both share one nature and can be considered one body, given that she has been fashioned from Adam's body. They are in one sense one but in another two: "It is thus evident what befits the union. For through this (union), [Christ's] natures that have been bound together constitute one *prosôpon* in accordance with the union. Just as what the Lord said about a man and his wife, that 'they are no longer two but one flesh,' we would also ourselves say in a similar way in regard to the term 'union,' so that there are no longer two *prosôpa* but one, with their two natures positively distinguished. For just as his assertion there that there is one flesh does not exclude the number two—for it is evident that they are for the [same] reason said to be one—so here also the unity of the *prosôpon* does not exclude the distinction of the natures."[71] Theodore uses this analogy, then, to emphasize how two different realities can be said to form a unity on a different level and how the *prosôpa* of the human and divine natures, while two, can still be united within one *prosôpon*, as Adam and Eve, while two, are also one body.

The Soul/Body Analogy

The third analogy compares the union of Christ's natures to that between the soul and its body. This is the most interesting and revealing of Theodore's analogies. Theodore probably bases this analogy on Romans 7:14–23, where Paul speaks about the conflict between the body and its soul or, as the following passage suggests, also from experience or general knowledge: "We have appealed to sufficient arguments about the soul and knowledge [about it] to [confirm] the truth of what is being sought. We seek to show here only this (truth). Nevertheless we also show abundantly that we make known not simply the distinction of natures from the Scriptures but also the significance of the body and the rational soul [for our inquiry]."[72] Whether or not this is the source of the analogy, there are two separate issues here. The first is Theodore's willingness to use this analogy to show (as in the previous analogy) how two natures can be considered different on one level and yet truly one on another. The second and more significant issue concerns how the soul interacts with its body. This provides insight into how the Word interacts with the assumed man in their common *prosôpon*. This second purpose will be discussed at length in Chapter 7, for it deals with the kind of union Theodore envisions between Christ's natures. At present, we want to focus on how the soul and its body can be both affirmed as two and yet truly one.

Granted there are serious weaknesses in applying this analogy. For instance, the soul and the body are incomplete natures, whereas Christ's na-

---

71. *TEP* 2:299–300. See also *THC,* 206/207; *CH* 8:14: "Moreover he has said of man and woman that 'they will not be two but one body.' And the man and the woman are not two because they are a single body. They remain two in that they are two, and they are also one whereby they are one and not two." I have relied primarily on the French translation, as I found the Syriac text illegible.
72. *TFS,* fol. 11b, col. 2/50.

tures are complete. Also, the soul comes into existence by necessity at the same time as its body, whereas the Word preexists from all eternity the birth of Christ's humanity and has also freely entered into this union. Theodore, moreover, opposes Apollinaris's use of the analogy to explain philosophically the organic unity of Christ's natures. The analogy, like all alalogies, is less than perfect. As with the other two analogies, the point here is to show that, just as the soul and its body are two different (incomplete) natures yet form one person, so are Christ's divine and human natures two different natures but at the same time one on the level of their union. This makes logical sense as long as one stays close to the point of comparison and does not attempt to explain it metaphysically. For, as Theodore recognized, the analogy ought not to be interpreted to signify that a "new" nature has resulted from the union. Moreover, as the divine nature is truly simple and incapable of being limited in any way, Theodore could not admit an organic, natural binding, as Apollinarius earlier proposed.

From what we have seen, Theodore understood *prosôpon* to signify how a person externally manifests who he or she is inwardly. Because a person has to be inwardly and outwardly—for this is one and the same person—every *hypostasis* must have its own *prosôpon,* except in the unique instance of Christ, who has two natures. Theodore therefore reasons that because the Word cannot be seen in a visible way, it stands to reason that Christ's humanity's *prosôpon* must share with the divine nature a common *prosôpon.* This common *prosôpon* describes the Christ portrayed in the New Testament accounts as "the one and the same" who acts in divine and human ways, but with the added notion that his exterior appearance and actions also reveal who he is inwardly—as one who is divine as well as human.

If one understands Christ's common *prosôpon* in this way, then we can contend that it is equivalent to Theodore's understanding of Christ as the visible "image of God." When we apply the roles that Christ's humanity plays as "God's image," we can expand our understanding of how Theodore understands the one *prosôpon* of Christ. His humanity not only reveals the existence of the Word dwelling within him but also binds all creation to his humanity as a head does to its body, for all creatures share in his spiritual and bodily nature as a human being. This insight shows that the term *prosôpon* also signifies that a person is more than an individual. It also suggests that a "person" has essential relationships to others. In other words, Theodore does not consider a person a self-subsisting individual in the metaphysical sense of a subject of his or her attributes and operations. Rather, he understands the term as the ways a person is known by his or her actions within a communal "body" or "bodies" to which he or she is essentially related. This is true too of the Trinity, whose Persons are known from the ways they relate to one another internally and the ways that each is portrayed economically as acting in Scripture.

The phrase "one *prosôpon*" is also meant to express why Christ's humanity can be the recipient of adoration because of his "exact" union with the Word. Divine worship is shown to Christ's humanity insofar as it images and manifests the Word's own *prosôpon*. Since a *prosôpon* presupposes a *hypostasis*—in this case, the Word's—adoration is offered to the Word's divine triune nature through adoration shown to the common *prosôpon*. There is, in fact, only one adoration, because Christ's humanity is essentially related to the Word in an inseparable and "exact" union, just as the body organically manifests its inner soul, since both constitute one person. This functioning of the two natures as one now needs to be discussed at greater length. For, just as the phrase one *prosôpon* suggests how the assumed man and the assuming One function outwardly in human and divine ways as one, it also clearly denotes how Christ's two natures function internally as one. Theodore expresses this unity as an "indwelling of good pleasure as in God's Son."

7. THE WORD'S "INDWELLING OF GOOD PLEASURE"

I N THE PRECEDING CHAPTER I tried to show how Theodore's phrase the one *prosôpon* sums up the visible
ways that Christ's divine and human natures are portrayed in the New Testament accounts as acting as one in human and divine ways. The question now to be faced is, what
does Theodore mean by the "exact union" of two natures in
one *prosôpon?* When pressed to explain, Theodore expressly
denies that it can be either a substantial or a purely moral, operational kind of union.[1] He delineates it rather in biblical
terms as an "indwelling of good pleasure as in the Son."
While he seems to have deliberately excluded any metaphysical kind of explanation by rejecting both a substantial and an
operational kind of union, his reply nevertheless has to be applicable to some philosophical category of union. As his adversaries have pointed out, his own manner of assigning pred-

---

1. This passage is found in Book VII of Theodore's *De Incarnatione.*
The present text is found in *TEP* 2:293–95.

icates to Christ's two natures and his common *prosôpon* provides a key to what he has in mind here.

I begin by ascertaining the source of Theodore's statement that the Word's union with Christ's human nature is an "indwelling of good pleasure as in the Son," so as to establish the context. I then look at what Theodore means when he speaks about the Word as the "Son of God by nature" and the assumed man as the "Son by grace," and the roles the Spirit plays both in the union of Christ's natures and in Christ's earthy life. Next I discuss how the Christian philosopher and theologian Nemesius, a contemporary of Theodore, can help us understand Theodore's analogy between the functional union of the Word and the assumed man and that of a soul and its body. Finally I analyze how and why Theodore assigns attributes to each of Christ's natures and to the common prosôpon—in other words, what is Theodore's equivalent to the classical *communicatio idiomatum*. This will prepare us for Chapters 8 and 9, where we will apply the insights derived from earlier chapters to reassess the excerpts cited at Constantinople II as grounds for condemning Theodore and his works.

An Inhabitation of Good Pleasure

As discussed in the previous chapter, Theodore adopts the phrase "one *prosôpon*" as the best way to express the union of Christ's two natures. When challenged to expand upon this union, Theodore turned, as one would expect, to Scripture for the terms and the ideas that best describe his view of the union. While it is hard to fault Theodore for resorting to Scripture, I am sympathetic to those who are convinced that his scriptural answer must ultimately be reduced to an ontological kind of union. This is, in fact, what the council fathers and most subsequent theologians have attempted ever since to demonstrate. They rely upon a passage from his work *On the Incarnation* as the best indication of his thought. Theodore expressly denies there that Christ's two natures can be joined in a substantial unity: "Therefore one can say that it is neither by substance nor by operation that the Divine has made a dwelling."[2] For a substantial union

2. Swete, in *TEP*, believes the *De Incarnatione* must be assigned either to the earliest years of Theodore's episcopate or to his earlier life at Tarsus (2:290). He relies upon the

would mean to him that the transcendent divinity can be limited to a specific location—an impossibility because he is present in all reality as its Creator. In his letter to Domnus, Theodore offers an additional reason. A substantial union occurs between two realities each possessing the same substance—a condition that does not apply here. For Christ's divine and human natures are wholly different substances: "Why is there need [to say] more? The reason for a union according to substance truly applies only [in the case of those natures that have] the same substances but is false in [the case of] those having another substance."[3] In other words, since Christ's two natures are substantially different from each other, they can be said to be two natures but not two in fact belonging to the same kind of nature. Analogously, we can speak of two apples, but these are not two in the same way that an apple and a pear are two kinds of fruit.

On the Incarnation also rejects an operational union of Christ's two natures. For God's power is present everywhere. But in his letter to Domus, Theodore appears to contradict this: "But by preserving the two natures unconfused and undivided, the kind of union according to 'good pleasure' affirms one person for both, as well as one will and one operation together with one authority and absolute rule."[4] If the Word is united to Christ's humanity in a union of "one will and one operation together with one authority and absolute rule," this kind of union would seem to place Theodore in a dilemma: either it must be an accidental one—which Theodore's critics are convinced is his actual position—or his acceptance of one operation in the union indicates that he holds for one resulting nature in the union, that of the Word. While I shall discuss this question more thoroughly later, suffice it to say that he appears to be asserting here that the divine and human wills, while still two, fuse into one within the common *prosôpon*. As we shall also see, Theodore believes that the union he is proposing is more than an operational one and yet not a strictly organic one, which would oc-

---

passage that Facundus (PL 67:321) cites from Theodore's introduction to his *De Apollinario et ejus Heresi:* "We have written the codex *De Incarnatione Domini* thirty years ago containing up to 15,000 lines in which work we have examined throughout the failures of Arius and Eunomius in this regard and also the vain presumption of Apollinaris."

3. Theodore, PG 66:1013.

4. *TEP* 2:295–96.

cur if there is only one resulting nature, the divine. But, as pointed out in the previous chapter, Theodore approaches the problem of the union of Christ's two natures not from any metaphysical perspective but from the existential way that Christ is presented in the Gospels as appearing to act as one "person" both outwardly and inwardly. His is a functional approach that presumes the presence of a true unity underlying the operational unity.

Theodore is aware in *On the Incarnation* of the need to state that the union of Christ's natures is more than an accidental one, because if the union occurs solely on the level of God's benevolent will, this would be similar to God's union with the saints. So, as an alternative to his rejection of both a substantial and an operational union, Theodore chooses to describe it as "an indwelling of good pleasure." But what kind of union is this, if it is neither substantial nor operational? It would appear to be incontrovertible, metaphysically speaking, that the union has to be either one or the other. His adversaries are confident that this becomes clear when he explains his "indwelling of good pleasure" as occurring "as in a son." For he immediately speaks about how Christ can be said to share in the honors of the Word. When this view is taken together with his many other statements affirming that the assumed man and the Word each act in accordance with their natures, his response appears to justify the conclusion that the graced union of Christ's two natures differs not in a radical way but only in an superior degree of grace and honor from that existing between God and his saints. Such an interpretation as this makes sense as long as the excerpts used to condemn Theodore are examined wholly apart from their own wider contexts and his overall theological synthesis.

The Meaning of the Term "Indwelling"

As all admit, Theodore chooses the word "indwelling" so as to stay close to Scripture. He prefers to use a biblical, descriptive word present in John and Paul rather than a metaphysical term, as Cyril's does with *hypostasis*. For instance, Theodore notes that John, immediately after asserting that "The Word became flesh" (John 1:14) describes this union as an "indwelling." John's intention here was to prevent misinterpretation, according to Theodore. "How, then, does the indwelling Word of God become flesh? It is evident that He has not been changed [into another nature] or translated [from one place to another]. Otherwise he would not also have said 'to indwell.'"[5] Theodore readily concedes that the word "indwelling" can be understood in different ways: "They should know that because the term 'inhabitation' is a universal, it does not indicate a particular kind of inhabitation. . . . For [example,] because a human being shares in the name of a living being, [it does] not [follow that] he is an ass, a bull, a sheep, a lion, a wolf (or bear), and a reptile, with whom a human being also shares [the designation as an animal]. [Each] is viewed as being one [species of a genus] but the understanding of each by itself is likewise also preserved."[6] For Theodore, his term is a specific kind of "indwelling."

Theodore specifies that the kind of "indwelling" he means is one of divine "good pleasure" or, perhaps better rendered in English, divine "benevolence." As such, it conveys the idea that a person is well pleased with another and does something explicitly to express that good will: "by good pleasure God is distant from some, and near to others. . . . For He becomes [close] by being very well disposed to those who are worthy of this nearness, and again far from those who sin."[7] In other words, a union of "good pleasure" essentially expresses God's own benevolent will for those who lovingly do his will. God manifests his good pleasure for Christ by uniting his humanity to his Son, the Word, so that they both become one: "But God the Word dwelt [within him] from [the very moment of his] fashioning in the womb of [his] mother, an inhabitation not according to a common inhabitation nor according to that grace understood [to be bestowed] on many, but according to a certain excelling (grace) whereby we say both natures are also united as one; and one person is brought about in accordance with a union of one."[8] The Word's indwelling within Christ's human nature is therefore a special graced honor exceeding that shown to the saints, because his human nature is inseparably united with the Word's nature.

In addition, Theodore understands that the word "indwelling" also excludes the idea of a union where Christ's natures are mixed: "By what we

5. Facundus has preserved this passage from Theodore. It is found in PL 67:762.
6. *TFS*, fol. 2a/35.   7. *TEP* 2:295.
8. Ibid., 2:307–8.

have said up to this point, we manifest the strength and excellence of the church's doctrine and speak aptly of an 'indwelling.' From the very words of Scripture we have capably shown that we are repeating what was previously said—that we rightly retain the word 'unity' and again reject the word 'mixture.'"[9] Theodore is reacting here against the Apollinarian interpretation of how "the Word became flesh." For if it is true that the Word has supplanted Christ's rational soul *(nous),* then this mixture of the human with the divine would be a hybrid. For Theodore, Apollinaris clearly interprets the Word's becoming human in much too literal a way: "John clearly says here: 'He became flesh' instead of 'He came to be in a human being.' For he said: 'He became.' He did not come to be [in the sense] that He was changed, but that He was believed to have been in appearance."[10] I quoted this passage earlier, when examining how Christ's humanity serves as God's true visible "image" and forms one common *prosôpon* with the Word's *prosôpon.* Theodore's primary point here is to reject the opinion of those who—he believes—cling literally to the view that Christ's humanity has been changed into the divine so that the Word has actually appeared in a visible way. Theodore insists that Christ's humanity visibly images the invisible Word. His visible appearance reveals God: "For it is impossible here on earth to see God."[11]

If the Word has not been changed in his nature, how then does the phrase "indwelling as in a s/Son" help to explain the union? As emphasized in Chapter 2, on Theodore's exegesis, he consults all other passages containing the same words to see to what extent they can provide him insight. So when Theodore elaborates on how the divine good pleasure lavished upon Christ's humanity differs from that shown to the saints, he

9. *TFS,* fol. 10b/44.

10. *TJA,* 33–34/23. Later in this passage, Theodore indicates the dates when he wrote his Commentary on John's Gospel and his work *On the Incarnation:* "If you earnestly want to learn more about this, you may go to the volume that we wrote about the human nature of Christ and then be accurately instructed concerning this verse as well as the whole subject treated there." When taken with Theodore's comment in his *De Apollinario et ejus Heresi* (noted in note 2 above), this means that John's Commentary was probably written in the 410s to 420s and *On the Incarnation* in the 380s to 390s.

11. Ibid., 39/27.

notes that this phrase is to be taken as it is "understood by Scripture in the customary way it has been confirmed there."[12] We find four passages in the New Testament where the words "indwelling," "good pleasure," and "Son," occur together: John's prologue, the accounts of Jesus' baptism and transfiguration, and Colossians 1:15–20 and 2:9–10. The last citation is particularly interesting, as we saw in Chapters 4 and 5, because Christ *qua* man is affirmed to be the "beloved Son" (Col. 1:13) who is the "image of God" (Col. 1:15), who is before all things and in whom all are bound together (1:17) and in whom (2:9) all the *plerôma* of the divinity dwells bodily *(sômatikôs)*.[13]

"An Indwelling as in His Son"

When Theodore speaks of the "indwelling of good pleasure" as being "in His Son" (ὡς ἐν υἱῷ),[14] the latter phrase can be translated in two equally correct ways. Since there is no Greek article before the noun "son," it is ordinarily translated in a generic sense, meaning "a son," which is how Kevin McNamara and Francis Sullivan have taken it.[15] But the article can also be omitted before a proper noun, in which case, we would read Theodore here as referring to the "Son of God." This is how Luise Abramowski understands it, translating the phrase "as in His true Son."[16] The first interpretation is difficult to make sense of in the context at hand, as witnessed by the relative silence of McNamara and Sullivan on this point.

Fortunately, we have a fragment from Theodore's *On the Incarnation* that indicates that the latter translation is the preferred one: "Therefore (the sacred writer) did not affirm that 'He spoke to us in *the* [the Greek ar-

12. *TEP* 2:294. The allusion may be to Matt. 11:25 and Luke 10:21, where Jesus praises his Father's gracious will for having chosen to reveal imself to the childlike.
13. In Köster's *Theological Dictionary of the New Testament,* abridged by Geoffrey W. Bromiley, Bromiley suggests an interpretation that can apply to Theodore's outlook on Christ's humanity: "The *sômatikôs* in this statement denotes the corporeality in which God encounters us in our world, i.e., the real humanity of Jesus, not a humanity that is a mere cloak for deity" (1147).
14. *TEP* 2:296.
15. Kevin McNamara, "Theodore and the Nestorian Heresy," *Irish Theological Quarterly,* part 2 (April 1953): 176–79; Sullivan, *Christology of Theodore,* 245–47.
16. Abramowski, "Zur Theologie Theodors," 293.

ticle expressed] Son' but 'in *a* [without the article] Son.' What is said absolutely [the latter case] could signify both [meanings] in this case, first of all, signifying the real Son. I call the true Son the One possessing Sonship by natural generation and also secondarily the one receiving it by designation who also shares the dignity because of his union with the Word."[17] Theodore repeats the same idea in his commentary on the letter to the Hebrews: "Therefore, he did not say: 'He spoke to us as in a son,' but 'in the Son.' For what is affirmed in an unconditional way can signify both [the specific and the unspecific] by the same [phrase]."[18] Theodore is even more explicit in connecting the idea of Christ's true sonship to his union with the Word, writing "because of his union to God the Word, he is honored as the true Son by all human beings."[19] It is clear from all this that when Theodore speaks of an indwelling ὡς ἐν υἱῷ, he intends the phrase in question to be translated "as in His true Son." For it is because the humanity of Christ is united by nature to the Word that he also shares in the Word's sonship, as Theodore understands it. It is somewhat similar to the way that those united to the human body of Christ can share in the immortality that he now enjoys in heaven.

The excerpt from *On the Incarnation* that speaks of "the indwelling of good pleasure as in His true Son" ends after Theodore affirms at some length that Christ as the Son shares in the honors of the Word. We can gain further insight into its meaning by interpreting it in light of Colossians 1–2. Christ is affirmed here to be the Son who is the "visible image" of God in whom "all the divine fullness *(plerôma)* was pleased to dwell" (Col. 1:19) and whom "the whole fullness *(plerôma)* dwells in a bodily way" (Col. 2:9). Applying these affirmations to Theodore's statement that God's "good

---

17. *TEP* 2.303.

18. Ibid. Theodore also uses this phrase as specifying Christ as the Son of God who shares in the Word's honors: "When he says likewise (in the Letter) to the Hebrews: 'He spoke to us in the [the article omitted] Son whom He appointed the heir of all' . . . he is clearly speaking about the human being whose words we have also heard . . . but He passes over to the divinity to confirm thereby the greatness of these things and again returns to the humanity, speaking in that part of the epistle about all things as though [proceeding] from one [person]." *TEP* 1:272–73.

19. *TJA*, 350/351.

pleasure" differs in the case of Christ in the flesh from God's graced presence in the saints "as in His true Son," Theodore is declaring that God's "good pleasure" toward Christ *qua* human differs radically in the way God manifests his pleasure to all others. For Christ's humanity alone has received the entire divine *plerôma* because of his "exact" union with the Word of God. This indicates a totally radical difference in kind, not in degree, from even the greatest grace that any saint has ever received.

The assumed man, therefore, surpasses even the greatest of saints because his humanity alone has received the divine *plerôma*. All others participate in his *plerôma* but in a limited way, depending upon what graces the assumed man, together with the Spirit, has apportioned them. All who are baptized become children of God but are not sons and daughters in the unique way that Christ is the true Son: "For the entire grace of the Spirit has been given to me, because I am joined to God the Word and have received true Sonship. For the grace that is [present] in me and to me, a limited portion will come upon you in order that you too may also be called children of God, although you are far removed from the honor bestowed on me as the Son. . . . This cannot happen to you, as you can acquire a small share—but one not at all equal to mine" (297–98/213). Christ *qua* man also differs from all others in that he has been gifted with supreme power over all creation: "That he is in his human nature truly much more exceptional than John [the Baptist] is clear both from his overwhelming power and from his union with God the Word, whereby he is elevated not only over all human beings but over all creatures" (44/31).

From what we have seen in the chapters regarding Christ's humanity's salvific roles as head of the Church and the universe, Theodore maintains that Christ *qua* man is fully present in both: "He also calls the church and indeed the universe to be the '*plerôma* of God,' insofar as he is in everything and is fully in everything." This makes sense if Christ's humanity is regarded as the head of a quasi-organic union and is far superior to all others, as the head is to the members of its body. In the previous chapters, I showed how his humanity alone serves uniquely as the sole mediating bond providing all other creatures access to God. Those, therefore, who regard Theodore's "indwelling of good pleasure as in His Son" as not sufficiently affirming how Christ in the flesh differs from the saints are judging, it seems, the passage at hand outside its scriptural context and Theodore's general theological framework regarding the roles of Christ's humanity in salvation.

Christ as the Son of God by Grace

If Theodore holds that Christ is a true Son of God, why does he distinguish between the Word as the "Son of God by nature" and Christ's humanity as "His Son by grace"? Theodore seems to be offering here clear proof that he does hold for two separate individuals. His guarded distinction appears to make his assumed man an adopted child of God, like those who are united to his body. It is true that they receive only a small portion of the graces that he has fully obtained by his sinless life, but he, like them, is in the last analysis only a son "by grace." Only the Word is truly God's Son by nature. Nonetheless, despite his clarification Theodore does insist that "Because of his union to God the Word, Christ is honored as a true Son by all human beings" (350/251). In fact, the reason why Theodore thinks Christ can be said to be a true Son of God is the fullness of grace bestowed on his nature because of his union with the Word: "For the entire grace of the Spirit has been given to me, because I am joined to God the Word and have received true Sonship. For the grace that is [present] in me and to me, a small portion will come upon you in order that you may also be called children of God" (297–98/213). This reception of the entire divine *plerôma* appears to be an early Pauline way of expressing Christ's divinity.

Theodore maintains that Christ in the flesh can truly regard God as his Father because of his humanity's shared "exact union" with the Word who is the Father's Son by nature: "Whence on account of the participation in the nature [that he shares], he says: 'my Father and your Father and my God and your God'; he has distinguished, however, his own person [the Syriac word for *prosôpon*] from these others, indicating the more excellent grace that he received whereby he is honored by all as the true Son on account of having been united to God the Word" (350/251). Of course, Theodore refers to the assumed man as a true Son of God by grace because of his need to keep Christ's two natures both intact and integral. Moreover, he cannot agree to any substantial unity between the Creator and a creature. Thus his stumbling block is how to justify a created human nature, even one so exalted as Christ's, being united in a direct way to an uncreated nature: "For it is not possible that the one who has come to be [can] be like that One who is from all eternity, because it is not possible that the one who has a beginning be like One existing from all eternity" (251/181). Theodore recognizes that the union can be accomplished only in an existential functional way because a unique grace from the Spirit makes it possible for Christ's humanity to function as one with the Word and to share in the attributes of the Word's nature, as the body does in the power and achievements of its soul. Before developing this point, we need to consider how not only the Word but His Spirit dwells within the assumed man.

The Indwelling of the Holy Spirit

Following Scripture, Theodore sees that the Holy Spirit plays two important roles in Christ's life: first, it enables Christ's human nature to be united to the Word at the Incarnation, and second, it leads and assists Christ in the flesh throughout his earthly life in being faithful to his union with the Word and in his roles as the mediator of graces to those who are united to him as a head to its body. First, Theodore holds that for Christ's humanity to be uniquely joined to the Word at the initial moment of his conception, the Spirit had to be involved. For it is not in the nature of Christ in the flesh to be united to God the Word. He needs the Spirit's mediation for the union to take place.[20] Theodore has doubtless reasoned to this from Luke's testimonial (1:35) of Jesus' birth, where the Spirit is said to have overshadowed Mary, so that the one born from her will be called the Son of God. While the Holy Spirit's assistance is required for Christ's humanity to be united to the Word, it is because of his union with the only begotten Son of God that Christ in the flesh can be called the Son of God and the sole mediator of the graces for those whom the Spirit regenerates at baptism: "'Christ in the flesh' is the first one to be generated in the Spir-

20. See *THC*, 82/83; *CH* 4:5.

it and, because of the Spirit's mediation, is united to the only begotten, from whom he has obtained the true dignity of Sonship and communicates to us the gift of the Spirit by whom we are also regenerated and are enumerated among His children according to the measure of each one's virtue."[21] Christ in the flesh is alone the true Son directly and immediately by the grace of his union and all others indirectly and mediately by the graces uniting them as living members to Christ as their head.

Theodore realized that the Spirit actively assisted in Christ's human life in three additional ways: through the supportive graces the Spirit provided Christ's humanity during his earthly life, through the Spirit's glorification of Christ's humanity at the resurrection, and through the Spirit's empowerment of Christ to rule over all of creation. Theodore summarizes the Spirit's activity in Christ's life as recounted in the Gospels: "For it is stated: 'He was being led by the Spirit.' Clearly this signifies that he was being ruled by him, strengthened by him for the power [to realize his] plans, led by him to what he ought [to accomplish], taught by him about what was right, bolstered by him in his thoughts so as to prevail in his vigorous struggle [against inordinate passions]."[22] The Spirit is, moreover, fully responsible for the power Christ *qua* man exercises over all of creation: "So it is fitting that he mentioned [here] the Spirit. For it was through him that he has received union, rebirth, and domination over all."[23] For his own part, Christ freely responded to these graces with exactitude: "After (Christ in the flesh) received the whole perfect grace at [his] anointing, he led [his] life in extreme exactness, in a way that human nature could not accomplish [on its own]" (296–97/212). The Spirit also plays a determining role in uniting the baptized to Christ. The Spirit empowers the members of Christ's body, the Church, to be joined to him as their head in a "natural union": "The assumed man now became the principle of all goods for all humans because of what has been fulfilled in him. All of us are going to share these, whether in [our] resurrection or in [our] ascension into heaven or in the kingdom or in glory. . . . And henceforth the congregation of [all] believers is also [to be] called the body of Christ and each one of us is

21. *TJA*, 47/33.   22. *TEP* 2:315–16.
23. *TJA*, 83/59.

a member of it and he is the head of all of us because by the power of the Spirit we receive, as it were, a natural union with him" (296–97/212).

One final point needs to be made about the role of the Spirit in the earthly life of Christ. When Theodore speaks of the indwelling of the Spirit in Christ and in others, he qualifies this as he has done in asserting that the Word dwells within the humanity of Christ. There cannot be a substantial union between a divine and a human nature. Just as Christ is Son by grace, so also those who receive the Spirit are not united to the Spirit as a divine Person but are the recipients simply of his graces: "Then we also understand by this that the 'Holy Spirit' many times does not designate the Person [qenômâ, the Syriac word for hypostasis] of the Holy Spirit and his nature but rather his operation and his grace" (162/115).

The Prosopic Union of Two Concrete Natures

Theodore is confronted with two difficult problems: how to maintain the full integrity of each of Christ's divine and human natures in a true unity, and how to explain the manner whereby the Word's divine nature and Christ's created human nature actually function together. First, because he insists that both the divine and the human nature are real, concrete, and freely able to exercise their powers, Theodore's adversaries accused him of holding for two sons and two lords. He denies this emphatically: "Because we speak about two natures, we are not forced to say that there are two lords or two sons. This would be naïveté in the extreme. For what has made all those who are two to be one in some way but one in another way does not destroy the distinction of (their) natures. Nor does this distinction between natures contradict the fact they are one."[24] For instance, that the fathers liked to point out that there are three Persons in the Trinity does not preclude their possessing one divine nature.

In the previous chapter, we saw that Theodore argued that two realities can exist independently on one level but be one on a different level. While this is generally true, how can the simple divine nature that cannot be lim-

24. THC, 206/207; CH 8:14. I have relied primarily on the French translation, as the Syriac text is difficult to read.

ited be joined to a creature? "For the nature of God the Word which is simple and simply not able to be contaminated cannot be composed."[25] How then do these two natures, each with its own *hypostasis*, interact in a way that they can be said to be existing in a true union, and what kind of union can this be? We can discover an answer in the analogy likening the union of Christ's two natures to that between the soul and its body. The following passage speaks directly to these questions.

> If then God the Word in His nature is the perfect Son of God, He is so by [eternal] generation from [His] Father. Therefore the one who does not share this [divine] nature is not so named by reason of his very own person [the Syriac equivalent of *prosôpon*] by itself, but is endowed with the name of the Son of God because of his exact union with God the Word. And what is said of God the Word is also clearly understood of the one assumed, even though he has been made perfect. And we are not forced because of this to say "two sons." For the soul and its body are two natures and are not like each other. This is evident, and these [heretics] also acknowledge [this]: namely, if the two natures [of soul and body] which are assumed are not like each other or like God the Word who has assumed [them], neither do they of themselves constitute another person [Syriac word for *prosôpon*] because of their union with God the Word.[26]

But how, then, do these two natures function in a true way as one?

Nemesius's Explanation

Robert Arnou and Kevin McNamara have called attention to the close similarity in language and thought between Theodore and Nemesius regarding the union of the soul and its body.[27] It is easy to establish a convincing connection. Nemesius was a Christian philosopher and a theologian who wrote at or near Antioch in the second half of the fourth century and doubtless alludes to Theodore in his own classical work *On Human Nature*, even though he couched his criticism in a restrained, respectful

---

25. Facundus of Hermiane, PL 67:755.

26. *TFS*, fol. 7a/39.

27. Robert Arnou, "Nestorianisme et Neoplatonisme: L'unité du Christ et l'union des'Intelligibles,'" *Gregorianum* 17 (1936): 16–31; and McNamara, "Theodore and the Nestorian Heresy," part 2 (April 1953): 172–91.

way when he rejected "the opinion of certain men of note . . . who maintain that the union is by divine favor."[28] He strongly objected that the
union of the divine and human natures in Christ ought to be "grounded in
nature" (299). Because Nemesius is opposed in other places to a Monophysite interpretation of how the divine and human natures in Christ are
united, his union "grounded in nature" seems to be asserting that the
union needs to be explained on a level deeper than one of "divine favor,"
in which two persons act in ways pleasing to each other. Thus it is not un-
reasonable to assume that Theodore was well aware of Nemesius's criticism of his "indwelling of good pleasure" and thus of his opinion on how
the soul interacts with its body.

Although Nemesius's *On Human Nature* is philosophical, Nemesius
does frequently appeal to fundamental Christian theological positions that
bolster his metaphysical stance. For instance, he describes the Word as interacting with Christ's soul and body in a way that is close to how the fathers at the Council of Chalcedon would later speak of the union of Christ's
natures: "the Word mingles with body and soul, and yet remains throughout unmixed, unconfused, uncorrupted, untransformed, not sharing their
passivity but only their activity, not perishing with them, not changing as
they change; but, on the one hand, contributing to their growth, and, on
the other, in no way degraded by contact with them, so that he continues
immutable and unconfused, seeing that he is altogether without share in
any kind of alteration" (301).[29] The use of negative words in this statement
brings out how Nemesius viewed the dynamic interplay between Christ's
two natures. Both the soul and its body have active roles to play within
their union with the Word.

Nemesius's discussion of how the human soul acts upon its body re-

28. Nemesius's *On Human Nature*; hereafter cited parenthetically in the text; Nemesius of Emesa, *Cyril of Jerusalem and Nemesius of Emesa*, ed. and trans. William Telfer,
Library of Christian Classics 4 (Philadelphia: Westminster, 1955), 303, 299. Telfer asserts
that Nemesius's use of the anonymous plural should not be understood as referring to
anyone other than Theodore.

29. The fathers at the Council of Chalcedon declared that the union ought to be "acknowledged in two natures which undergo no mixture, no change, no division, and no
separation" (Tanner, *Decrees of the Ecumenical Councils*, 86).

veals that he accepts the Neoplatonic principle that a spiritual reality can impart a life-giving energy to those material beings capable of receiving its power without its own spiritual nature being compromised: "it is the nature of the *intelligibles* both to be capable of union with things adapted to receive them and to remain, nevertheless, unconfused with them while in the union" (295). Nemesius does grant, however, that a soul can truly feel sympathy for its nonequal partner: "the vital power which is prerequisite to feeling is acknowledged to be derived by the body from the soul. It is, therefore, legitimate to speak of the soul's 'sympathy' with its body, thus recognizing that while the soul and body are not partners on equal terms, in this respect they are partners" (297). The reason whereby a soul can interrelate "sympathetically" with its body is: "to wit, the community of feeling which is throughout the living creature, because it is one subject" (296–97). In other words, a human soul can and does share in a sympathetic way in what its body experiences because both are joined as one in the same living organism.

Nemesius also regards the active "sympathy" that the soul extends to its corporeal partner as habitual in nature: "Therefore, if the soul is said to be in a body, it is not affirmed in the sense of being located in a body, but rather as being in a habitual relation of presence there, even as God is said to be in us. For we may say that the soul is bound by habit to the body, or by an inclination or disposition toward it, just as they say that a lover is bound to his beloved, not meaning physically, or spatially, but habitually" (299). This habitual kind of union, of course, does not define the metaphysical union that exists between a spiritual and a material nature. It simply describes the functional way (or the *how*) a spiritual being is continually disposed in a loving way toward its corporeal partner but is not altered in the process.

Using Nemesius as a backdrop, we are in a position, I believe, to understand Theodore's analogy of how God's good pleasure can dwell in Christ's humanity without the divine nature in any way being altered: "Therefore what we have said suffices for this [way of speaking] where we have shown both the difference between the natures and the unity of the person; that is, in regard to [the difference of] the natures, this one receives the favor, the former gives it, with a fixed unity established whereby honor is fully shown in an undivided way [to both] by the whole creation. We have employed sufficient arguments about the soul and knowledge to [confirm] the truth of what is being sought. We seek to show here only this. Nevertheless we also have shown at great length that we do not simply teach from the Scriptures but also from the implication of the [union of the] body and the rational soul the distinction of [their] natures."[30]

William Telfer, who has edited Nemesius's work, observes that despite Nemesius's criticism of Theodore, there is a similarity between Nemesius's "soul suffering out of compassion" for its bodily companion and Theodore's "inhabitation of good pleasure": "We may compare Nemesius' notion of the soul's indwelling in the body by habit of predilection with that of Theodore of Mopsuestia that God indwells in the righteous, not by omnipresence, but by his good favor (eudokia)."[31] In other words, Telfer believes that Nemesius's way of speaking of the habitual relationship between the soul and its body and Theodore's union of good pleasure are describing in different words how the Word acts habitually upon Jesus' humanity, from the moment of conception throughout their inseparable union together. They affirm that, while the Word is not directly altered by his contact with Jesus' human nature, it is continually disposed to act sympathetically on his be-

---

30. *TFS*, fol. 11b, col. 1–2/49–50.

31. Nemesius, *Cyril of Jerusalem*, 299n8. In his *Christ in Christian Tradition*, Alois Grillmeier criticizes Nemesius's Christological stance as operational and not at all substantial: "However much (Nemesius) may continue to stress the conjunction of substance with substance he can achieve no more than a *'co-action.'* . . . Here the unity in Christ transcends the unity of soul and body, as in the latter the soul is affected because it is not completely free from material and corporeal elements (PG 40:601AB)" (*Christ in Christian Tradition*, 1:390–91). This is a valid criticism and can be aimed at Theodore as well. Granted that the analogy between the union of a soul and its body and that between the Word and the assumed man limps in a number of ways, I think, however, that Nemesius and Theodore are stressing the presence of some sort of an quasi-organic unity in which the spiritual and the material can interact as one. This is difficult to conceive, for it is a mystery that the human mind cannot fully grasp. But it is just as much a problem for those affirming that the Word is the personal subject of Christ's human attributes and operations. For how does the Word who has appropriated Christ's human nature act in such a way that Christ's human will truly acts in a free way? They presume, of course, that the Word appropriates Christ's human nature in a way that respects its integrity and ability to act freely.

half, as a lover would toward his or her beloved, and supplies the vitality and energy for Jesus' humanity to act and respond. The point, however, is that this union occurs within a personal and, if one can push the analogy, quasi-organic union similar to that between the soul and its body.

Nemesius thus helps to elucidate how Theodore appears to have conceived of how the Word acts on Christ's humanity such that each nature can be different and yet function as one, without either's integrity being compromised. This analogy is common to the fathers. It clarifies, too, how Theodore envisions the role Christ's humanity plays as God's "image."[32] It suggests that Christ's humanity visibly reveals the Word just as the body manifests its soul. Nemesius offers another illustration of the relationship between the soul and its body and between Christ's humanity as the visible "image" and the Word as its inner reality. He says that a ray of light embodies the sun from which it has emanated. As the source of this light, the sun differs from the ray but is illumined in it: "The presence of the sun transforms the air into light, making the air effulgent by uniting light with air, at once maintaining them distinct and melting them together, so likewise the soul is united to the body and yet remains distinct from it."[33] This expresses well how Theodore conceives of the way Christ's humanity reveals the presence of the Word dwelling within him: "But through those things that we witness, we accept him truly as the only begotten Son. For those things we see are such that they abundantly declare the greatness of that one who has been seen, because they can be from no other than the only begotten, who has an exact likeness with [His] Father."[34] Norris captures this superior/inferior relation when he notes, "It seems evident that Theodore attaches great significance to the relationship of subordination between the Word and the Man which, as he sees it, makes an organic unity of a 'conjunction' between two subjects. . . . His point seems to be that there is a single source (though not a single subject) of all that Christ is and does, and that this source is the divine Word who dwells in the Man."[35]

32. See Kelly, *Early Christian Doctrines*, 98.
33. Nemesius, *Cyril of Jerusalem*, 298.
34. *TJA*, 34–35/24.
35. Norris, *Manhood and Christ*, 228. He also repeats this idea on p. 231: "When Theodore speaks of Christ as one πρόσωπον he means that, because of the union

We can sum this up by saying that Nemesius's and Theodore's Christo-logical approaches function by emphasizing how the divine and human natures of Christ interact with each other, not in a static but in a dynamic way. They at least imply a model similar to the organic unity between the soul and its body. It is a different approach from that of Cyril and his followers, who seek a unity that justifies such linguistic statements as that Mary is the mother of God. Since Cyril holds that the Nicene Creed affirms that the Word and the Lord Jesus Christ are one and the same, he can logically substitute the Word for Jesus and state that Mary is indeed the Mother of God. While one can accept in faith that the creed expresses truths of revelation, this approach does not address the quandary that Theodore was most concerned about: how can Christ's human will act freely in an integral, existential way within its "exact" union with the Word? He reasons that the external unity Jesus manifested in his earthly life as a common *prosôpon* signals the presence of a true personal unity that underlies their ability to function as one. I am tempted to call this underlying union a substantial one except that Theodore so connects the term "substance" with "hypostasis" that he would regard the union as "natural." So, while one can find fault with Theodore's "indwelling of good pleasure" for not expressing the substantial unity that has to exist between Christ's natures if there is to be a true unity, this does not justify the conclusion that he denies such a unity. He is dealing with the issue of unity on a different level from Cyril. For while Cyril's approach has its strengths, it has trouble explaining how Christ's divine and human natures, both with their own separate wills, function together within a single Person who is the subject of all their attributes and operations, at least in a linguistic, if not in an ontological, way. Theologians describe this as an appropriation of Christ's human nature by the Word in such a free way that the Word allows the human nature to act according to its nature in a truly free way within their substantial union. But this is the area where Theodore was struggling to express and integrate the functional unity of Christ's two separate natures.

---

between the Word and the assumed Man, the Lord presents himself to the world and to the believer as a single object of knowledge and faith and a single agent of reconciliation with God."

The Word's Initiative

While Theodore strenuously defends the full integrity of the human and divine natures in the union, he does acknowledge, as we have seen, that it is the Word that initiates and completes the activity in the union: "as regards the natures, this one receives the favor, the Former gives it, with a certain unity established whereby honor is fully displayed in an undivided way [to both] by all creation."[36] This statement must be understood, nevertheless, in light of Theodore's defense of Christ's human freedom. His human reception of divine favor must be seen as leaving him humanly free in a nondeterministic way: "There is always present to me the power of operating whenever or howsoever I will want [to act]."[37] "I also act whenever I want, as there is no set time for those things to be done by me for human salvation. And just as (the Father) has the power of operating, so do I. . . . For I also have power to act in an equal way whenever I want."[38] Yet this freedom has to be reconciled with the Word's power: "If, therefore, (Christ) affirms that such great power has been bestowed upon him, consider who it is who dwells in him, whether he is perfectly like the One who works everything He wants and as He wants through His own innate power."[39] So this ability of Christ's human will to act freely while being empowered by the Word places us at the heart of the mystery of how the human and divine wills can be said to be truly one.

When Theodore speaks of "one will and operation" in Christ, he appears to be referring to how the human and divine wills function as one in their common *prosôpon*. Since Christ is portrayed as one person in the gospel accounts, this must mean that there is present one will internally, that is, that the human will always freely chooses to be one with the di-

36. *TFS*, fol. 8b, col. 2/50.

37. *TJA*, 56/39.

38. Ibid., 104/74. The same idea is expressed in 56/39: "There is always present to me the power of operating whenever or howsoever I will want [to act]."

39. *TJA*, 270/193. Theodore also expresses the preeminence of the divinity in the following: "When we look to the union, then we proclaim that both natures to be one 'persona' with the humanity receiving from [all] creation the honor belonging to the Divinity and the Divinity completing in (the humanity) everything that is needed." *TEP* 2:299–300.

vine: "By preserving the natures unconfused and undivided, the union of good pleasure shows [that there is] one person for both and one will and one operation with the accompanying one authority and absolute rule. . . . For by being thus conjoined to God the Word by means of His good pleasure, as we have said, that temple who is born from the womb of the Virgin remained undivided, having the same will and the same operation with him in all things, than which nothing can be more conjoined."[40] In brief, while Christ's humanity derives its power to act because of the Word's initiative and empowerment and forms one will with the Word, still Theodore considers that all this is done in a mysterious free way. Otherwise, Theodore would be espousing a monoenergistic or Monothelite view of the unity in Christ—a view he roundly rejects.

'Communicatio Idiomatum'

The *communicatio idiomatum* is a technical theological Latin phrase Christians use to indicate whether one is correctly attributing predicates to the Person of the incarnate Son of God. In its classical form, it justifies the direct application of human properties to the Word as their personal subject. According to this standard, one can rightly state that "the Word died on the cross" and that "Mary is the mother of God." Its rules evolved out of the twelve anathemas that Cyril issued against Nestorius and their modified form as found in the Pact of Reunion that Cyril later signed with John of Antioch.[41] They have been motivated too by the conciliar decrees declaring Christ to be the Person of the Word who subsists in a divine and a human nature. As such, the *communicatio idiomatum* justifies traditional liturgical and creedal statements about Christ as the Word. During Theodore's lifetime, however, these rules were not commonly accepted. Theodore can assert that "When they ask whether Mary was the mother of the man or of God, let us reply that she was both," but with the added qualification, "the first by nature and the second by the Word's relationship to

40. *TEP* 1:300.

41. J.N.D. Kelly describes the effect of the pact thus: "A form of *communicatio* was sanctioned, but a much less thorough-going form than the one for which (Cyril) had contended" (*Early Christian Doctrines,* 329).

the assumed humanity."[42] But when he is pressed to affirm unequivocally whether the Word was born of Mary, his response is clear: "For it is indeed unthinkable to affirm that God was born of a virgin. For this is nothing other than to say: He is [born] from the seed of David, brought forth from the substance of the virgin and formed in her."[43] Theodore, like Diodore before him and Nestorius after, rejected the literal view that "Mary was truly the mother of God" and that "the Word suffered."[44] To avoid such a literal reading, Theodore insisted on the need for nuance. He distrusted any formulation that could be so misinterpreted as to suggest that there was only one single nature in Christ and that Christ was not a fully human being, lacking a rational soul and a free human will. For him, the chasm between the Creator and all creatures must be defended.

First, we need to confront some confusion and ambiguity in Theodore's statements about who Christ is. In such passages as that of Ephesians 1:7–16, the term "Christ" appears to signify primarily his humanity,[45] but in others, such as Philippians 2:8, the emphasis is upon the indwelling Word. As a general rule, however, Theodore speaks of Christ as the concrete expression of the union of human and divine natures. Its specific meaning is to be understood in each context. When Theodore tries to be exact in his statements about Christ, he speaks of "Christ in the flesh" or reverts to his favorite phrases, where he refers to the Word as the "assuming One" and Christ's humanity as the "assumed man," thus indicating that one nature cannot exist apart from the other and that the presence of one implies the presence of the other. In this regard, Theodore would be content with the statement in the Pact of Union of 433, which asserts: "We

42. Theodore, PG 66:1012D–13A.

43. *TEP* 2:310. For an English translation of the whole passage from which this sentence has been taken, see Richard A. Norris Jr., trans. and ed., *The Christological Controversy*, Sources of Early Christian Thought (Philadelphia: Fortress, 1980), 121–22.

44. Cyril explicitly denies that he holds this view literally in his third letter to Nestorius, which contains his twelve anathemas: "Neither do we say that his flesh was changed into the nature of the divinity, nor that the ineffable nature of the Word of God was laid aside for the nature of flesh; for he is unchanged and absolutely unchangeable." Percival, *Seven Ecumenical Councils, NPNF,* 14:202.

45. For example, see *TEP* 1:126. Theodore writes: "It should be noted in this place that of all of the things that (Paul) says of Christ, he says of the assumed man."

confess, therefore, our Lord Jesus Christ, the only begotten Son of God, perfect God and perfect man composed of a rational soul and a body, begotten before the ages from His Father in respect of His divinity, but likewise (το αὐτόν) in these last days for us and our salvation from the Virgin Mary in respect of His manhood."[46]

Theodore cautiously assigns attributes to each of Christ's two natures and to the ego of his common *prosôpon*. As we have seen above, Theodore considers the common *prosôpon* to be the one person of Christ that is visible to others and that images his inner divine and human natures acting not only in divine and human ways but also as one. While Theodore insists that divine activity must be assigned to the Word and human activity to the humanity, still he grants that one can refer divine and human attributes to the ego of Christ's common *prosôpon*. Theodore's view is sharply etched in those passages, especially in John, where Jesus speaks of himself as one with the Father. These Johannine statements are especially challenging for Theodore because of his lifelong commitment to be faithful to a literal, rational interpretation of the text. For example, when Theodore explains Jesus' statement about being one with his Father, he insists on the necessity of examining carefully what Jesus actually says: "You [Pharisees] say [to me]: 'You blaspheme' because I said: 'I am God.' But since [this] charge was said only by them, he said: 'I and my Father are one.' But there is an immense difference between this and that [statement]. By [his] distinction, he seeks to show it would be a blasphemy for a human being to be called by the name of God. So when he adds the distinction that we are one, he is [making] a huge distinction here. So [fearing] that they might believe he intends by the word 'one' to be without a beginning as the Father is, he pointedly added that 'I am the Son of God,' signifying that, although he says he is one with Father, he does not at all affirm that he is without a beginning like that One without a beginning, but that he is the Son because of his relation to the Father [of the Word] who has a perfect likeness to Him through generation."[47]

46. The Pact of Union can be found translated in Kelly, *Early Christian Doctrines,* 328–29.
47. *TJA,* 216/154.

Theodore, as pointed out earlier, applies the name of "God" in an absolute sense to the Father—which is not unusual among the early fathers. This means that when Christ asserts that "the Father and I are one," he does not understand this to mean that he is wholly the same as God the Father, who is ungenerated. Nor can the Word as Word be said to be one with the Father in this sense, for he has been eternally generated from the Father. Rather, Christ's "I" expresses the union of Jesus' humanity with the divine nature of the Word, who shares the same nature as the Father. This signifies that Christ's humanity participates in the Word's sonship because of his graced union with the Word in their common *prosôpon* and thus is indirectly united to the Father. Though the assumed man differs by nature from the Father and the Word, his humanity can still be said to be truly one with the Father. This relationship is evident in the following passage, where Christ's humanity is said to participate in the Word's role as the Creator and in his power, majesty, and authority: "For like him, I am greater than all [others] by being like him in that I am also the Maker of creatures like he is, and I have created them with him and am equal to him in power. For we are one, the Word and I, in majesty and authority. For this reason no one can take [all these] from my hands, just as [they can] not [take them] from the hands of the Father."[48]

Theodore uses the above distinction to explain the remarks in Philippians 2 about Christ Jesus taking on "the form of a slave": "When he indeed speaks about whatever ought to be said of the divine nature, he also joins in one and the same person those (remarks) proper to the humanity about a growth in humility. . . . For from the fact he has said everything about one person, he shows in a sufficient way the union. Indeed in a passage where there is a dispute about Christ, he says in general everything as [belonging] to one person; and those [attributes] that virtually differ [from one another] due to the division of natures, he gathers into one so that he may keep the personal union without division."[49] Theodore therefore detects no difficulty in asserting what is proper to each of Christ's human and

---

48. Ibid., 213–14/152. For a discussion of this, see Theodore of Mopsuestia, *Theodor und das Nicänum*, 250–51n684.

49. *TEP* 1:220.

divine natures as truly applicable to Christ's common *prosôpon*. For his ego expresses their unity: "For when (John) would speak of those two (natures) as one, he was revealing the unity of [their] person."[50]

Theodore's way of explaining the scriptural passages about Christ's oneness with the Father certainly suggests a model of organic unity. While the Father and Son in the Trinity are one by nature, they are two as Persons, the Father being ungenerated and the Son generated. The Word and the assumed man are also one by sharing one *prosôpon* in a way similar to how the different natures of soul and its body share in one organic person, but not in the sense that the two become one nature, as do the soul and the body. The assumed man, therefore, is one with God the Father because he is one with the Word. This can be confusing, but it does preserve the different natures intact in a manner that clearly maintains the union of the Father, the Word, and the assumed man as "one." Theodore affirms this when commenting on Paul's remark about the intense conflict between the flesh and the spirit in Romans 8: "When he spoke of the two natures as two diverse things, aptly according to the difference of natures, he posited this 'I' [as belonging] to each one of them as one; i.e., he speaks of the two of them as [pertaining] to his person because of the union the body has with its soul. So also our Lord, when speaking of his humanity and his divinity, posited this 'I' [as pertaining] to [his] common person. And in order to make known that he is speaking in all these instances not of one and the same nature, he showed [this] by distinguishing his words" (167–68/119–20).

In other words, when confronting Christ's common *prosôpon*, one must carefully ascertain what pertains to the divinity and the humanity in the union and determine from the context what pertains to each: "In both of these (cases), whether it is a question of divine or human (attributes), he posits this 'I' in a way that the intent of [these] words is [to be] understood from the context, the different natures being [recognized] from the different words [spoken]. From the fact then that he speaks about himself in both cases as one, he manifests a personal union [of the natures], which

50. *TJA*, 113/81.

unless it would be exactly [so], there would be no honor at all for the one assumed, insofar as he clearly shares in everything because of the One dwelling in him" (270–71/193–94). Theodore is confident that his way of speaking about Christ's two natures and personal unity is accurate and prudent: "Indeed, as I have stated, he prudently refers all things to the one person, collecting into one those [attributes] which differ virtually because the natures are divided, so as to draw from both what was useful for exhortation."[51]

Theodore also uses the analogy of the soul and its body forming one person to justify his formulation of Christ's individual natures and person:

Since, however, a human being is said, according to us, to consist of a soul and a body, we also say that these two natures, the soul and its body, are, in fact, one human being composed of both. In order to claim the two as one, is it proper to confuse the natures and affirm in an inverted way that the soul is flesh and the flesh soul? Since the former is indeed immortal and rational but the flesh is truly mortal and irrational, shall we affirm by reversing [the two] that the mortal is immortal and the irrational rational? But we are not taught this by divine Scripture, O most wise of all. Neither does anyone else say this nor [any] of those today who have a sane human mind. . . . For whatever things differ according to one [level] achieve unity according to another. They preserve their own reason for differing while keeping their unity intact. . . . In the same way, even though some realities differ by nature, it [can] happen that they are truly united in another way. They thus do not lose their distinction by nature [while still] having their own unity, just as the soul is united to the body, [with] one human being resulting from both. There remains a division of natures, the soul indeed being one and the flesh truly another, [with] the former immortal and the latter mortal [and with] the former rational and the latter irrational. Yet both are one human being. A human being in se is never affirmed to be in an absolute and proper sense to be one [e.g., the soul] or the other [the body], unless perhaps with some addition, such as an "interior man" and an "exterior man," not a human being in an absolute sense but [one who

51. *TEP* 1:221–22. Theodore repeats the same idea in his commentary on Col. 1:17: "For we have shown that the apostle has done this when writing to the Philippians where he says 'who is existing in the form of God, etc.' Evidently there the apostle has passed from divine matters to the human and is indeed speaking of all things as of one and the same" (*TEP* 1:272).

is] interior and exterior. So we also say in the case of Christ [our] Lord, O amazing one, that the form of the slave exists in the form of God, nor is the assuming One the one who is assumed. The unity of the assumed one with the assuming One is inseparable, incapable of being sundered in any way.[52]

One can infer from this passage that Theodore regards the union of Christ's nature in one common *prosôpon* as a quasi-organic unity, similar to the functional organic union between soul and body. While it is difficult to determine what is truly like and unlike in an analogy, we know that Theodore rejected Apollinaris's organic unity in a metaphysical sense and therefore that he was espousing a functional unity in which the divine and human natures act as one in the organic way that the soul and its body act as one person. This explains what Theodore intends by his statement that Christ in the flesh shares in the name and power of the Word as the Son of God by nature. In other words, as long as one relies upon such titles as "Incarnate Word," the "assumed one," the "assuming One," and "Christ" (denoting the union of his two natures), one can assign both human and divine attributes to this personal unity.

Theodore's Christological position was shaped primarily by his commitment to the Antiochene tradition of safeguarding the distinction between a transcendent God and all creatures, including Christ's full humanity, his commitment to a literal, rational form of exegesis, and his opposition to the Apollinarians. He was not unaware of or insensitive to the need to maintain a true personal unity of Christ's divine and human natures. But his attention was chiefly focused on expressing and defending the unity in such a way that it preserved the full integrity of Christ's humanity in light of the scriptural witness, above all the exercise of his free will. The aim of this and the previous chapter has been, first, to clarify exactly what Theodore means by the personal unity of Christ's divine and human natures as a common *prosôpon* and by the phrase "indwelling of good pleasure as in God's true Son." Theodore's Christological terms show that his "person of unity" (which he called one *prosôpon*) sums up the visible way that Christ acts as one "being" in human and divine ways. These two kind of activities point to the inner presence in Christ of a human and a divine nature that

52. Ibid., 2:318–19.

not only function as one but are one in a union where Christ's humanity shares in the Word's honors, much in the way the body shares with its soul an organic kind of union.

Theodore derives his language and thought about the union as an "indwelling of good pleasure" from both the New Testament and his understanding of how a soul and its body relate functionally to each other as one "being." This is not a metaphysical explanation that will reassure theologians and philosophers. Rather, he simply asserts an existential fact he found revealed in the Gospels: Christ is the one in whom the Father is well pleased and the one who acts in truly human and divine ways, enabling him to serve as the perfect mediator between God and his creation. His humanity is also the visible image of God and the dwelling in whom the divine *plerôma* fully resides and whose graces are dispensed with the aid of the Spirit to other creatures in different measures. In brief, Theodore's Christology is best understood as a functional one that mirrors the Synoptics'. While he does mention the terms *physis, hypostasis,* and *prosôpon,* he does so to respond to his adversaries, especially Apollinaris, in terms that do justice to the scriptural evidence.

Theodore recognized that his scriptural description of the union of Christ's natures as an "indwelling of good pleasure as in the true Son" could be misinterpreted, for God is also pleased with others who fulfill his will. Theodore answers, I believe, in light of how Paul described the Word's indwelling in Christ's humanity in Colossians. Like Paul, Theodore relates the indwelling to how Christ in the flesh is the visible "image" of the invisible Word and the bond who fully recapitulates in his humanity the spiritual and material worlds, the head of the body of all those who belong to his Church, and the one in whom the divine *plerôma* dwells in a bodily way. Only Christ's humanity wholly receives the fullness of grace because of his exact and perfect union with the Word. It is this unique union that enables him to be truly God's Son, while all others become God's adopted children insofar as each becomes a member of Christ's body. By being united to Christ, they too receive through his acquired fullness what they need for salvation, but not in the full and direct way that Christ's humanity has been so blessed.

The previous chapters, on the roles that Christ in the flesh plays in salvation as the head of his body the Church and the cosmos and as the "image of God," enable us to enlarge our view of how Theodore understood Christ's humanity's *prosôpon* and its role in the history of salvation. Not only does Christ's human *prosôpon* play a unique pivotal role in its union with the Word's divine nature within one common *prosôpon,* but also a critical role in the salvation of all creatures, spiritual powers, and material beings, as well as humans. Theodore considered the term *prosôpon* to connote a communal and corporate aspect as well as an individual designation. It also embodies the relational unity between a person's outward and inner self and between all those who share Christ's human nature. While it is true that Theodore rejected Apollinaris's organic view of how the Word has united itself to Christ's body, he does appear to have conceived of the presence of a quasi-organic relationship between the Word and Christ's humanity similar to that between Christ's human nature and those of the angelic and material worlds. He likens these unions to the union between the human soul and its body in one true substantial being. As such, Theodore's affirmation of a unity in Christ needs to be interpreted and judged not on an ontological level, where a union is asserted as either substantial or accidental, but on a practical level, where one's personal activity reveals a person's identity and the dynamic way that a spiritual reality can act together with a material one in an uniquely organic unity. Theodore simply accepts the mystery of how Christ's two natures form one true unity, but with each nature remaining intact and integral in a way that enables Christ, as the person of the two natures, to be the true mediator between God and creation.

8. THE CHARGES AGAINST THEODORE

S O FAR WE HAVE CONSIDERED how Theodore understood the mediating roles that Christ's humanity plays
within universal salvation, as well as the assertions
that the union of Christ's divine and human natures occurs in
a common *prosôpon* and is described accurately as "an indwelling of good pleasure as in God's Son." All of these roles
overlap with each other and reinforce the view that Theodore
evolved a soteriological synthesis in which Christ *qua* man
serves as a true mediator, for his humanity is united by nature
to all creation and by an "exact," inseparable union to the
Word of God. In all of this Theodore is thoroughly faithful to
what he interprets as the New Testament's inspired revelation
and to his Antiochene tradition. I want now to examine the
main charges of heresy leveled against Theodore's Christological approach by the Second Council of Constantinople in 553,
which condemned not only Theodore's writings but his very
person.

I begin with a detailed summary of what is contained in the seventy-one excerpts cited in the *acta* of the Council as examples of Theodore's heretical thought and the creed that he supposedly composed. I shall also note the charges advanced in two other documents that are found there. This will provide background for understanding the principal points of the Council's anathemas against Theodore. Because Theodore's adversaries in the fifth and sixth centuries left little or no explanation of what they found heretical in Theodore's thought, I rely on the arguments of Kevin McNamara and Francis Sullivan for Theodore's heterodoxy and on those of Facundus of Hermiane and Paul Galtier for his orthodoxy.

The Charges

After Theodore died in 428, his enemies amassed collections of what they considered Theodore's heretical statements. The fathers at Constantinople II took seventy-one excerpts from these and judged them prima facie evidence of Theodore's impious teaching. From the documents we have at hand, they apparently made no effort to read these excerpts in their own contexts.[1] We have some hints—in the résumés attached to the excerpts in the version attributed to Pope Vigilius, and in two addenda included in the *acta*—that the fathers shouted out in absolute horror when these extracts were read to the assembly. Evidently they took for granted that Theodore regarded Christ as a human being. But our strongest evidence of what disturbed the fathers are the anathemas they issued against Theodore. While these records are helpful, even invaluable, we nevertheless lack the full texts and historical contexts of these extracts. Nor are we certain when most of them were written or whether there might have been an evolution of Theodore's Christological outlook. But even if there had been, his critics were and are still persuaded that the remaining excerpts and creed show a consistent pattern of thought and furnish more than sufficient grounds for judging Theodore's Christology. The general, indeed almost universal, consensus of the past fifteen hundred years is that the fathers at Constantinople II were correct to condemn Theodore and his works.

1. At the ecumenical councils, the fathers would listen to a reading of the Nicene-Constantinople Creed and then judge whether a controversial writing conformed with this and, if not, whether it was to be rejected as heretical.

The Conciliar Excerpts

The critical edition of the *acta* of the Second Council of Constantinople[2] contains seventy-one excerpts and one questionable creedal statement from all of Theodore's extensive literary output. These were drawn from much earlier florilegia, or compilations of supposedly heretical passages that his adversaries (most likely the Apollinarians) had culled from his writings. While all the original florilegia have been lost, we do possess four compilations containing in varying arrangements and numbers the fragments presented at the Council. These are the acts of the Council itself, the work of Leontius of Byzantium,[3] a collection of sixty attributed to Pope Vigilius, and those discovered in a Monophysite manuscript entitled the British Museum codex 12156. Except for that of Leontius, who alone provides a Greek text, the others are all translations; BM 12156 is in Syriac and the other two are preserved in Latin. Since no one collection includes all seventy-one excerpts, they have been compiled so as to supplement one another and arrive at a critical text.[4] Modern theologians grant that, except for the fragments from Theodore's *Catechetical Homilies* and his *Commentary on John's Gospel* (both copies have survived in Syriac versions), his other works provide no context for judging Theodore's attitude or beliefs. In those cases where a full work is available, there are only two instances where one can argue with any plausibility that Theodore's thought has been distorted.[5] While conceding that one must proceed with caution in

2. *Concilium Universale Constantinopoltanum Sub Justiniano Habitum,* 44–72.

3. Leontius of Byzantium's Greek collection of the fragments is found in Theodore of Mopsuestia, PG 66:972–93.

4. There are also individual fragments drawn from Cyril of Alexandria's two volumes, *Contra Theodorum,* from Severus of Antioch, a moderate Monophysite (who drew from Cyril's work), and from the catenae. In regard to the excerpts taken from Cyril's first volume, Sullivan, *Christology of Theodore,* believes it likely that "Cyril based his [work] not on a first-hand study of his [Theodore's] works, but on a florilegium of extracts supplied to him, and that the mistake [that he made in applying the three fragments found in the Council's *Acta* and five of those in his response to the ten that he obviously thought were Theodore's excerpts] was due to the fact that while this florilegium contained texts of both Diodore and Theodore, Cyril took them all to be the works of Theodore" (39–40).

5. See Sullivan, *Christology of Theodore,* for specifics, 104–6 and 110–12.

evaluating these fragments, theologians today readily acknowledge them as authentic.[6] They believe that these, together with Theodore's other surviving writings, provide more than enough data for assessing his Christological thought in light of Cyril of Alexandria's twelve anathemas, which became the standard employed against Nestorius and Theodore, first by the Council of Ephesus and then, more than 125 years later, by the Second Council of Constantinople. It must be pointed out that while Cyril's first two letters were authoritatively accepted, his third letter, which included the anathemas, was not definitively approved.[7]

A critical examination of the seventy-one extracts used at the Council reveals that three (#28, 44, and 45) are spurious.[8] These are now acknowledged as belonging to Diodore (d. before 394) rather than to Theodore.[9] The creed cited also appears to be spurious in the opinion of Richard Norris Jr., who sums up the literature on this point: "Considering that it most certainly is not the symbol which Theodore employs as the basis for his Catechetical Lectures, this Creed can be ascribed to him only with the utmost hesitation. Its source is best considered doubtful."[10] Thirty-one other excerpts can be judged to be of only relative importance. While most reinforce the principal arguments that swayed the council fathers against Theodore, they appear to have been selected to highlight how suspect also were his exegetical interpretations.[11] Specifically, #62 deals with the literal

6. Such as Rowan Greer, in his *Theodore of Mopsuestia,* who writes: "Sullivan in his *Christology of Theodore of Mopsuestia* discusses the critical problems involved in the use of these sources in what must be considered a definitive way" (10).

7. It was Cyril's second letter that was approved by the Council of Ephesus as consonant with the faith of Nicaea.

8. See Sullivan, *Christology of Theodore,* 119.

9. The Acta of Constantinople II contain ten extracts attributed to Theodore with responses by Cyril of Alexandria. Three of them—#2, 4, and 5—are found among the seventy-one fragments (on pp. 74, 75, and 76, respectively, of Straub's edition). These three and the five contained in Cyril's response are now attributed to Diodore.

10. Norris, *Manhood and Christ,* 241n3.

11. In his article "'A Letter that Killeth,'" John J. O'Keefe accepts Leontius of Byzantium's charge that Theodore's method of exegesis did violence to the nexus between the Hebrew and Christian sacred books. O'Keefe argues that "Antiochene exegetes were so bent on following the rules of ancient grammar and historiography that they failed to grasp both the significance and the necessity of Christian figurative and theological reading of the Old Testament" (85). While one can assert that Theodore's rhetorical back-

interpretation Theodore offered regarding the flaming sword that prevented Adam and Eve from returning to Paradise (Gen. 3:24); he believed that the sword was literal rather than allegorical. Also, in #63–71, Theodore maintains that the Book of Job was derived from pagan literature and that the Canticle of Canticles was a secular love poem unworthy of inclusion in the canon.[12] As is evident today, Theodore was insisting on the need to establish the background and context of a scriptural passage and agreed-upon norms for authenticating an inspired work of Scripture. (It is significant to note that Vigilius's sixty extracts do not contain the above excerpts that reflect Theodore's exegetical interpretations.) Numbers 19–24 reveal Theodore's firm opposition to allegory. The fathers also seem to have taken exception to Theodore's unwillingness to concede the presence of direct messianic content in the Psalms, save in only four cases.[13] But it is hard to see, at least today, why these excerpts provide solid arguments for declaring Theodore an impious heretic on a level with Judas.[14]

More serious are excerpts #6–7, which list those New Testament passages where Christ is affirmed to have, humanly speaking, required the Holy Spirit; #11 and 41, which address the immortality Christ achieved after

---

ground influenced his exegesis, especially of the Psalms, apparently composed when he was twenty years old (see Zaharopoulos, *Theodore on the Bible,* 82 and n. 18, 33–34, and esp. 49–52), this did not prevent him from affirming a link between the Hebrew and Christian Scriptures. For he did acknowledge the presence of typical/archetypal relation between the two, even granting that Psalms 2, 8, 45, and 110 can be considered messianic (see Zaharopoulos, *Theodore on the Bible,* 149). To have this kind of typical relationship, he insisted that both the type and the archetype had to be historical realities and that their mutual relation had to be also explicitly approved within the New Testament. He believed that the Scriptures themselves had to confirm God's inspired intent. As a result, he rejected allegorical interpretations as being the imaginative speculations of the exegete. Theodore may be conservative on this question, but his position is hardly heretical.

12. For a further treatment of Theodore's position on the Canticle, see Zaharapoulos, *Theodore on the Bible,* 33–34, 49–52. Theodore's opponents interpreted his rejection of an allegorical interpretation of the Canticle as an attack against tradition and the Holy Spirit. This exemplifies Theodore's willingness to differ with other fathers over how to interpret Scripture.

13. These are Psalms 2, 8, 45, and 110. Theodore regarded most New Testament references to the Psalms as accommodations. See Zaharopoulos, *Theodore on the Bible,* 145–48.

14. See *Concilium Universale Constantinopoltanum Sub Justiniano Habitum,* 56.

his resurrection; #14, which refers to the question of whether the disciples received the Spirit when Jesus breathed upon them; #17, which likens the adoration of Christ to that of an emperor's image;[15] #25, which deals with the faith confessions of Nathaniel, Peter, and Martha; #26 and 33–34, which address passages regarding Christ as God's "domesticus"; #40, which compares Christ as God's beloved Son to other sons; and #55–61, which discuss Theodore's theological framework, whereby he envisaged the presence of two stages of existence in the human journey to salvation: the present world of sin and death and the future world of immortality, immutability, and sinlessness. His adversaries seem to have taken exception to Theodore's comments about sin's educational value.

The remaining thirty-seven fragments raise far more weighty questions about Theodore's Christology than those previously cited. The principal objections to Theodore appear to be those highlighted in the short critiques appended to the excerpts found in the compilation attributed to Pope Vigilius. These can be roughly grouped under three major and overlapping headings. In the first,[16] Theodore allegedly presents Christ as a mere man whose mother is Mary and who, with the aid of the Spirit, overcame his struggles against inordinate passions and became perfect. The second group is similar to the first but the stress is on passages in which Theodore's "assumed man" acts so independently that he appears to be an individual person in his own right. This means that despite all claims to the contrary, Theodore can be said to hold for two different sons, the Word as the Son of God by nature, and Christ as the true Son by grace. The third array groups together those excerpts that address what Theodore meant by an "indwelling of good pleasure." Since he rejects a substantial union and one of operation between Christ's two natures, the phrase is perceived to be, if not something in between, then certainly an accidental union. His explanation of how God's "good pleasure" differs in the cases of Christ and the saints has led many commentators to see it as a voluntary, moral unity,

15. This passage will be discussed in the context of the principal criticisms raised against Theodore.

16. For the extracts that emphasize Jesus as a mere man, see especially from the Vigilius collection #1, 4, 6–7, 8, 11, 16, 18, 20, 28, 29, 31, 35, 38, 40–42, 44–46, 48, 50, 53–54.

for Theodore cannot affirm unconditionally that the eternal Word became man and suffered and died on the cross.

In Johannes Straub's critical edition there are also a number of very brief introductions to #15–17, 26, 28, 30, 50–54, 61–63, 66, and 68, and a paragraph criticizing Theodore's creed. But, unlike the short comments in the Vigilian collection, there is no explicit indication of what the council fathers found heretical and meriting anathematization. This is exemplified in what can be described as a "lynching refrain" in a passage inserted between #27 and #28 in Straub's edition: "And while Theodore's blasphemies were being read, the holy synod exclaimed: 'These are what we have already condemned! These we have already anathematized! Anathema to Theodore of Mopsuestia! Anathema to Theodore and his writings! These are all foreign to the Church! These are foreign to the Orthodox! These are foreign to the Fathers! They are brimming with impiety! These are foreign to the synods! These impugn the divine Scriptures! Theodore and Judas are one!'"[17] This outburst implies that there was no discussion about what Theodore meant to assert in these excerpts. Nor is there any indication that anyone dared to stand up and object to these emotional cries for condemnation of Theodore's writings and person, least of all after the emperor Justinian had declared them heretical.

The *acta* also contain ten fragments alleged to have been taken from Theodore's works, each with a concise refutation by Cyril of Alexandria. After examining these, Francis Sullivan concludes that there is "a serious problem as to the authorship of the five extracts said by the council to be taken from the first book of Cyril against Theodore. The fact is that three other sources attribute some, or all, of these five texts to Diodorus, rather than to Theodore." Sullivan believes that contrary to Cyril's assertion that he derived all his citations from the original works of Theodore, he actually gathered them from a hostile florilegium containing suspect statements of Diodore and Theodore.[18] Presuming rightly, however, that Diodore's and

---

17. *Concilium Universale Constantinopoltanum Sub Justiniano Habitum,* 56.

18. Sullivan, *Christology of Theodore,* 37. At least five of the citations (#2, 4, 5, 7, and 8) that are cited by Cyril are found among the Council's seventy-one extracts. See also 39–40 and 49–50.

Theodore's basic positions mirror each other, we can assume that what Cyril says can be attributed also to Theodore. Cyril finds fault in these excerpts with Theodore's insistence that the titles of Christ as a son of Abraham, of David, and of Mary should be applied solely to the assumed man as a man and not to the Word. Cyril then appeals to passages from the New Testament to justify his contrary position that the Word is the sole subject of Christ's human attributes.

The *acta* also include a document entitled "The Sentence Against the 'Three Chapters.'"[19] It is primarily a justification of Theodore's condemnation as a person and attacks his steadfast refusal to attribute the Jewish prophecies to Christ and anathematizes his statements that there exist two Sons and two Christs, claiming that: "This has been very clearly shown to be the case by us in our acts from the works of Cyril and Proclus" (111).[20] The document also mentions Theodoret and explains at considerable length why the "so-called" letter written by Ibas was also condemned. What is particularly illuminating is the brief statement made in passing: "When all the blasphemies in (Theodore's) works were exposed, we would not even have allowed the official reader of these blasphemies to continue, since each blasphemy was worse than the one before in the extent of its heresy and shook to their foundation the minds of their listeners" (109). Again, there appears to have been little or no discussion about what Theodore actually held in each excerpt.

Conciliar Anathemas

The conciliar decrees can be grouped under five headings. They are drawn from the list of seventy-one extracts and indicate what the fathers found most offensive. The first concerns the Council's insistence that there is only the one "subsistence" of the Word and not two. This means that the Word is identically one and the same as Christ. The second finds fault with Theodore's inability to declare in an orthodox way that the Word has two

19. This is found in *Concilium Universale Constantinopoltanum Sub Justiniano Habitum*, 208–15. For an English translation, see Tanner, *Decrees of the Ecumenical Councils*, 107–13.

20. For Proclus's letter, see *Concilium Universale Constantinopoltanum Sub Justiniano Habitum*, 85–86.

births, one eternal and another from Mary, who is properly and truly called the Mother of God, and that the Word is the One who performed miracles and truly suffered. The third group revolves around the nature of the union between Christ's two natures. The fathers rejected a union affirmed to be of grace and of affection, wherein there exists an equality of honor, power, and authority, wherein the Word can be said to exist separately in Christ as in another, wherein each nature has its own subsistence (as do a husband and his wife), and wherein the assumed man can receive adoration (as does the statue of the emperor). The fourth grouping excludes Theodore's statements that Christ—whom the Council insists is the Word and not the man—was baptized as a man, received special graces to overcome human passions and desires, progressed in good works and merited thereby his sonship with the Word, and received immutability after his death and resurrection. The last grouping rejects three scriptural interpretations: that Christ's breathing upon his apostles in John 20:22 did not signify the imparting of the Spirit but was simply a sign of it, also that Thomas's exclamation "My Lord and my God!" was an expression of astonishment, and, worse than this, that Theodore, in his lost commentary on Acts, compared Christ to Plato, Manichaeus, Epicurus, and Marcion, as men who offered their own teachings and had followers named after them.[21]

The principal argument summing up these anathemas is that Theodore separated Christ and the Word into two different persons, when they are really one and the same in a union of hypostatic subsistence. All other charges are made to clarify that Theodore only pretends "to speak of one person and one Christ when the reference is to his title, honour, dignity or adoration" (115, anathema 4). To appreciate this argument, let us turn to two contemporary studies that rely upon Theodore's excerpts and other extant books to back up the Council's condemnation of Theodore. We shall then look at two others, which interpret his writings in a very different light, and summarize the reasons why they dispute this conclusion.[22]

21. These anathemas can be found in Tanner, *Decrees of the Ecumenical Councils*, 114–20.

22. Other studies worthy of consideration are the lengthy articles by Amann, "Théodore de Mopsueste," and above all John Romanides, "Highlight in the Debate over Theodore." Romanides provides a concise, accurate critique of the arguments of those

Before beginning, however, we need to address two separate but inter-related issues. Some reject Theodore's claim to orthodoxy on the grounds that the excerpts culled from his writings do in fact demonstrate that he considered Christ and the Word two independent "persons" and therefore different Sons of God. Others accept the sincerity of his avowals but believe that in the final analysis he failed gravely in his attempts to explain the union of Christ's natures as being a true substantial unity in one Person. Their point is that Theodore speaks of Christ in such human terms that he has really envisioned Christ—and not the Word—to be the personal subject of his human attribution and operations and that, as a result, the union is a moral one. The first denounce Theodore's Christological thinking and personal character; the second are persuaded that, despite his many pleas to the contrary, Theodore's written statements about the unity in Christ are flawed and must be considered heretical.

Kevin McNamara's Critique

We turn now to Kevin McNamara's two-part article in the *Irish Theological Quarterly*.[23] McNamara readily concedes that Theodore died at peace with the Church and was widely hailed as one of the outstanding scholars of his era and a man who sought to remain faithful to the Christian Scriptures and authentic tradition (2:188–89). He praises Theodore for his zealous efforts to vindicate the doctrine of Christ's perfect manhood. He admits, furthermore, that those who initially drew up the florilegia of suspect opinions in Theodore's writings misrepresented his thought in a few instances and that the charge of impiety against him as a person was hardly justified (1:257, 2:188–89). McNamara even concedes that the ecclesiastical standard for speaking correctly about the unity of Christ's natures was established after Theodore's death. After acknowledging all this, however, he concludes that Theodore held for the existence of two separate "per-

who reject and defend Theodore's orthodoxy. I also recommend Henry Chadwick's "Eucharist and Christology in the Nestorian Controversy" for the questions it raises about the relationship between Antiochian Christology and its sacramental thought.

23. McNamara, "Theodore and the Nestorian Heresy," part 1 (July 1952): 258, hereafter cited parenthetically in the text.

sons" in Christ, at least by the Scholastic definition of "person" as an *"individuum completum subsistens in se"* (1:263–64).

McNamara reproaches Theodore for his failure to recognize that Christ's humanity was specially endowed with the gift of personal integrity. He is elaborating here upon the charge made in Constantinople II that because the union of the natures is centered solely in the Person of the Word, the Word has to be also the subject of operation for Christ's humanity, such as Jesus' miracles. But if this be so, then Christ ought to have been free from every kind of moral struggle involving inordinate sensible appetites, to the point that he was incapable of sinning (1:263–64). McNamara argues in addition that since Christ's human nature has to be perfectly allied with the Word's Person, Christ could not have truly grown, as Theodore believed, from an intellectual and moral state of imperfection to one of perfection. Nor can Christ be said to have "merited" in any way this perfection, humanly speaking, through his own efforts.[24]

McNamara scrutinizes Theodore's interpretation of "person," *prosôpon* (1:266). He recognizes the root of Theodore's failure here as his inability to perceive a distinction between a concrete and an abstract nature. For him, all "concrete" terms are those referring to a *suppositum,* or a nature with all its respective properties in an independent center to whom attributes can be assigned (1:269). "Abstract" terms, conversely, "signify the nature or property considered in itself, i.e., prescinding from its subject of attribution." Because he failed to make this distinction, McNamara argues, Theodore ended up making Christ's abstract human nature concrete and thus an actual individual "person." This failure had the result that Theodore's language cannot be rightly reconciled with the declarations of the ecumenical councils that the divine Word is the one who can be said to have been born of Mary and to have suffered and died (1:270).

McNamara justifies these conclusions by enumerating the various ways in which Theodore personalized the humanity of Christ. He discerns this in the same contexts in which Theodore contrasts the two natures in such a

24. McNamara, ibid., believes that the notion of the perfecting of Christ is strongly Pauline, but that "Theodore has given it a meaning it never had for St. Paul" (part 2 [April 1953]: 175).

stark manner that they appear to be two equally independent subjects of attribution (1:272). He asserts that Theodore fails to make "a very clear-cut distinction between that which is the agent of a set of experiences and that which is merely the sphere of these experiences, i.e., between the principium quod and the principium quo" (1:273). He readily concedes that Theodore probably "did not think of [a person] as possessing its own being, the distinctive note of personality, quite as vividly as we think of a person possessing its being" (1:273). When McNamara comes to his concluding judgment, however, he is convinced that one is left with the clear impression that the man and the Word are each a distinct subject of attribution, metaphysically independent of one another (2:189). This same discord "pervades his whole Christological teaching and must doom to failure any attempt to rehabilitate him as an orthodox thinker" (2:173).

McNamara expends considerable effort in analyzing what he holds to be Theodore's understanding of how a prosopic union is, in fact, "an inhabitation of good pleasure." He points out that Theodore himself describes this as signifying a special relationship whereby God acts in and with those whom he loves according to the "good pleasure of His will" (2:178). Since Theodore is excluding a substantial union (such as that present among the Persons of the Trinity) and a union of a simple operation whereby God's power maintains all created beings in their existence, he has to propose a union that expresses the preferential treatment God shows to all those who are pleasing to him. God's benevolent will toward particular humans indicates the existence of a special kind of a moral relationship between God on one side and Christ and all those fulfilling his will on the other (2:178–79). But McNamara points out that this puts Theodore in a quandary: how can he explain that there exists a real, radical difference between God's benevolence toward Christ *qua* man and his benevolence toward the saints?

McNamara subjects to careful scrutiny Theodore's explanation of how God's good will differs in regard to Christ and the saints. For Theodore, the difference abides in the fact that the Word dwells in Christ "as in a son." Instead of elaborating on this, McNamara points out that Theodore holds that the Word's indwelling takes place in the area of the will instead of nature, in order to stress that the Word was not necessary to this union by his nature but freely decided to enter this union (2:177). McNamara takes this as evidence that Theodore realized that he had to address the ontological structure of the union rather than the causal reason that was motivating it. So when Theodore insists that the assumed man shares in the full honor, dignity, and power of the Word, McNamara concludes, "we cannot say that, when it comes to the final analysis, he has in mind a difference not only in degree but in kind" (2:178). In other words, Jesus as the *homo assumptus* is fundamentally a son of God no different from all others who are sons and daughters of God. He is superior only in the degree to which he is a son of God.

McNamara also considers Robert Arnou's astute observation that Theodore's description of the union resembles that proposed in the Christian philosopher Nemesius's work *On Human Nature* (2:179). As we have seen, Nemesius follows the Neoplatonist theory that a spiritual reality can be united to a material body that is capable of receiving it. This occurs not in any local sense but takes place because of the soul's close relationship, inclination, and disposition to its bodily partner (2:180). McNamara contends that if this is how Theodore understands his "indwelling of good pleasure," then it follows that "the Hypostatic Union would be a union of essences, but not in essence," that is, a union of two realities rather than a true unity within one person (2:180). It would also be "a circumincession of two activities," that is, a union between two activities working together. But this does not fulfill the requirement that the union between the Word and Christ's humanity must be one where the Word as the Person of the union appropriates the two natures and acts in a personal way in each (2:181).

From here, McNamara delves more deeply into the kind of relationship that Theodore saw existing between a *prosôpon* and a *hypostasis*. He notes that *prosôpon* is "the only word used by Theodore to express the concept of *per se individuum*. . . . or some kind of a real unit presenting a single undivided appearance" (2:182). As such, it appears to connote a sense of personality rather than a person understood in a philosophical sense. This difference is highlighted by the distinction between "having" and "being" a personality. The latter concept suggests an independent subject of attribution (2:184), and the former suggests all the physical, psychological characteristics that a person exhibits. In this sense the Word and the *homo assumptus* can be conceived of as having a single personality, "the wonderful and perfectly harmonious personality of the God-man Christ" (2:184). But this kind of unity would be based only upon a moral unity of wills rather than on a substantial, ontological unity, and thus is one more indication of Theodore's failed Christology.

Francis Sullivan's Critique

Francis Sullivan makes a similar argument. He too insists that one must distinguish "between what is predicated of the Word in His nature as Word, and what ought to be true of him as the ultimate subject to whom the humanity and its operations belong by reason of appropriation of human nature in the Incarnation."[25] He believes that since Theodore could not adequately separate the notion of "person" from "nature" (a distinction not definitively realized until the time of Justinian),[26] he was not able to predicate human attributes to the Word and was thus forced to regard the Word and the assumed man as two completely independent subjects of attribution (198). Sullivan then raises what is the most decisive question: "If, in order to defend the transcendence of the Word, one must constantly distinguish between the Word and the man, how can there be 'one Lord Jesus Christ'?" (201).

To present Theodore's position in as balanced a way as possible, Sullivan analyzes Theodore's term *physis* as it is applied to Christ's human nature (203–4). For Sullivan, *physis* designates the "concrete, individual human nature that was assumed by the Word in the Incarnation" (205). From his detailed examination of how Theodore attributes Christ's human oper-

---

25. Sullivan, *Christology of Theodore*, 197, hereafter cited parenthetically in the text.

26. Grillmeier, *Christ in Christian Tradition*, 2:428–29. Grillmeier sums up well the traditional relation between a *hypostasis* and a *physis*: "the divine *hypostasis* creates this spiritually ensouled human nature for himself, for the purpose of being hypostasis for it and to exist humanly in it as divine *hypostasis*. Fundamentally this is a good *concrete* explanation of the insubsistence or *enhypostasis* of Christ's human nature in the hypostatic Logos. (2:436).

ations and sufferings to the assumed man as an ultimate subject, Sullivan concludes that Theodore regarded the assumed man as both a nature and a *prosôpon* in his own right. But when Theodore applies *physis* to the Word, Sullivan finds no clear evidence that he "meant to establish a distinction between what could be said of the Word, and what could be said of his divine nature" (207). This inability to distinguish between a "person" and a "nature" "undoubtedly has contributed largely to the unfavorable opinion held of Theodore by his critics" (218–19).

Continuing his inquiry into Theodore's use of terms, Sullivan observes that the term *prosôpon* "is not used in a strict, philosophical sense, but in a much more elastic meaning" (224). In general, it can connote either the one "who" is speaking, or "of whom" one is speaking, or "for whom" one is speaking. Understood in these senses, this "who" or "whom" is not necessarily a person in the strict sense; it can be an individual, a group, or even the whole human race (225). In other words, *prosôpon* can be understood in both a communal and an individual sense. Sullivan also interprets Theodore's explanation of John's verse that the "Word became man" to mean that the Word "became a man in the opinion of those who think he is merely a man" (231). This suggests that *prosôpon* implies simply a "mere appearance" (232). One can add to this that Theodore failed to recognize that "the term 'man' can be understood in a broader sense to mean 'one possessing human nature'; one who has made human nature his own" (235). Sullivan believes that Theodore looks upon the Incarnation as "nothing more than an extraordinary presence of God the Word in man" (239).

Sullivan considers what Theodore meant when he said that the one *prosôpon* uniting Christ's two natures is "a union by inhabitation." Sullivan detects what he believes is a fundamental flaw in Theodore's reasoning here, for Theodore looks upon Christ's common *prosôpon* "as being *effected* by the union of the two natures" (245). In other words, this common *prosôpon* flows from the union rather than functions as the subject in whom and from whom the two natures draw their subsistence. Theodore's inhabitation appears to Sullivan to be a merely moral, or dynamic, union between the Word and man. If so, it would seem to follow that Theodore's "one person will be no more than a moral or dynamic person" (245). Sullivan finds a corroboration of this in those passages where Theodore describes the Word's inhabitation as one of "good pleasure."

Sullivan regards Theodore's "inhabitation of good pleasure" as "an attitude on the part of God whereby He is willing to grant special assistance, special cooperation, to those in whom he is pleased" (246). While granting that Theodore has maintained that the Word was united with the *homo assumptus* from the first moment of his conception, Sullivan points out that "still it was only subsequent to his death and resurrection that he had God the Word accomplishing absolutely everything in him, so that he had no activity apart from him" (253). From this Sullivan concludes that Theodore's divine inhabitation of good pleasure "seems to be a divine cooperation superior in duration and in degree, but not in essential character, to that cooperation which characterizes the inhabitation of God 'by good pleasure' in other saints. . . . in all this we do not see anything which is essentially superior to that cooperation which God grants to other men in whom he is well pleased. This factor of 'working through the man' does not seem to involve anything essentially superior to a moral, dynamic union; an extraordinary cooperation of God with a man" (254–55).

Sullivan also insists that it is highly doubtful that Theodore's description of the union as "one" in a common *prosôpon* can be said to be equivalent to Cyril of Alexandria's union in one *hypostasis* (259). He points out that since, for Theodore, the Word and the "man assumed" form one common *prosôpon*, every action of the humanity or the divinity has then to be referred to the common subject, and not simply to the Word as the real subject. This way of speaking about the natures of Christ is likened to the union of the body and soul. Just as one attributes to a human being what is true of either his body or his soul, the same can be affirmed of Christ's common *prosôpon* in relation to his divine and human natures. But this union "does not warrant saying of the Word what pertains to the man assumed, any more than the union of soul and body warrants saying that the soul becomes a body or becomes mortal" (282). From all this it follows that Theodore's asserting the existence of a common *prosôpon* in Christ does not necessarily imply the real presence of a true individual subject who is a "person" in the strict philosophical sense of the word (263). Thus when Theodore insists that he is holding for only one Son, he seems in actual fact to be proposing only a moral kind of unity: "scil., a 'Son' who really includes two persons, a natural Son of God and an adoptive Son" (269). Sullivan has no doubt that the *homo assumptus* is an adoptive son, although far higher in dignity than all other believers. But he is nonetheless in the last analysis merely a human being (273). Sullivan's final assessment is that "It cannot be denied that Theodore of Mopsuestia, despite his orthodox intentions, was indeed what he has so long been called: the Father of Nestorianism" (288).

Paul Galtier's Critique

Of those few who have written in support of Theodore's orthodoxy, Paul Galtier presents by far the strongest theological defense of Theodore's Christology. He argues in a long two-part article that Theodore's real thought was badly misconstrued by Cyril and the fathers of the Second Council of Constantinople. He questions whether it is either logical or just to judge Theodore's language by Cyril's.[27] He insists that Cyril's language has to be widened to include the viewpoint contained in the tome of Pope Leo 1 (440–61). In other words, Theodore's Christology ought to be assessed in light of the Christological balance that the Council of Chalcedon (451) sought to introduce into the embittered controversy between the Orthodox and the Monophysites.

Galtier points out that Theodore's use of *homo assumptus* should not be considered wrong in se, for similar wordings can be found in the writings of other orthodox fathers (165). He notes too how fluid was the understanding of the basic Christological terms of *physis, hypostasis,* and *prosôpon* in Theodore's day (167) and also how Theodore concedes that Mary can be said to be the mother of God, but with the proviso that she bore the assumed man who is united to the Word (172). Galtier argues at great length to show that Theodore's union was never a simple union of cooperation and rejects the view of those who claim Theodore tried to de-

27. Galtier, "Théodore de Mopsueste," part 1, 161–86, part 2, 338–60, hereafter cited parenthetically in the text.

fine the nature and the mode of union between Christ's divine and human natures in a strict ontological way (177–83). Theodore was simply following the lead of the New Testament writers, who continually distinguish Christ's two natures while at the same time asserting that they act as one and are one (185, 350).

In the second part of his article, Galtier discusses how Theodore understood the Word as the One who works everything in the assumed man and therefore the one to whom activities are attributable (338). He maintains that Theodore understood his common *prosôpon* to be the subject to whom properties and activities belong and ought to be predicated, but he is also convinced that Theodore never dreamed of doing this. To charge, therefore, that Theodore actually held for the existence of two "persons" in Christ corresponding to the two perfect natures in Christ makes sense only if each one is viewed abstractly (180). No one can speak concretely of the real existence of two *prosôpa* in Christ, for the natures of Christ have never been divided from the moment of his conception. Since it is the Word that has united himself to the assumed man, Galtier believes that it is the *prosôpon* of the Word that is the unique *prosôpon* of the union (351–52). As for the further question of whether Christ's designation as the Son of God by grace is to be understood to be the same as that of believers being sons and daughters of God, Galtier is emphatic. Because of his union with the Word, the assumed man's Sonship is wholly other (344). As all others have become adopted sons and daughters by their participation in the plenitude of Christ's graces, his filiation can indeed be said to be a true filiation and theirs an adoptive one (345).

Facundus's Defense

After Theodore was condemned at the Council of Constantinople II, a schism occurred in Africa and Aquileia that was not finally resolved until around 689 under Pope Sergius I. These two churches regarded the Council at Constantinople—despite Justinian's strenuous efforts to the contrary—as a repudiation of the Council of Chalcedon. From the period after the council, we possess one lengthy response by the sixth-century African bishop Facundus of Hermiane, who defended Theodore, Theodoret's works against Cyril, and the letter of Ibas, as all orthodox.[28] A number of Facundus's points are worth mentioning, for he appears to have had in hand most, if not all, of Theodore's works. He asserts in forceful, impassioned language: "Like wolves and dogs, the heretics have not preserved whole the sentences of Theodore. . . . they have snatched a few obscure words from his sayings. . . . We, however, as you see, choose to draw closely from the spectrum (of his works) rather than incur the suspicion of fraud by being brief and obscure" (745B). He also points out enigmatically that "some of his books were corrupted by the heretics" (780C), which raises a troublesome question in light of Sullivan's long-accepted defense of the authenticity of the fragments used to condemn Theodore's works.

Facundus also notes that no word of praise was allowed to be introduced in defense of Theodore despite his being one of the outstanding theologians of his day. "For 45 years Theodore shone brightly in his teaching and fought every heresy" (710C). Nor were any opinions favorable to Theodore, such as those asserted by the beloved John Chrysostom, permitted to be mentioned at the council sessions (705CD). Facundus also questions why Theodore is singled out as a heretic when other fathers have erred in their writings: "Can one justly condemn only Theodore and not also Ignatius, Eustathius, Athanasius, Basil and the two Gregories, Flavian, Diodore, John Chrysostom, Ambrose, Amphilochius and Atticus, and ten thousand others?" (711C). He also raises the troubling question of why one ought to condemn a leading churchman 125 years after he died fully at peace with the whole Church. "If we want to better interpret those who have piously and religiously died at peace with the Church, we do so by excusing human beings, in order that we may accuse (their) errors" (753C).

Facundus also complains that the fathers at Constantinople II did not want to confront the truth that the fathers at Chalcedon had accepted the letter of Ibas as orthodox. To avoid this, the fathers at Constantinople acquiesced in the subterfuge that the fathers at Chalcedon had accepted Ibas but not the "so-called" letter attributed to him. In reply to all this, Facun-

---

28. Facundus of Hermiane, PL 67:527–878, hereafter cited parenthetically in the text.

dus notes, "The synod of Chalcedon believed more the testimony [of those eminent fathers of the Church] seeing that it did not judge heretical the epistle of Ibas in praise of Theodore" (705C). Facundus is interesting also for several of his replies to the charges raised against Theodore. He responds to those who often pounced on his use of the words "alius et alius" (one and another): "Theodore does not introduce two sons; for just as he most evidently teaches here, God the Word is other by nature; however, the one assumed is other but yet is discovered to be the same person. . . . Perceive, august one [the emperor Justinian], that he is speaking not about a 'person' but rather a nature—that the assuming one is other than the assumed one; and he wants this to be understood of the natures which differ in many ways. It is for this reason that it is proper to say that the assumed one is not the same as the assuming One. But he is asserting of the person that the assuming One and the assumed are the same" (749BC). Facundus adamantly maintains that Theodore's references to Christ as having two concrete natures does not mean that he taught that Christ was two persons: "Just as we say that the interior man who has been fashioned to the 'image and likeness of God' is other and that the exterior man (2 Cor. 4:16) . . . is another. It is not that there are two persons but two natures" (750A). Facundus expresses this more clearly when he affirms that "When someone considers the natures, he discovers that there is necessarily one and another (nature). Nor do I think these contradict this reality [of the two being one reality] because God the Word is by nature other than what is assumed—whatever that may be is conceded to be another. But still the person itself is found to be the same, with the natures in no way confused" (747C–48B).

Taking into account all the various charges raised at Constantinople II against Theodore's orthodoxy, we can summarize the most serious ones in the form of ten questions that will be addressed in the following chapter: (1) Are some of Theodore's exegetical interpretations truly suspect? (2) How does Theodore understand a *prosôpon,* a *hypostasis,* and a *physis?* (3) What does he mean by a common *prosôpon* that is *effected* by the union of Christ's two natures? (4) How does this common *prosôpon* relate to Cyril's *hypostasis?* (5) What is an "indwelling of good pleasure as in His Son" and is it simply one of circumincession, where the Word and the assumed man harmonize their wills in the ways a husband and wife are united? (6) Does Theodore actually hold for the existence of two independent persons who are one and another? (7) Does he regard the assumed man as a true son or an adopted one? (8) What is the correct way to speak of the Word's and Christ's sonship? (9) Can Christ's humanity be truly adored, like the statue of an emperor is? (10) Does the integrity of the union preclude an intellectual and moral growth in the assumed man, and does it exclude even the possibility that the assumed man could sin?

9. A REASSESSMENT OF THE
CHARGES AGAINST THEODORE

N THIS CHAPTER I want to examine the principal
charges leveled by the fathers at the Second Council of
Constantinople and modern-day theologians against
Theodore's orthodoxy. These will be considered in light of
previous chapters, particularly on how Theodore understood
the mediating roles that Christ's humanity plays within universal salvation, as well as what he intended by asserting that
the union of Christ's divine and human natures occurs in a
common *prosôpon* and is described accurately as "an indwelling of good pleasure as in God's Son." These roles overlap with each other and reinforce the view that Theodore
evolved a soteriological synthesis, for Christ acts as a mediator in these roles because his human nature is united to all
creation as well as existing in an "exact," inseparable union
with the Word of God. Ever faithful to what he believed to be
the New Testament's inspired revelation and his Antiochene
tradition, Theodore was committed to protecting the chasm

between the Creator and everything created as well as Christ's integral humanity and his divinity in their union within one *prosôpon*. I want now to consider whether Theodore's soteriological approach provides a context and perspective for reassessing the charges of heresy not only against Theodore's writings but against his very person. Before beginning this reassessment, however, I shall examine Theodore's own defense of his orthodoxy.

Theodore's Protests

Throughout his extant works, Theodore frequently protests against the accusations by his adversaries that he proposed that Christ was a mere man. First, he insists plainly that he never looked upon Christ as simply a human being: "For no one at any time has heard us assert these things [that Christ is a pure man]."[1] He acknowledges that if the union he proposes is not a true unity, then Christ would be a mere man: "For [those speaking differently] do not consider that they are dividing the perfect participation that the one assumed has with the assuming One. For if this union is abolished, the one assumed is seen to be nothing other than a simple man like us."[2] He considers the term "Christ" to express the union of his two natures: "(Christ our Lord) was not God only nor a man only; but he truly is naturally partaking of the two of them, being also God and also man."[3]

Theodore is even willing to call Christ "God," but with an appended reservation: "But if indeed someone will want to ask what I finally call Jesus Christ, I say 'God and Son of God.'"[4] He adds the phrase "Son of God" because he reserves the title "God" for the Father alone. To those who assert that Theodore is infected with the Christological error of Paul of Samosata, Theodore strongly condemns him because he made Christ to be a mere man: "For it is evident that Paul of Samosata was the bishop of the Church of the Lord God at Antioch and suffering from the error of Theodotus and Artemon who have said that the Lord Jesus Christ was a pure man, not recognizing him [to be] God the Word and existing as the Son of God in his own substance before the ages from God the eternal Fa-

---

1. *TEP* 2:293.
2. *THC*, 134/135; *CH* 6:3.
3. *THC*, 186/187. *CH* 8:1.
4. *TEP* 2:306.

ther."[5] Theodore also declares in his preface to John's Gospel that John saw the need to write his Gospel in order to complete what was lacking in the Synoptics: "(John) again said that (the Synoptics) were right in what they wrote about the coming of Christ in the flesh, but they nonetheless had failed to speak about his divinity. . . . the burden was placed on him to write about those matters that have been omitted by the others."[6]

The following citations provide us with some general notions of what Theodore rejects explicitly in other writers. His comments furnish us with the parameters of his thought. First, Theodore explicitly rejects paganism and those philosophers who advocate it and mentions Paul of Samosata, the Arians, and Apollinarius: "We must consider as angels of Satan all those who are devoted to profane wisdom and who spread the error of paganism into the world. Clearly angels of Satan are all the poets who increase the worshippers of demons by their fables and restore to health the error of paganism through their wisdom. Angels of Satan are [also] those who in the name of philosophy have established pernicious doctrines and corrupted the multitude . . . Paul of Samosata is also an angel of Satan who says that Christ our Lord is an ordinary man and denies the divine subsistence (qenômâ/hypostasis) of the only begotten Son generated before the ages. Arius and Eunomius too are angels of Satan for daring to maintain that the divine nature of the Unique Son is created and therefore has not existed from the beginning. . . . Also Apollinaris, who corrupted [our Christian] confession of faith in the Father, Son, and Holy Spirit and under the appearance of orthodoxy decided our redemption was imperfect and said that our intellect was not assumed and did not share, like the body, in the reception of grace."[7] Clearly Theodore is opposed to pagan philosophy and those Christians who do not consider Christ to be both truly and fully human and truly and fully divine, at least in some sense. These passages also help to explain why he so emphasizes the human nature of Christ in his writings. He does so to counteract the growing influence of those he thought were overemphasizing either the divinity or the humanity of Christ. He was seeking to find and establish an orthodox middle ground.

5. Ibid., 2:318.

6. TJA, 7–8/3–4.

7. THC, 378–82/379–83; CH 13:8–9.

The Charges

The charges brought against Theodore, detailed in the previous chapter, and the questions raised at the end of that chapter, can be summarized under five headings. Theodore's teaching is rejected in regard to his understanding of (1) a union of a common *prosôpon;* (2) the union of Christ's natures as an "inhabitation of good pleasure as in a Son"; (3) his method of assigning attributes to Christ's two natures and to the ego of the common *prosôpon,* especially by referring to the Word as the Son of God by nature and the assumed man as the Son of God by grace, and by rejecting Mary's title as the mother of God; (4) the ramifications of Christ's personal integrity in regard to what Christ can humanly know and morally do as well as in what areas he can grow, humanly speaking; and (5) his interpretation of two scriptural passages and his comparison of Jesus Christ to Plato, Manichaeus, Epicurus, and Marcion, who had evolved their own teaching and had their followers named after them.

Theodore's Prosopic Union

Theodore's adversaries understand the term "person" first in a logical, linguistic sense as justifying the creedal and liturgical attributions of human qualities to the Word and then later in a reflective metaphysical sense as a complete, self-subsisting individual who is the subject of Christ's personal unity and of divine and human operations. There has been a subtle but major shift here in the understanding of whom and what a person is— away from the view of a person as expressing a substantial unity in ordinary speech to one seeking an ontological definition. The same can be said of the time it took to distinguish how the term "person" differs from "nature" and a "concrete nature" from an "abstract" one. There was also a shift from regarding the divine nature as the source of activity in the Trinity to maintaining that the person rather than nature is the source of human activity in Christ. What complicates the Christological controversy even further is the conviction that if one cannot affirm unreservedly that the Word is truly the One who was born of Mary and suffered and died, then he or she is contradicting the true substantial unity that the Christian faith requires for a true unity of Christ's two natures. It is presuming that language fully and adequately describes the underlying reality. While Cyril was doubtless firmly convinced of this, Theodore approached the unity of Christ's natures from a notably different perspective, and at a time of major disputes on how to express this. Like other fathers, Theodore was struggling to express who Jesus Christ is as God and as a man.

As Luise Abramowski has pointed out, Theodore understood his main term for "person," *prosôpon,* in a double sense: first as related ontologically to a *hypostasis,* and then as an object of liturgical adoration.[8] In the first sense, which Theodore treats only in passing, he looks upon every *hypostasis* (or real, complete, existing nature) as having its own *prosôpon.* In the second sense, Abramowski points out how worship could be shown to God through Christ's common *prosôpon.* As I have argued in this study, these two senses are interrelated. Probably influenced by the Synoptics' portrayal of Jesus as the Christ, Theodore realized that the human and the divine *hypostaseis* (Christ's two real, complete natures) manifested themselves in visible ways to others. These would be the outward appearances (the *prosôpa*) of the interior human and divine natures of Christ. Because Christ's two *prosôpa* fuse together into one common *prosôpon,* Theodore regarded these two activities as revealing how Christ's natures could function together as a true unity internally as well as externally, for, as noted above, a *prosôpon* is ontologically related to a *hypostasis* as the outer person is to his or her inner personhood. In other words, if the New Testament reveals Jesus as the Christ who acts as one in human and divine ways, then there exists a true interior unity. While this is, in fact, a functional union, it presumes a deeper union, in a similar way to how the Jews cannot conceive of a body without its soul and philosophers maintain that the soul and its body form an organic unity.

Admittedly, Theodore's references to Christ's human and divine natures as each having its own *prosôpon* but both together comprising one common *prosôpon* are confusing. But this is understandable in his conceptual framework. He arrived at this conclusion because Christ alone has

8. Abramowski, "Zur Theologia Theodors," 263–66.

been revealed as uniquely having a divine as well as a human nature. All other natures have but one *hypostasis* with its own *prosôpon* (excepting of course the Trinity in orthodox Christian dogma). But Christ's two natures require two *prosôpa* that reveal and express their inner unity. While one may retort that such a union can be interpreted as merely voluntary, this does not mean that the opposite cannot be true. Theodore in fact maintains that his "exact" union of Christ's two natures ought to be regarded as a true unity. If this is rejected out of hand, then the Synoptic portrayal of Christ ought also to be rejected as insufficient.

Besides having the above revelatory meaning, the term *prosôpon*—as seen in Theodore's view of the roles that Christ's human nature plays in salvation—also connotes the relational roles that Christ's human *prosôpon* exercises with other humans and all other creatures. The same can be asserted of the Word, the divine *prosôpon* which implies not only the ways he reveals himself to others in a visible way but also his essential relationships to his Father and his Spirit. To see Jesus as the Christ is also to see the Word in his essential relations to his Father and his Spirit. It is for this reason that all spiritual beings can and ought to worship God through his visible "image," but not in the sense that his image merely points to God. The reality of the Word truly resides internally within the humanity in an "exact" union.

While there is a weakness in Theodore's functional approach, the same can be said about Cyril's emphasis on the union in the Word's *hypostasis*. If the Word is to be regarded as the sole logical, linguistic subject of Christ's human attributes and operations, it is difficult to grasp how he has safeguarded a role for Christ's human freedom in the union. For Cyril's formula, when stated baldly, is open to Apollinarian, Monophysitical, and Monothelite kinds of interpretations. One can postulate that the Word appropriates the human nature in such a way that while it subsists in the Word's *hypostasis,* it can still act humanly and freely. Yet, as the Neo-Chalcedonians felt impelled to do, one needs to clarify the statements that the Word was born of Mary and was crucified on the cross by adding that this occurred *qua* man. Even Cyril agreed to the distinction made in his Pact of Reunion with John of Antioch in 433: "We confess, therefore, our

Lord Jesus Christ [was] . . . begotten before the ages from His Father in respect of His divinity, but likewise . . . from the Virgin Mary in respect of His manhood."[9] While Cyril grants that human attributes can be assigned to the Word as a Person but not to the Divinity as an abstract term, the question can be raised as to whether Theodore and Cyril are close in their understanding of the real underlying union of the natures.

The problem, of course, resides in the distinction between *hypostasis* and nature. As pointed out in Chapter 6, *ousia* and *hypostasis* were linked together in the codicil to the Nicene Creed. While it seems that the fathers at Nicaea included the two terms to counter a charge of Sabellianism, the impression is given that *hypostasis* connotes the presence of an *ousia* and nature. Cyril's formula presupposes at least a logical distinction between a person and nature, though they are one in the existential order. In fact, it was really not until the time of Justinian, 125 years after Theodore's death, that this distinction was definitively established. Justinian had insisted on the distinction because he thought it would enable the non-Chalcedonians to agree with the Chalcedonian decree that there exists one divine Person *(hypostasis)* subsisting in two natures. This distinction allowed those following Cyril to avoid the charge that by centering the unity of the natures in the *hypostasis* of the Word they were in reality asserting the presence of only one nature in Christ.

If one does not distinguish the terms "person" and "nature," it appears inevitable from a logical point of view that one will evolve into a form of Monophysitism. This would certainly happen if one holds an extreme form. For this would mean that Christ's human acts spring from the divine nature and are not attributed to the Word as the subject of unity. Theodore, by contrast, insists that Christ's human acts have their source in Christ's human nature. He may have been influenced too by the traditional view that the Trinity's activity flows from its nature. With this kind of outlook, he would be sorely troubled by those who insist that the Word is the subject of Christ's human operations. Like many others, he might not have been able to grasp a distinction between the Word as a logical, grammati-

---

9. This translation is taken from Kelly, *Early Christian Doctrines*, 328–29.

cal subject and as the actual subject who is willing and acting through Christ's humanity. Even if he could have, he would probably have foreseen the eventual need for a Constantinople III in 680–81 to proclaim the real existence of two will faculties and operations within the one person of Christ.

One can understand, therefore, why Theodore believes that the unity of Christ's natures is expressed better in one common *prosôpon* than in the *hypostasis* of the Word. But much depends on what is meant by the person of the Word being the subject of unity. Theodore would readily accept the Word as the One who initiates his union with Christ's human nature, continuously activates it, and takes the lead in their common activity. For the Word is the Savior God. Theodore, however, would want to elaborate upon this by adding that God has deigned to effect his salvation through the humanity of Christ. This is why he is so emphatic about the need to include the humanity of Christ in his concrete statements of who Christ is. He would insist on making clear the salvific role of Christ's humanity within his Christological formulation. To insist that Christ is the Word who subsists in a divine and human nature certainly brings out Christ as a true individual, but it does not do full justice to his mediating role as fully divine and fully human and his twin salvific roles as the head of the body of the Church and the cosmos and as the true visible "image of the invisible God." In other words, Jesus plays a communal as well as an individual role as the Christ of salvation. Theodore's stress on one common *prosôpon* brings this out more clearly and emphatically than does Cyril's emphasis on the term *hypostasis*.

One may criticize Theodore's understanding of a prosopic union as Kevin McNamara has done when he asserts: "While explicitly upholding the doctrine of one Christ and the one person, he implicitly but indubitably denied it, by according independent existence to Christ's human nature."[10] If we are correct, Theodore's formula of union basically expresses how he sees Jesus as portrayed in the Gospels as acting as one in human and divine ways. He presumes that this reveals an inward "exact" union similar

10. McNamara, "Theodore and the Nestorian Heresy," part 2 (April 1953): 189.

to how the Word is united as one to his Father and how one's spiritual soul combines with its body in one organic unity. One may assert that Jesus has a real human existence, but it must always be considered as one with the Word, just as the body exists as one with its soul. This unity is exemplified in his constant references to the "assuming One" and the "assumed one." If we insist that Theodore always be precise in speaking of Jesus as the Word, then we must find fault with many statements of the Synoptics and many others. Moreover, such insistence does not take into account Theodore's thought framework, which forbids any possibility that the Creator can be substantially united with a creature, including Christ's humanity. To interpret his functional approach to Christology as a merely moral union runs counter to what Theodore clearly seems to espouse.

Francis Sullivan objects to Theodore's understanding of a prosopic union because it is *effected* by the natures rather than being the Word assuming a human nature. But this needs to be evaluated in light of Theodore's perspective. Theodore certainly grants that the Word is preexisting and acknowledges the fact that the Word does assume the initiative in the union and has empowered the humanity to act. This is exemplified in his frequent designations of the union between the Word as the assuming One and Christ in the flesh as the one assumed. It is the Word that is the active One and humanity the receptive one. Theodore is not saying here that the unity of natures is *effected* by the union. He is not asserting that the common *prosôpon* is caused by the coming together of his natures. Rather, he is expressing here how the revelatory abilities of Christ's divine and his human natures fuse to appear in a visible way as one to those who have encountered Jesus in the Synoptic accounts. In other words, when Theodore affirms that his one common *prosôpon* is "effected" by the natures, he is simply contending that it is the "product" of the Word's *prosôpon* and that of Christ's humanity when their *prosôpa* are viewed as one visible appearance. The natures do not cause the union. The Word, which comes to dwell within Christ's humanity in an "exact, inseparable union" is the cause. In brief, it is not established as a fact that Theodore's attempt to explain the union as one common *prosôpon* should be understood as clearly expressing a union of two independent natures in a moral union.

A Union of Indwelling of Good Pleasure

Theodore's phrase a "common *prosôpon*" sums up the union of Christ's natures as "one." When he addresses how the Word relates to the humanity as "one" in an interior way, he rejects both a substantial and an operational kind of union. He describes it "as an indwelling of good pleasure as in God's true Son." His opponents believe that he is caught in an obvious dilemma when he asserts this. For the union of Christ's natures has to be either one or the other, metaphysically speaking. It is impossible, however, for Theodore to approve of a substantial union between a transcendent divine nature and a created one, even Christ's. So, as McNamara argues, Theodore's indwelling of "good pleasure" seems to be—despite his resolute rejection of an operational kind of union—actually a moral, voluntary union. To cut the apparent knot here, one must keep in mind that Theodore is not concerned about seeking a metaphysical term that expresses the unity. Rather, he accepts as fact that Christ is portrayed as one "person" when acting in both divine and human ways within the New Testament. He interprets this union in a way that he believes does justice to such passages as those describing the union in John's Prologue, in Jesus' baptismal accounts, and at his transfiguration, as well as in his role as the visible "image of God" as amplified in the first two chapters of Colossians. Theodore appears to have formed, from these passages, the conviction that the union is best stated as a graced kind of unity where the Word freely enters into a unique union with Christ's humanity. He seems to be alluding to the way that Colossians speaks of the Word's divine *plerôma* dwelling entirely within Christ's humanity in a bodily way. Such a union is made possible because at the Incarnation the Spirit provides the necessary grace so that Christ's humanity is enabled to be "exactly" united as one with the Word in a way similar to how a rational soul is united as one with its body. In this unity, Christ's human nature can share in such honors as the Word's sonship and power because he participates with the Word in a way similar to how one's body shares fully in what belongs to its spiritual nature. Though they are different by nature, they exist as one person.

Admittedly when Theodore speaks of a union of good pleasure, he appears to be talking about some sort of a graced union where God is pleased with Jesus' free actions, as he is well disposed to those who heed his will. This is surely not expressing a metaphysical union as such. Rather, Theodore's interest is in how a created nature can benefit from its relationship with a transcendent spiritual nature and act together with it in a "corporate" kind of true personal unity. The phrase "an indwelling of good pleasure," therefore, indicates for Theodore how the Word freely initiates a loving union wherein he establishes a truly unique, inseparable relation with Christ's humanity, which, thanks to the Spirit's grace, enables it to function as one with the Word without either the divine or human nature being jeopardized. Thanks again to the Holy Spirit, the entire divine *plerôma* of the Word has so permeated Christ's human nature that Christ in the flesh is able to bestow these graces in measured ways to others. Because his human nature is so "exactly" united to the Word and his Spirit, Christ *qua* man serves as the mediating bond both between God and humanity and between God and the rest of creation. In other words, Theodore's phrase "an indwelling of good pleasure as in God's true Son" indicates the role that God has chosen for Christ's humanity to play in salvation history. To interpret this phrase, then, as indicating that Theodore regards Christ as a mere man who has received superior graces (but not of a different kind from the saints) simply distorts his thought.

The closest Theodore comes to offering a philosophical solution of the union is his likening of the union of Christ's natures in one *prosôpon* to that between the soul and its body in one person. His appeal here is intriguing and provocative. Since Theodore repudiates Apollinaris's analogy between the Word and Christ's body with that of the soul and its body in an organic unity, it appears surprising that he too presents an analogy here. If Theodore rejects Apollinaris's organic unity because it implies that Christ has only one nature, how can we explain his own use of the analogy? He employs it first to illustrate how two natures can be different but yet one, and, second, to show how a spiritual and a material nature can act in concert as a true unity without the spiritual Word's nature being in any way compromised. As with all analogies, one must attend carefully to what is being claimed and what is being repudiated. Theodore seems to be claiming that the unity of Christ's natures ought to be understood in accordance with a functional quasi-organic model. This would be an extension of the kind of union he maintains exists between Christ in the flesh as the head and the Church and the universe as both "living" members of his "body."

When Theodore speaks about how Christ in the flesh participates in the Word's sonship, powers, and honors, his critics assume that he means a voluntary union. They are convinced of this because Theodore distinguishes between the Word as the true Son of God by nature and Christ in the flesh as the true Son by grace. This indicates that he cannot assign these honors directly to Christ as the Word. Theodore, however, has to reason as he does. For he cannot concede that Christ's human nature can be united substantially with God's uncreated nature and, therefore, that Christ *qua* man cannot be considered God's true Son by nature and cannot have divine powers and honors that flow from his own nature. In such a conceptual framework, Theodore is able only to affirm that the assumed man is the true Son of God by grace. Later Scholastics solve this problem by affirming that humans can share in a union with God in a subsistential way, in that sanctifying grace elevates and therefore divinizes Christ's human nature. These theologians regard the act of perfecting Christ's human nature to be not an efficient cause but a quasi-formal cause whose perfection is intrinsic to the assumed human nature, but "with an assumption that in itself is not accidental but substantial and subsistential."[11] This is a difficult distinction, but I think that such a viewpoint would have intrigued Theodore. The best he could do given his circumstances, however, was to maintain the integrity of Christ's human nature and its true unity with the Word in a graced union where the Word's full *plerôma* dwells within his human nature, so that he can *qua* man be called God's true Son, and all others who share his human nature can become God's adopted children. Again, one must take care not to misunderstand Theodore's functional method of reasoning, especially if it is drawn from and dependent upon the early chapters of Colossians.

11. For an extended treatment of the idea of subsistential union, see Emile Mersch, *The Theology of the Mystical Body* (St. Louis: Herder, 1951), 202–26, esp. 206. Mersch discusses the Scholastic understanding of a "quasi-formal cause" at 208–10. Quotation at 209.

Theodore's 'Communicatio Idiomatum'

Since the traditional way of applying the *communicatio idiomatum* is employed against Theodore, we need now to compare and contrast this with his method of speaking about Christ's two natures and his common *prosôpon*. As we saw in Chapter 7, an ecclesial consensus on how to speak correctly about the unity of Christ's two natures had not yet been established in Theodore's day. He wrote at a time when the Arian controversy was finally being resolved in the Eastern Empire. The theologians of the 380s were able to agree on how to speak about the Trinity as three Persons subsisting in one divine nature. But there was no clarity regarding the unity of Christ's two natures. For the Orthodox this was not settled until the Council of Constantinople III in 680–81. To judge Theodore's Christology, therefore, by a standard based on Cyril's twelve anathemas against Nestorius is anachronistic. It would be fairer to employ the "Symbol of Reunion" that Cyril and John of Antioch signed in 433 to terminate the bitter dispute at the Council of Ephesus. As J.N.D. Kelly has observed, this pact has truly moderated and added nuance to the strict wording of the *communicatio idiomatum* based on the anathemas: "A form of *communicatio* was sanctioned, but a much less thoroughgoing form than the one that [Cyril] had contended."[12] Kelly spells this out in his earlier treatment of Cyril: "As he explained, the Word did not actually suffer in His own nature; He suffered as incarnate, i.e., in respect of the human nature which was truly His, while remaining Himself as immune as the fire into which a red-hot bar which is being hammered is plunged" (322). Theodore could readily agree that the incarnate Word suffered and died.

Given that the phrase "one *prosôpon*" expresses for Theodore the external as well as the internal ways that Christ functions as both human and divine, it is not surprising that he would take exception to the argument that only the Word is the personal subject of attribution. He believes that one must take into account the role that God has assigned to Christ's humanity in the union and salvation. It is not hard to understand, therefore,

12. Kelly, *Early Christian Doctrines*, 329, hereafter cited parenthetically in the text.

why Theodore's adversaries have trouble interpreting him correctly. For them, his references to Christ as the Lord Jesus Christ or the assuming One or the assumed man signal that he does not hold the Word and Christ to be "one and the same" and thus does not center the true unity of Christ in the Personhood of the Word. This is, of course, to apply Cyril's formula to Theodore's statements on the basis of a logical and ultimately a metaphysical standard. It is not, however, sensitive to how Theodore simply accepts the union in an existential way. For if Jesus as the Christ acts as truly one in human and divine ways, then his inner human and divine natures must be one, as we have seen, in a way similar to how the soul and its body are truly one. This is not a unity of nature but, to Theodore's mind, of a person. One may argue that this approach does not conform to Cyril's standard, but Theodore's intent is clear. He wants to maintain the integrity of Christ's human and divine natures as not only functioning but being one, even though they are two natures.

Theodore sees the unity of Christ's two natures as a functional one that presupposes an "unknown" center of unity, or at least one not expressed other than as the ego of the common *prosôpon*. Such an approach, one can argue, does justice to the integrity of the two natures but leaves vague their substantial unity and the best way to express this. Cyril, by contrast, uses the term *hypostasis* to express this unity. But this is ambiguous concerning the relationship between the Word and Christ's humanity, in that Cyril admits that both the divine and human natures are real and present in the union and that the Word is the logical, linguistic subject of the substantial unity of the natures. This view is later expanded to explain how the Word appropriates Christ's human nature and provides it subsistence.

We can clarify the difference between Theodore's and Cyril's approaches by probing the meaning each attaches to the phrase the "Lord Jesus Christ." Both agree on what the New Testament and the Nicene Creed affirm. But Cyril looks upon the Word as "one and the same" with the "Lord Jesus Christ." In other words, the Lord Jesus Christ *is* the Word. For Theodore, by contrast, "Lord Jesus Christ" means the Word and Jesus as *together* being one real being. As noted earlier, Theodore would not object to the way that Cyril restricts the title to the Word, if it were explained simply as signifying that the Word takes the initiative and empowers the humanity to act. For the Word is the Savior who employs Christ's humanity as the medium of salvation. But he would doubtless prefer to remain with such titles as the "Lord Jesus Christ," "the assuming One," "the assumed one," the "God-man," and even "Christ" (as it sums up the presence of his two natures). For all these titles bring out in a clear, generally scriptural way that Christ is human and divine. One may argue that Theodore's understanding of Christ's natures as concrete rather than abstract ends up making the humanity of Christ into a real person separate from the Word. But this ignores what Theodore means by a concrete nature, namely, that it is a real and existing one. Theodore is considering Christ's humanity and its union with the Word as existing in an existential, not in an abstract, order and being one in the way that the body is one with the soul.

Theodore's manner of assigning attributes to the individual natures and their union as one *prosôpon* underscores his sensitivity to the ambiguity of so centering Christ's unity in the Word that one can logically profess that the Word suffered. For he is convinced that a person's activity proceeds according to one's nature. Like Nestorius, he would be concerned that Cyril's statement could be interpreted in an Apollinarian sense, namely, in the sense that there Christ had only one nature, the divine. Had he been aware of Cyril's decision to place the unity in the Word's *hypostasis* (a term he thought included the notion of a concrete existing nature), Theodore would be alarmed that this would be taken in the same way, as in fact the Eutychians did and later the Monothelites did. They did so by rigidly applying Cyril's anathemas as if they were "gospel" approved as the only way for expressing the personal unity of Christ. Theodore would doubtless have viewed such an approach as an assault against the traditional Antiochene defense of Christ's integral humanity. It would also have caused problems for his explanation of how universal salvation is to be achieved. For it runs counter to the contrast Theodore saw between the typical and archetypical roles that Adam and Christ's humanity play *qua* humans in God's plan for salvation.

Theodore does not oppose the concept of an underlying unity on a level deeper than his functional union, but he chooses to remain on a level where Christ mediates salvation because of the union of his divine and human natures. He would certainly denounce Cyril's way of expressing the union as "one incarnate nature of the divine Word" as vigorously as he opposed Apollinaris's use of this formula. Theodore would prefer a clearer designation, such as the "incarnate Word." For him, this is the safer way to ensure the essential integrity and role of Christ's human nature in the Incarnation and in God's plan for salvation. He would have been aghast at the charge that he holds for a union of two separate individuals, for this would destroy Christ's role as a true mediator between God and creation.

In brief, Theodore is deeply conversant with the problem regarding the unity of natures in Christ, though of course not with its later "solutions." When he professes that God has been pleased to gracefully unite Christ's humanity to his Son in an "exact" union, he accepts as a fact what Scripture reveals about Christ operating as an "ego" in both human and divine ways within a common *prosôpon*. Theodore does not explain how the wills and natures function in tandem with each other as one operating agent, for this lies at the heart of the mystery whereby the natures can be two yet one. Theodore's position would be that only God can understand this. The most Theodore can maintain is that the Word provides the initiative and power for the human nature to act in a free way. He seems to have had the very good sense to conclude his reasoning where he did. For Theodore, if the Scriptures do not provide an answer, then this is as far as one can and ought to go.

Integrity

In his criticism of Theodore's thought, Kevin McNamara began by arguing that Theodore failed to do justice to what ought to characterize the Word's integrity as the Person of the union. He sees this failure as a logical consequence of the premise that the Word is the subject of Christ's human attributes and operations. If Christ's human nature is so united with the Word as the personal subject of unity, one can draw the logical conclusion that Christ's human intellect must have shared in what is called the "beatific vision" and, through this, known all that there is to know, including his divinity, from the first moment of his conception. Moreover, his human will would be so intimately allied with the divine will that it could never be tempted by evil in any way. Christ's humanity, by this reasoning, would have been not only sinless but perfect. Theodore, however, saw no contradiction at all in speaking about how Christ grew in human knowledge, virtue, and grace; this, after all, is what the Gospels reveal. He was even willing to admit that although Christ as the assumed man never sinned, he was able, in his humanity, to experience inordinate desires and temptations and thus could have yielded to these and sinned.[13] Theodore doubtless found justification for this position in Hebrews 4:15, where Christ is said to be like us in all things but sin. Since Theodore was so willing to concede human development in Christ's human nature, his opponents charged him with failing to appreciate the integral unity that had to exist between Christ's two natures and with portraying Christ as merely human.

While it is disingenuous, to say the least, to judge Theodore by a standard of integrity that evolved after his death, it is clear that Theodore draws his statements about Christ growing in truly human ways from a literal reading of the Synoptics and the letter to the Hebrews. These provided him with plenty of support for his position—for example, Luke's remark (2:52) that Jesus "progressed in wisdom and age and favor [which can also be translated as 'grace'] before God and man"; Mark 13:32 about Jesus' apparent ignorance as to the time when the universe, as we know it, will end: "But concerning that day or hour, no one knows, neither the angels in heaven nor the Son, but only the Father"; and Hebrews 4:15: "For we do not have a high priest who cannot sympathize with our weaknesses, but one who has likewise been tested in every way, yet without any sin." Had Theodore been aware of his opponents' arguments regarding integrity, he would probably have countered that the New Testament was on his side.

We are fortunate to have passages in which Theodore discusses how Jesus grew in human ways. In commenting on Luke 2:52—"And the child grew and became strong, being filled with wisdom, and the grace of God was upon him"[14]—Theodore acknowledges that Jesus grew not only phys-

13. For a brief summary of Theodore's thought on these points, see McNamara, "Theodore and the Nestorian Heresy," part 1 (July 1952): 262–63.
14. This is how Theodore cites Luke 2:52.

ically and intellectually but also even in grace: "For he grows in age with the passage of years, in wisdom by gaining understanding with the passage of time, and in grace by seeking virtue in conformity with understanding and knowledge. There came to him an increase of grace with God, with God witnessing to this and cooperating in what has come to pass."[15] This point needs some elaboration, as Theodore's critics point out that the Word as the subject of operations for Christ's humanity would not need the Spirit's grace, since he was all-powerful in his own right. But as Theodore concluded from the scriptural passages that speak of the Spirit's presence in the life of Christ, Christ's human nature also needed graces beyond that of the union. For it is only when Christ has ascended to heaven and attained immortality and immutability for his bodily nature that his human growth process ceases. In the meantime, his humanity requires the assistance of the Spirit to be faithful to his union with the Word, which God foreknew would always be true. For Theodore, moreover, such growth is attested to and approved of in the New Testament.

Many scholarly studies have reexamined, in light of the New Testament witness, those theological theories that have evolved over the centuries concerning Christ's human knowledge. For example, the late Raymond Brown, while acknowledging that there is a dogmatic issue here as well as an exegetical one, points out that "the biblical evidence does not decide the theological problem or conclusively support one theory over another [regarding what Christ knew in a human way]."[16] Yet, after a careful examination of the passages dealing with Christ's human knowledge, he concludes, "if theologians should ultimately come to accept the limitations of Jesus' knowledge that we have seen reflected *prima facie* in the biblical evidence, then how much the more shall we understand that God so loved us that He subjected Himself to our most agonizing infirmities."[17] This is a qualified statement, but it shows that Theodore's statements about Jesus' growth in human knowledge reflect a reasonable interpretation of the New Testament

15. *TEP* 2:297.

16. Raymond E. Brown, *Jesus: God and Man; Modern Biblical Reflections* (New York: Macmillan, 1967), 42.

17. Ibid., 104.

evidence. It also undermines the position of those who believe that Theodore's remarks on how Christ grew in his human knowledge ipso facto indicate that he held Christ to be a man wholly independent of the Word.

As for the question of whether Christ could be prey to inordinate desires and temptations, Theodore argues that Satan strove to tempt Christ because he regarded him as a human being: "For if he knew [he was] God the Word, (the devil) would not have attempted [to tempt him]. For God according to His substance *(ousia)* is unknown to all, but he was according to the flesh truly both hungry and tempted."[18] Theodore also holds that the assumed man was tempted to show that he was sinless: "He was tempted by the devil, in the way the devil wanted, in order that he might be clearly seen to be sinless, not because he was not tempted but because after having been tempted he remained [without sin]."[19] This passage strongly implies that Christ's humanity was truly tempted by the devil. We are at the heart here of the Christian mystery of how Christ can be both fully God and fully human. Theodore could imagine, in a way that his adversaries could not, that Christ's humanity was capable of acting freely. While he does not really explain how the two natures function, Theodore's intention was clearly to preserve Christ's full human nature and his human role in salvation as the sole mediator between God and creation. As we have seen, he saw that it was critical to maintain Christ's human free will as a counterbalance to Adam, who freely sinned. Because Christ in the flesh was always faithful to the will of God, from his youth to his death on the cross—a death to which he freely agreed, with the assistance of the Holy Spirit's graces—God chose his human nature as the gifted one in whom the Word's *plerôma* would dwell and who would enable others to be redeemed and exalted. His whole human life serves, therefore, as the inspiring example for all other humans.

McNamara saw Theodore's implicit denial of Christ's impeccability as a major weakness in his Christology.[20] If the Word as the subject of Christ's

18. Theodore of Mopsuestia, *Replica a Guiliano Imperatore,* 80.

19. Ibid., 82. For a discussion of Theodore's views regarding Christ's temptation, see ibid., 142–44.

20. McNamara, "Theodore and the Nestorian Heresy," part 1 (July 1952): 264.

will acts, then it would seem to follow that Christ's human will is always in full agreement with the Word's and could not be attracted to sin. In fact, he would be impervious to any and every inordinate movement of the sensible appetites. This whole issue is, of course, theoretical, for Theodore is emphatic on the point that Jesus never sinned: "Our Lord had no need for (John's baptism) because he was completely free from all sin."[21] This controversy nevertheless goes to the heart of the questions of how intimately conjoined were Christ's divine and human wills and to what extent his human will could function freely. In other words, how can one reconcile the belief that the Word is the personal subject of the union with the fact that Christ also enjoys true full human freedom? While those who emphasize the Word as the personal subject of Christ's humanity concede that his humanity functioned in biological and emotional ways befitting his human nature, the question becomes troubling when dealing with Christ's human faculties of knowing and willing in a spiritual and voluntary way.

Theodore's position on the divine *plerôma* dwelling within Christ might appear to support the argument that Christ's human will would be so enchanted by the goodness residing in this human nature that it could not be discouraged from always fulfilling God's will. But this is exactly where the mystery resides in regard to how Christ can be humanly free within his union with the Word. Though Theodore does not expand on his opinion that God foreknew that Christ would live a sinless life, this presumes that Jesus freely resisted all temptations. Because of this, God sent his Son, the Word, to dwell within Jesus' humanity in an inseparable, "exact" union, using this union as the way for all creation to come into union with himself: "He received from the Legislator the reward of victory [that is, immortality] for having kept the commandments of the Law. By this means, he achieved for his whole race this blessing that the Law promised to those keeping it."[22] Jesus' freedom was so strengthened by grace that he could confront temptation in any form and resist it. This shows us how close was Jesus to our human situation and experience of inordinate passions.

On the question whether Christ *qua* human could sin, Theodore never

21. *THC*, 450/451; *CH* 14:23.
22. *THC*, 150/151; *CH* 6:10–11.

implies, at least not in his extant works, that Jesus overcame temptation by his own power. He is not a Pelagian. For, as elaborated above, Theodore maintains that the Spirit provided the humanity of Christ with the graced assistance it needed to be faithful to his union with the Word throughout his earthly life. Theodore saw this truth in Luke's statement that Jesus grew in grace as well as in wisdom and age. But Theodore would vigorously maintain that Christ's human freedom was never coerced by grace. This is why he writes as he does about Christ's having "merited" not only his union with the Word and his own salvation but also the salvation of all others whom he recapitulates in himself. But this does not occur apart from Christ's union with the Word from the moment of his earthly conception and the graces that his humanity received from the Spirit. This is why Theodore is so insistent on the active roles that God's Spirit played in Christ's human life and ministry for universal salvation.

Theodore's emphasis on Christ's human growth in knowledge and virtue is received more sympathetically in contemporary circles than it was in his own day, thanks in no small part to the interest that Scripture scholars and theologians have expressed in the historical Jesus.[23] This has stimulated a desire to balance the dogmatic pronouncements of the Councils of Ephesus and of Constantinople II with the Councils of Chalcedon and Constantinople III. This last Council is highly relevant here for the Orthodox and Roman Catholics because its fathers decreed the existence of two natural wills and operations in Christ that are not to be divided, changed, separated, or intermingled.[24] It is a position that Theodore struggled strenuously to maintain and defend in his own theological synthesis. Since he always stayed close to the gospel accounts, his observations about Christ's human growth are as relevant today as they were in his own day.

23. For contemporary theologians who stress the humanity of Christ, see Lane, *Reality of Jesus;* John F. O'Grady, *Models of Jesus Revisited* (New York: Paulist Press, 1994); and Frank J. Matera, *New Testament Christology* (Louisville: Westminster John Knox, 1999). For a profound examination of the contemporary Christological issues, see Karl Rahner, "Current Problems in Christology," in *Theological Examinations,* trans. Cornelius Ernst (Baltimore: Helicon, 1961), 1:149–200; and Walter Kasper, *God of Jesus Christ,* trans. Matthew J. O'Connell (New York: Crossroad, 1986).

24. Tanner, *Decrees of the Ecumenical Councils,* 86.

The Adoration of Christ's Humanity

The fathers at Constantinople II specifically anathematized the statement that Christ *qua* man is to be adored like the statue of an emperor. But, as discussed in the chapters on "image" and *prosôpon*, he is adored not merely as a man or as if he were an image of an emperor. Rather, Christ reveals in a true visible way the transcendent Word dwelling in his humanity: "For this was the greatness of the assumed man, that God dwelt in him; and believing this, we also likewise adore him. And if it is not [so], who is so foolish to adore a man *qua* man?"[25] Not only humans but all creation are invited to adore him because of the Word who assumed his humanity and made it one with him: "For the Word assumed the likeness of a slave, exalted him by a union with himself and extolled him and had all creation adore him. . . . This one was assumed in grace by the (Word) and on account of [this] grace he is adored by all creation."[26] This includes all of the spiritual powers: "now we know he is to be adored by men as well as by spiritual powers."[27] This adoration can also be equally shown to the humanity, because there exists a true unity of the natures: "he becomes Lord of all by his union with the divine nature and is equally adored as having the rank of Lord by all creation."[28] The objection raised here comes from Cyril of Alexandria's eighth anathema, which interpreted adoration shown to Christ's humanity as God's visible "image" and implies a separation of Christ's humanity from the Word. In other words, Cyril insists that it is not Christ as the Word who is to be adored but (logically) simply the Word. As our discussion of "image" has affirmed, those who charge that Theodore taught that Christ's humanity was to be worshipped as God have not grasped how Theodore regards Christ's humanity in its salvific role as the perfect, visible "image of God."

25. *TJA*, 310/222.
26. *TFS*, fol. 13a/47. The same idea is expressed in the following: "It is evident that it is not the term 'name' that he is speaking about but the [underlying] reality that he acquired [namely, that he is Lord]. . . . For (God) bestowed on him this (name) in order that all might adore him and that all might confess Jesus Christ fashioned in the glory of God the Father is God . . . because of his union to the only begotten" (*TEP* 1:222–23).
27. *TJA*, 251/181.   28. *THC*, 576/577; *CH* 16:27.

The fathers at the Second Council of Constantinople cited in their twelfth anathema that they condemned Theodore for his analogy between the adoration that the assumed man receives to that shown to the image of an emperor. We saw earlier the passage at which they took undoubtedly took offense. We ought to judge this passage, however, in light of the point that Theodore makes when he likens Christ's humanity as God's image to that of the statue of an emperor. Theodore does not intend a pictorial image of the Word and the emperor or even a symbol of the regal person and power of both. Rather, his meaning ought to be interpreted in light of the revolt of the citizens of Antioch against the onerous taxes imposed by Emperor Theodosius I in 387. The mobs destroyed Theodosius's imperial image within the city. Theodosius considered this a personal attack and desecration, a *lèse majesté* against his official role as emperor.[29] If one takes Theodore's analogy in this sense, his point is to illustrate for his readers how Christ's humanity visibly manifests in a personal revelatory way the transcendent Word. But even beyond this, he does not intend to affirm any real separation between the humanity and the Word.

Understood in this specific sense, Theodore's view of "image" is sacramental in a way similar to how the visible "elements" in the Eucharist are believed to be truly the body and blood of Christ. A Catholic attending an all-day exposition of the blessed sacrament is not thought to be offering two adorations, one to the host and the other to the Word. Likewise Theodore looks upon Christ's divinity and humanity as constituting a single "person" or a common *prosôpon:* "He affirms: 'You yourselves judge in a bodily way'; because you judge these things as pertaining to a visible body, so you do not know that One by whom these marvelous deeds are accomplished."[30]

Responses to Theodore's Scriptural Interpretations

The Second Council of Constantinople relied on the seventy-one extracts and the creedal statement submitted to the council fathers as proof

---

29. Downey, *History of Antioch,* 428–29.
30. *TJA,* 165/118.

of Theodore's heterodoxy. It may be significant to observe again that Pope Vigilius's collection of sixty extracts does not include those dealing with Theodore's exegetical interpretations. Of those exegetical excerpts included in other collections, the fathers at Constantinople chose three for particular condemnation. The first challenges Theodore's assertion that when Thomas touched the resurrected Christ's wounds, he merely expressed astonishment and not an admission that Christ was God: "Since Thomas earlier did not believe that [Christ] has risen from the dead, does he now regard the Savior Lord and God? It is not likely. For behold Thomas, the doubting disciple, does not call him Lord and God. For the sign of [his] resurrection did not teach him that the one who rises is also God. Rather he was praising God for the miracle worked, dumbfounded on account of the miracles he saw. Grace was given to the believing disciples three times: in the mission to the Gentiles, after the resurrection, and at Pentecost."[31]

Theodore's unwillingness to affirm that Christ is God is an instance where his theological outlook has certainly affected his interpretation, preventing him from interpreting John's obvious literal meaning. But one must recall that for Theodore the term "God" is reserved for the Father. As we have seen, he has no trouble affirming that "the Father and I are one" and that "Christ is God and the Son of God." In fact, he asserts that Christ is truly divine, but not in the sense that the Father is God. But taking Theodore's interpretation by itself, one can see that it is plausible, for Jesus' resurrection does not necessarily denote that he is God. Just as one spontaneously utters "My God!" at a surprising event, one can argue that this was the reaction of the doubting Thomas, especially after his refusal to accept the other apostles' claims that Christ had risen. Theodore's interpretation, of course, differs utterly from that of modern Scripture scholars. Theodore misses how John structured his Gospel around seven weeks, signs, and "I am" statements, leading up to the incident that affirms Christ to be God.

The above exegesis is hardly Theodore at his best and is rightly open to criticism. But as an interpretation, one can contend that it is reasonable within his theological framework—though one may characterize it as a ra-

31. Ibid., 358/256.

tionalization. My interest here is in the way the fathers at Constantinople II took Theodore's interpretation to mean that he did not believe Jesus to be God. This is true in the sense that he could not affirm Christ to be the "Father" or God by nature. Yet this only reminds us why we must be familiar with Theodore's semantic understanding, his theological framework, and his equivalent theory of the *communicatio idiomatum.*

The fathers at Constantinople denounced two other of Theodore's interpretations, his view that Christ's breathing upon his disciples is not to be taken as a bestowal of the Spirit, and his analogy, in his commentary on Acts, between Jesus and Plato and others as founders of schools whose members have been named after them. Mention ought also to be made of the accusation that he undermined the close nexus between the Old and the New Testaments. These passages were chosen doubtless to highlight two points—that the passages cited seem to substantiate the charge that Theodore really regarded Christ to be a mere man, and that his exegesis was suspect because of his rejections of almost of all of the messianic prophecies in the Hebrew Scriptures and of the canonical status of the Canticle of Canticles.

Regarding the first of these charges, two things must be kept in mind. First, for Theodore, one cannot receive the very Person of the Spirit but only his graces. Like the Word, the Spirit cannot be united with a creature in any substantial way. One must also remember what Theodore means by a sign. For Theodore, a "sign" is to be understood as equivalent to a symbol and a type. A sign is intrinsically related to the reality that it points to, participates in its power, and guarantees its fulfillment. To maintain, therefore, that Theodore considered Jesus' breathing as merely an empty sign, without any imparting of the Spirit and its graces, misconstrues what he means by a typical sign. In the present case, Theodore may in fact be alluding to the graces the Spirit will bestow at Pentecost.

As for the last of the three charges, the fathers want to establish here that Theodore considered Christ to be simply a mere man, like Plato and others. All three of these anathemas appear today to be excessive. After all, as the Acts assert, it was at Antioch that the followers of the Way were first called Christians. This appears to be an example of how Theodore's enemies sought out any passage that could be interpreted as implying that he regarded as Christ as a mere man. They probably advanced the argument that all the passages taken together point in the direction of heresy. But, as I hope I have shown, these passages can be interpreted in a different light.

Regarding the criticism leveled at Theodore for weakening the bond between the two Testaments, it is hard today to be critical of Theodore for raising serious theological questions about what ought to be the nexus between the two Scriptures. Theodore considered the Hebrew Testament inspired and accepted the Hebrew canon as the primary inspired text recording God's intervention in Jewish and salvation history. He did not underestimate its value for Christians, but he was wary of those who found what he considered to be messianic prophecies in the Hebrew Testament that could not be justified in a reasonable theological way. He was especially harsh toward allegorical interpretations. While Theodore was admittedly grudging in his willingness to admit the fulfillment of messianic prophecies in the New Testament, he certainly held that the two Testaments were linked. This is seen in the way that he understood and applied his typology, especially in regard to Adam and Christ. But on the whole, it is undeniable that Theodore was more interested, at least in the last part of his life, in what the New Testament, especially Paul, revealed about God's plan for Christ as the mediator of salvation.

In summary, we can see that the charges against Theodore can be interpreted in markedly different ways. Since Theodore adamantly denies that he regards Christ as a mere human, I think that the burden of proof lies upon those who consider him a heretic. Theodore has been judged primarily by a linguistic, logical standard that does not take into full account his Christological synthesis and framework. The question, then, is whether a later standard of orthodoxy ought to be applied to establish his own thought.

10. CONCLUSION

WHAT SPECIFIC CONCLUSIONS can be drawn from this study? First, do the salvific roles that Theodore ascribes to Christ's human nature provide us with insights into his understanding of the unity of Christ's natures and, therefore, of his orthodoxy? Is it possible, that is, to reassess the charges against Theodore on the basis of what we have learned about how Christ *qua* man serves as the head of the "bodies" of both the church and the universe, and as the visible "image of the invisible image of God"? These roles certainly indicate how Christ's human nature can be seen as the mediator between God and creation, for all are recapitulated under his leadership, as all the members of a body are to its head. But how does Christ function as the mediator from the side of God? Cannot Christ fulfill this as a man, much as Abraham and Moses served as heads of Israel and her mediators, by God's grace? If one accepts the interpretation offered in this study of what Theodore means by a common *prosôpon* and the point of his analogy between the union of Christ's divine and human natures as one "person" and that of the soul and its body in one person, then one can see that Theodore asserts a much stricter union than a merely moral one. As we have seen, he contends that Christ *qua* man can bring salvation to all of creation because of his inseparable, "exact" union with the Word in a real common *prosôpon*. Since he argues that Christ's human nature is united directly with the Word's uncreated nature, in a way similar to how the spiritual soul can interact with its own material body in an organic unity, it is clear that Theodore believed that Christ was both human and divine and, therefore, a true mediator. Theodore admits that the Word, like the soul, takes the initiative and supplies the power for the humanity of Christ to act freely in accordance with its own nature, but always in agreement with the divine will. The Word is the one who saves, but he achieves this through the ways that all of creation is united with Christ's humanity—and also indirectly with God himself—and is able to share in what Christ's human nature now enjoys.

The dispute over Theodore's intentions reminds me of the age-old controversy between Lutherans and Catholics over whether faith alone or only faith with works ensures salvation. As recent ecumenical discussions have brought out, both sides emphasize essential aspects of how one is saved by God's love. God is the Savior who in his love reaches out to a sinful humanity. But God also expects a response of loving faith that leads one to live virtuously. As the saying goes, God will not save humanity apart from humanity. In the present instance, Cyril's formula highlights how it is the Word who saves, while Theodore wants to incorporate in his formulation the concrete mediating role that God has chosen for Christ's humanity.

Theodore believes that his way of stating the union as an "indwelling of good pleasure" is found in the New Testament. I have argued that this "indwelling" needs to be evaluated in light of Colossians 2:9, where Christ *qua* man is said to be the visible "image of God" in whom the entire *plerôma* of the divinity dwells "in a bodily way." This is recognized as an early scriptural way of stating that Christ is divine as well as human.[1] To be com-

1. Matera, *New Testament Christology*, believes that "'All the fullness' is best taken as a circumlocution for God, especially the wisdom and glory of God" (143).

pletely taken over by the Word's divine power and love in such a way that Christ in the flesh can be said to be the true Son of God is a union totally surpassing what any other human, even Abraham and Moses, can ever claim. To condemn Theodore, therefore, on the grounds that his "indwelling of good pleasure" differs only in degree but not in kind from the graces that the greatest saints have received, is to judge him on the basis of an isolated fragment wrenched from the context of his overall thought. One can object that his Christological synthesis does not adequately explain what one may require of a metaphysical substantial unity, but it may also miss his intent to portray Christ as fully divine as well as human and the role that Christ's humanity plays within salvation.

In addition, it is difficult to attack Theodore's orthodoxy on the grounds that he approved offering divine worship to Christ's visible humanity. This requires an understanding of what he meant by his teaching that Christ in the flesh serves as the true and perfect visible "image" of the invisible Word. For him, to see and encounter Christ in a visible way is to see and encounter the Word dwelling within him. This is clarified and strengthened by his understanding of Christ's common *prosôpon*. For his common *prosôpon* manifests that he is truly divine as well as human. His humanity embodies the Word in an analogous way to how one's external self discloses one's inner self in an exact, inseparable union. To claim, therefore, that Theodore countenances the adoration of a mere man goes against not only his own clear statements but against his explanation of how Christ's humanity functions as the true perfect "image of God" within a *prosôpon* that is inseparably linked as one with that of the Word. It is similar to how Catholics show adoration to the exposition of the blessed Sacrament at benediction. They are not adoring the host, but God, whom they believe is really present there. The host is not pointing to the reality of God but is imaging its presence.

Those who assert that Theodore considered Christ a mere man can cite fragments to substantiate their conclusion about Theodore's orthodoxy when judged in light of Cyril's twelve anathemas. But this raises the question of whether they are reading their own theological viewpoint into these texts. Their method can be exemplified by an appeal to a Scholastic-like syllogism. Its major would be that one is a true heretic who cannot affirm that the Word of God is the sole subject of Christ's human attributions and operations, its minor that Theodore has never affirmed this without a qualification, with the conclusion inexorably following that he must be considered heretical. The problem here lies in the fact that one can challenge the major premise. Is it an absolute statement that allows no other theological formulation as justifiable about Christ? For instance, since it presumes that the term for "person" (a *hypostasis*) is distinguished from "nature," does the major hold for those, like Theodore and the Synoptics, who portray Jesus Christ as a person in a functional sense, under a composite title such as the "Lord Jesus Christ"?

As Cyril himself grants, the phrase "the Word of God" has to be understood mainly existentially and concretely. For if it is taken abstractly as referring to the divine nature or the Godhead, then one has to distinguish clearly between what belongs to the divine nature as such and what pertains to the humanity. If not, we are confronted with a form of Monophysitism. This was, in fact, Theodore's primary concern. He differs from Cyril in that his personal subject of unity stresses how the divine and human natures function as one and *are* one, whereas for Cyril the Word alone is the subject who so subsists in Christ's natures that he can call each his own. Cyril's approach justifies assigning human attributes to the Word. Theodore, on the other hand, expresses better how the Word and Christ in the flesh both know and will according to their own natures in a functional way that presumes an inward union and unity as one person. The point is that one cannot simply condemn Theodore as a heretic because his manner of affirming the union does not conform to Cyril's syllogistic way of affirming the union. There are differences that cannot be circumscribed within a syllogism.

Theodore is also chided for an inability to distinguish clearly between an abstract and concrete nature, and in fact for using the two interchangeably. Because he regarded every existing nature as concrete and the source of its own proper actions, he appears frequently to speak of the assumed man and the Word as though they were two separate individuals. He is, of course, more concerned with maintaining the integrity of both natures. Theodore adheres to the patristic view that sees the actions of the Trinity as flowing not from the Persons but from their nature. He seems to be applying the same view as true for Christ's two natures, especially as he believed that Christ's natures are both real. Within this framework, Theodore would be confused, to say the least, by those who insist that the Word's *hypostasis* is the subject of unity. Since he could not separate *hypostasis* from "nature," he would necessarily have to interpret this as affirming that the Word is the source of every human action of Christ, including his biological, psychological, and spiritual activity. He would doubtless cite passages from the Gospels where Jesus appears to be acting solely as human in support of his way of speaking about the assumed man.

If the Gospels present Jesus as acting in human ways, one can ask how valid is the view of those who assert that Theodore is heretical because some of his assertions about Jesus are not linguistically correct according to what later became the *communicatio idiomatum*. One can question too whether it is fair to judge Theodore by a standard established after his death. Moreover, in criticizing Theodore's statements, his critics discount his constant, careful references to Christ as the "assumed one" and the "assuming One" and other such paraphrases as inadequate expressions of Christ's unity of natures. If one must always be sensitive to how one refers to Jesus as the Christ, it would seem that one should also criticize all those passages in the New Testament that present Jesus as simply human, and replace these by the term "Word." The same should be asserted of any others who speak solely of Jesus or the Christ. If we accept that such references ought to be interpreted in their context, it seems presumptuous to demand that Theodore be always exact. In fact, this is what he regularly attempts to do when he refers to the Word as the assuming One and Christ in the flesh as the assumed one. It is his way of expressing that these are not two wholly separate and independent persons.

The present study has, I hope, made sense of the way Theodore assigns attributes as he did. His *communicatio idiomatum*, as it were, differs from what has become the traditional one. He insists that human attributes ought to be imputed to Christ's human nature and divine attributes to the divine, while allowing both attributes to be assigned to the ego of the common *prosôpon*. As I have argued above, Theodore's way of speaking seems grounded in a quasi-organic unity similar to the union between the soul and the body. It admittedly differs from the traditional *communicatio idiomatum,* but not to the point that it can be labeled heretical. Like all of Theodore's statements, its wording should be taken within its own framework and context. To recall but one example that ought *prima facie* to reveal whether or not Theodore views Christ to be a mere man, our discussion of how Theodore interprets the Johannine statement that "the Father and I are one" bears this out. Theodore admits that they are one in power. He cannot say that he is one with the Father who is ungenerated. But he goes on to explain that because his human nature is one with the Word's divine nature, he is thereby united as one with his Father. His human nature is directly united with Word and indirectly with his Father. Theodore cannot attest to this unity as taking place on a substantial level but on a level similar to how the soul and its body are one in an organic unity, where the body shares in the power of its soul. His explanation is admittedly awkward, for he is striving linguistically to preserve and defend the integrity of both the divine and human natures within the union in a way that remains truly faithful to the gospel accounts of who Jesus Christ actually is and what is his role in salvation as the true mediator between God and creation. One can argue strongly here that Theodore complements Cyril's approach rather than opposes it.

The Condemnation of Theodore as a Person

Not only have Theodore's works been rejected, but also his very person. It is hard to understand, from a theological perspective, why this is so. While one may contend that the fathers at the Second Council of Constantinople were justified in their belief that Theodore saw Christ to be a mere man, it is less easy to see how they could have anathematized his person. Theodore may indeed have been an independent thinker, but he was sincerely convinced that he was always faithful to Scripture and the Christian tradition as he knew it. The glowing eulogies delivered at his death attest to his reputation. Even Cyril was hesitant to speak out publicly until several years after Nestorius's condemnation at the Council of Ephesus. Even at the Second Council of Constantinople, Pope Vigilius initially did not want

Theodore to be explicitly named in the conciliar anathemas. The emperor Justinian, however, was unbending. For he realized he had to placate the non-Chalcedonians, who refused to accept the Council of Chalcedon because the fathers there had not objected when Theodore was praised in the "so-called" letter of Ibas.

Justinian was caught in a dilemma. Since he could not deny the orthodoxy of the Council of Chalcedon, he was forced to find a way to win the assent of the non-Chalcedonians to Chalcedon. The irony is that his condemnation of Theodore as a person failed to reconcile the Orthodox and the non-Chalcedonians. Many theologians today are embarrassed by the harsh condemnation of Theodore as a person 125 years after his death. While Justinian may have been firmly convinced that Theodore was truly a heretic, one must not lose sight of his political and nationalistic agenda. The personal condemnation seems unduly excessive and unmerited today, as does the peremptory anathema leveled at Constantinople II against those who might attempt to explain and defend Theodore.

What Standard Should Be Used?

One can debate whether Theodore has adequately explained the unity of Christ's natures within the functional framework that he employed.[2] As Paul Galtier has observed, the question of Theodore's orthodoxy ought to revolve around what standard should be used to judge it. Galtier believes that it should not rest solely on the doctrinal affirmations of the Council of Ephesus (or, we might add, Constantinople II). It ought to include too that of Chalcedon (and Constantinople III). Instead of being applied as "a line drawn in the sand," the standard might be better imagined as a square box that sets the parameters within which Theodore ought to be evaluated—whether as a heretic or as an orthodox theologian. If this "box" is accepted as a realistic standard, two of the opposite sides facing each other would

---

2. John A. T. Robinson, for one, in his *Human Face of God* (Philadelphia: Westminster, 1973), has attempted to integrate a functional Christology along with what he describes as a "mythological" and an "ontological" model. He believes that this will reveal the human side of Christ for modern-day Christians. I am thankful to Rowan Greer for pointing out the similarity between Robinson and Theodore.

be the dogmatic decrees of Ephesus and Constantinople II, while on the other pair of opposing sides would be those of Chalcedon and Constantinople III. The first two stress the personal unity of Christ's natures. Without minimizing this unity of the divine and human natures in the Person of the Word, the latter two conciliar decrees insist that the humanity, especially Christ's free will, must be acknowledged. One can argue, then, that those who formulate a Christology that falls within these parameters ought to be regarded as orthodox, at least in intention, though one may challenge their articulation as weak when it is subjected to theological and philosophical scrutiny. I think we see this viewpoint exemplified in the sources that the fathers at Chalcedon relied on when they defined the unity of Christ's divine and human natures. They based their definition on two of Cyril's letters, the Symbol of Reunion in 433 between Cyril and John of Antioch, Pope Leo's *Tome,* and the patriarch Flavian's profession of faith.[3] Though they did reiterate Ephesus's anathema against Nestorius, they saw no need to condemn Theodore and in fact remained silent, apparently, when Theodore was praised by Ibas.

Richard Norris contends that the council fathers at Chalcedon meant their decrees to be taken in their ordinary—not philosophical—meaning.[4] Their dogmatic decrees ought to be understood in second-order terms: "What our historical analysis suggests is that the definition's terminology can be best treated as *second-order language.* Functionally considered, the nature-substance terminology reflects not a metaphysic but something more elementary: a view of the logical structure of the normal sentence."[5] In other words, a statement's wording is one step removed from a person's experience and is never able to exhaustively express the reality in se. The formulas of the conciliar decrees are second-order statements that, no matter how carefully crafted, cannot wholly communicate the reality underlying their words. This becomes even more complicated when we recall that

3. Kelly, *Early Christian Doctrines,* 340–41.

4. See Norris, *Manhood and Christ,* 209, as well as his "Toward a Contemporary Interpretation of the Chalcedonian Definition," in Norris, *Lux in Lumine,* for his argument that the fathers at Chalcedon did not intend to favor any philosophical opinion regarding the meaning of "person."

5. Norris, "Toward a Contemporary Interpretation," 76.

the church fathers and theologians are dealing with a central Christian mystery of how two complete natures, one divine and the other human, can still be "one." It is inherently difficult to assess Theodore's thought, especially when his fragments are judged solely by how well or poorly they concur with a dogmatic formulation based on a different view of a "person."

For all the awkwardness of Theodore's qualified statements on this matter, he is attempting, as best as he can, to be faithful to what the Synoptics, John, and Paul assert of Christ as both divine and human. Like them, he goes as far as he believes he can to affirm the mystery of how the Word takes the initiative in the union and supplies the energy Christ's humanity needs to act. In this sense, Theodore can agree that the Word is the subject of Christ's human operations. But, like Cyril and his followers, he cannot demonstrate in greater detail how Christ's human will can act freely in this unique union. On this question, it may be necessary to undo the Gordian knot, as the Roman Curia did in 1607 when it ordered the Dominicans and the Jesuits to end their acrimonious controversy over grace and free will. Both sides were forbidden to brand the other as heretics. One can go only so far when speaking of the fundamental divine mysteries. One may attempt to explain them but must always be sensitive to the limit beyond which one cannot reasonably go.

Contemporary Interest in Christ's Humanity

After the condemnation of Theodore at the Second Council of Constantinople, emphasis on the humanity of Christ faded in favor his divinity. Christ's humanity, of course, continued to be maintained and even at times emphasized, such as during the medieval period under Saint Francis and later in the sixteenth century under Saint Ignatius, when the humanity of Christ was stressed. But because of the emphasis on Christ as the divine Word, Christ was portrayed most often as the Pantocrator, the all-powerful Creator of the universe who knew all things even as an infant and was incapable of being tempted. Such a strong accentuation upon the divinity was not satisfying, however, for those who felt a need to relate devotionally to Christ as a brother. This outlook also contributed to the widespread opinion that one encounters God by rising above one's bodily life through discipline, asceticism, and attaining to what was later labeled an illuminating stage that prepares one for a mystical level. When this "road to spiritual perfection" was connected to an understanding of "original sin" as also involving bodily concupiscence, the role of the body, even of Christ's, was considered of secondary value, if not a negative factor, to that of being joined spiritually to God in mystical union. Even now, with the continuing emphasis on the sanctifying and divinizing nature of grace, it is still difficult for many to realize that the body has always been intended by God to play a purposeful role in salvation. This overemphasis on Christ's divinity left most ordinary believers, as well as theologians, at a disadvantage when scholars began to employ modern critical historical methods to establish the identity of the true historical Jesus.

The renewed interest in Christ's full humanity, at least among Catholics, can be dated to 1951, when the Church celebrated the fifteen-hundredth anniversary of the Council of Chalcedon and emphasized the need to balance the two natures of Christ.[6] When taken in concert with the Third Council of Constantinople's (680–81) affirmation of two natural wills and operations in Christ that are not to be divided, changed, separated, or intermingled, theologians sought new ways to place Christ's humanity to its rightful place in an orthodox Christology. This effort helped to address the issue of the relationship between the "Jesus of history" and the "Christ of faith." It also promoted what is dubbed a "low" Christology, as distinct from the "high" Christology that emphasized the divinity of Christ. It is in this kind of setting that Theodore's approach can be better appreciated.

The Role of the Body in Salvation

In addition to reexamining the questions of Theodore's approach to Christ's humanity and his orthodoxy, this study has attempted to elucidate his understanding of the central roles that the "body" plays in God's plan for salvation. We saw this in the role that Theodore attaches to the "body"

6. One can, of course, argue that the interest in Christ's humanity derives, at least in part, from the scholarly efforts to determine in a systematic way who is the Jesus of history as distinct from the Christ of faith.

of a scriptural text and his emphasis on understanding the literal meaning of a text. Theodore is firmly convinced of the intrinsic connection between the outer and inner meaning of a text. Since most contemporary biblical scholars employ the historical critical method to determine as fully as possible the meaning of a word or a passage, they find Theodore's approach appealing and agree with him that one ought to attend to what the critical text says and not what one may imagine it to mean. The postmodernists may dismiss this attempt to know a sacred writer's actual intention, but they accept the received text, believing that the meaning a reader derives from this is what is meaningful and valuable. For all, the text "incorporates" its inner meaning as Theodore believed.

Theodore also draws upon Paul's statements about salvation and knits them together into a coherent system. Relying upon Paul's emphases on the body's resurrection and immortality, Theodore understands salvation as a passage from a state of living in an earthly mortal body to an immortal existence in a heavenly union with God. He holds that the passage from one stage to the other occurred at Christ's bodily resurrection. This transformation has affected all who share Christ's human nature, not only all other human beings but also the spiritual powers who are akin to his human soul and the material world who are related to his human body. But to enjoy an eternal heavenly union with God, humans must also be joined to the body of Christ as bodily members are to their head. As such, the body fulfills an essential role in the attainment of salvation. It highlights too how salvation is a communal endeavor in which Christ recapitulates all creation within his human nature and enables all to participate in not merely his achievements but also his union with God. This kind of perspective explains more clearly the body's role in the attainment of salvation than that affirming salvation in terms of divinization. While this latter approach is explained in different ways, it is basically a personal sharing in God's divine life and nature here and in a future life. It expresses well how the sacraments are spiritually effective in an incarnational way here and now. But its emphasis upon an individual's present spiritual life deemphasizes the need and role for the body in the attainment of salvation. It misses, too, the communal and cosmic dimensions of both faith and salvation.

We need to balance in a complementary way Theodore's communal approach with the highly personal approach of Cyril and to incorporate Theodore's defense of the full integrity of Christ's two natures with Cyril's justification of a substantial unity in the Person of the Word.

Because today's age is highly materialistic, image-conscious, and scientifically inclined, we are more open and sensitive to the role that the body plays in human life not only in general but also in the way that all creation is intertwined as one. If creation began with a "big bang," we can see in Theodore's synthesis a theory that not only incorporates what Christian revelation has revealed about the unity of creation but also speaks to contemporary concerns. This is witnessed in the fascinating way that he regards how the spiritual and material worlds are bound in Christ to form one "body." In his view the body is not to be esteemed as merely a supplement or an appendage to its soul but as a constitutive and essential element in God's universal plan for the salvation of the cosmos. His understanding of how the whole universe is recapitulated in Christ gives meaning to those who speak of the cosmic Christ as the one who sums up all creation and serves as their chief spokesperson and mediator in salvation. Christ in the flesh represents all of creation, and as God he offers salvation and union with the divine nature. If one grants that the unity Theodore promotes between creatures and Christ's humanity and between the Word and Christ's humanity is a corporate, quasi-organic unity, we have here a convincing statement that speaks in a theological way to contemporary ecological concerns. Although Theodore does not say that human beings have any responsibility to care for other creatures, it would be implied in their role as the bond of the universe. For if all created beings form one "body," then one ought to be sensitive to the well-being of a fellow "member." Other beings may not be created as God's "image" as such and are, therefore, not sacred; still, humans cannot abuse them any more than one's head can disregard or manhandle other parts of its body without suffering harm to itself.

Theodore's synthesis also highlights in a striking way the real, symbiotic relationship between humanity on one side and the spiritual and material worlds on the other. It furthermore accentuates how the human body serves as the medium par excellence for intimate relationship and dialogue not merely with other humans but also with nature itself. For example, a spiritual kind of love needs the body to express itself in a true symbolic way. This view is close to that proposed by Eastern religions and American Indians who teach the need and duty to exist in harmony with nature and its spirit. Such a bond escapes the understanding of all those who are so imbued with a materialistic, scientific outlook that they regard matter as simply something to be used for human pleasure. Theodore's theory of how Christ's human nature recapitulates all of creation widens the notion of "body" but also that of "atonement." This can be understood in the root meaning of atonement as an "at-one-ment" between humans and God and between humans and other creatures, so that all form a "body" that is at "one" with itself.

Theodore stands out, too, as a theologian who explains and defends the unique role that the humanity of Christ plays in human and cosmic salvation. He maintains that it is only through and in Christ that all other creatures can come into a true union with God. For his human nature is in direct and immediate union with the Word. All others are mediately and indirectly united to God. Theodore does not address, at least in his extant works, the question of what happens to those not joined to the body of Christ as members of his Church. But in his understanding of how Christ is fully present in all beings through his *plerôma,* there seems to be a way that those who in good conscience live a virtuous, loving life can be considered embodied in Christ. This perspective also provides an insightful answer to the question often raised against those mystics who profess an immediate ecstatic union with God: what role, if any, does Christ *qua* man have in this experience? In her autobiography, Teresa of Avila responds to this question, insisting explicitly on the absolute necessity that Christ's humanity be present in this experience: "I can see clearly, and since that time have always seen, that it is God's will, if we are to please Him and He is to grant us great favours, that this should be done through His most sacred Humanity, in whom, His Majesty said, He is well pleased."[7] Though Theo-

7. Teresa of Avila, *The Life of Teresa of Jesus,* trans. and ed. E. Allison Peers (New York: Image, 1960), 212–13. For those using another edition, the citation is found in chap. 22.

dore does not address this issue, we can say that he would probably regard a mystical experience as a conscious awareness of one's bodily union with Christ's humanity and thereby of one's own union with the Word and the Father. In other words, Theodore offers a theoretical outlook that can offer a reasonable justification of the role Christ's humanity plays within a Christian mystic's experience of an immediate union with God.

How then ought we to sum up Theodore as a biblical theologian and as a person? He was a pivotal as well as a tragic figure in biblical exegesis and Christology in the late fourth and early fifth centuries. He was hailed as an outstanding advocate of literal exegesis and the preeminent critic of Origen's allegorical method. Like Origen, he was devoted to ascertaining and using the critical text as the inspired medium of God's revelation. But he differed with Origen over how to determine the relationship between what the text affirms and what God intended. Besides his competence as a renowned exegete, Theodore stands out as a brilliant, innovative, systematic theologian who evolved his synthesis of God's plan for salvation from what he found expressed in Scripture. This is seen in the way he explored the soteriological ramifications of the typology between Adam as the head of mortal existence and an "image of God," at one end, and Christ's humanity as the head of a new immortal existence and as the true perfect visible "image of God," at the other. He proposed here a well thought out, coherent, and highly insightful synthesis drawn from the Scriptures. His sober, precise style may not be as passionate as that of John Chrysostom or Gregory of Nyssa, but his thought concerning Christ as the cosmic mediator for all creation is impressive and illuminating.

In conclusion, we can only speculate as to how Theodore would respond to the charges raised against his writings and person were he alive today. But we can be fairly certain that Theodore would remain committed to what a strict literal exegesis discloses about the New Testament revelation. For him, the Gospels indicate how Christ has acted as one in human and divine ways. He might therefore simply state that Colossians (1:15–18, 19–20 and 2:9) best expresses who Christ is for him: "He [the Christ] is the image of the invisible God, the firstborn of all creation. For in him were created all things in heaven and earth, the visible and the invisible. . . . He is before all things, and in him all things are bound together. . . . to reconcile all things through him, making peace by the blood of the cross, whether those on earth and in heaven. . . . because all the fullness of the Godhead dwells within him in a bodily way." While such an explanation may be hard to defend as a metaphysical unity, it is equally hard to find fault with.

It is a tragedy, therefore, that history has cast Theodore as one of the most prominent Christian heretics. His tireless effort to defend the traditional role played by the full humanity of Christ in its union with the Word's divine nature and in salvation deserves a better fate, perhaps at least along the lines of the esteem in which most scholars today hold Origen for his attempts to be a pioneer systematic theologian when the Christian faith was beginning to be articulated and defined through speculative reflection and controversy. As some modern-day theologians have concluded, it seems anachronistic to brand Theodore a heretic on the basis of later hostile assessments of isolated passages culled from his writings. Perhaps the best way to conclude this study of Theodore's Christological approach is to quote Theodoret of Cyr's view of the controversy between the Antiochenes and the followers of Cyril of Alexandria as a wrenching apart of the Christian Church that ought never to have happened:

> What does it matter whether we style the holy Virgin at the same time mother of Man and Mother of God, or call her mother and servant of her offspring, with the addition that she is the mother of our Lord Jesus Christ as man, but his servant as God, and so avoid the term which is the pretext of calumny, and express the same opinion by another phrase? And besides this it must also be borne in mind that the former of these titles is of general use, and the latter peculiar to the Virgin and that it is about this that all the controversy has arisen, which would to God had never been.[8]

8. The English translation is from Theodoret of Cyrrhus, "Letter XVI to Bishop Irenaeus," NPNF, 3:255–56. The original text, with a French translation, can also be found in *Théodoret de Cyr Correspondance*, ed. and trans. Yvan Azéma, Sources chrétiennes 98 (Paris: Cerf, 1964), 58–59.

BIBLIOGRAPHY

Primary Sources

Ambrose. "On the Decease of Satyrus" and "On Baptism." In *Nicene and Post-Nicene Fathers,* 2d ser., vol. 10. Ed. Philip Schaff and Henry Wace. 1896. Reprint, Peabody, Mass.: Hendrickson, 1994.

Augustine. "In Johannis Evangelium Tractatus CXXIV." In *Aureli Augustini Opera,* part 8. Corpus Christianorum, series Latina 36. Brepols: Turnhout, 1954.

Conciliorum Oecumenicorum Decreta, 3d ed. Ed. Josepho Alberigo et al. Bologna: Scienze Religiose, 1973.

Concilium Universale Constantinopoltanum Sub Justiniano Habitum. Ed. Johannes Straub. Acta Conciliorum Oecumenicorum. Tome 4, vol. 1. Berlin: De Gruyter, 1971.

Cyril of Alexandria. "Epistle 72 Ad Proclum." PG 77:344–45.

Cyril of Jerusalem. "Oration on Holy Baptism." In *Nicene and Post-Nicene Fathers,* 2d ser., vol. 7. Ed. Philip Schaff and Henry Wace. 1894. Reprint, Peabody, Mass.: Hendrickson, 1994.

Diodore of Tarsus. *Diodori Tarsensis Commentarii in Psalmos.* Ed. Jean-Marie Olivier. Corpus Christianorum Series Graeca 6. Turnhout: Brepols, 1980.

Facundus of Hermiane, PL 67:527–878.

Gregory of Nyssa. "Against those who deferred baptism." PG 46:415–32.

Irenaeus. "Adversus Hereses." Ed. Alexander Roberts and James Donaldson. Vol. 1 of *Ante-Nicene Fathers.* 1885. Reprint, Peabody, Mass.: Hendrickson, 1994.

Išoʿdad of Merv. *Commentaire d' Išoʿdad of Merv sur l'Ancien Testament, I. Genèse.* Trans. C. Van den Eynde, Corpus Scriptorum Christianorum Orientalium 156/Syr. 75. Louvain: Durbecq, 1955.

John Chrysostom. *Commentary on Galatians.* PG 61:531–32.

———. *Nicene and Post-Nicene Fathers,* 1st ser. 9:159–71. Ed. Philip Schaff and Henry Wace. 1889. Reprint, Peabody, Mass.: Hendrickson, 1994. 159–71.

Marshall, Alfred. *The Interlinear Greek-English New Testament,* 2d ed. London: Bagster, 1964.

Narsai. *Homélies de Narsaï sur la creation.* Ed. and trans. P. Gignoux. Patrologia Orientalis 34/3–4. Turnhout: Brepols, 1968.

———. *Narsai's Metrical Homilies on the Nativity, Epiphany, Passion, Resurrection and Ascension.* Ed. and trans. Frederick McLeod. Patrologia Orientalis 40, fasc. 1. Turnhout: Brepols, 1979.

———. *Narsai doctoris syri homiliae et carmina.* 2 vols. Ed. A. Mingana. Mosul, 1905.

Nemesius of Emesa. *Cyril of Jerusalem and Nemesius of Emesa.* Ed. and trans. William Telfer. Library of Christian Classics 4. Philadelphia: Westminster, 1955.

Nestorius. *The Bazaar of Heracleides.* Ed. and trans. Godfrey L. Driver and Leonard Hodgson. Oxford: Clarendon Press, 1925.

The New American Bible. St. Joseph ed. New York: Catholic Book, 1987.

The Seven Ecumenical Councils. Ed. H. R. Percival. *Nicene and Post-Nicene Fathers,* 2d ser., vol. 14. 1900. Ed. Philip Schaff and Henry Wace. Reprint, Peabody, Mass.: Hendrickson, 1994.

Sozomen. *Historia Ecclesiastica.* Trans. Chester D. Hartranft. *Nicene and Post-Nicene Fathers,* 2d ser., vol. 2. Ed. Philip Schaff and Henry Wace. 1890. Reprint, Peabody, Mass.: Hendrickson, 1994.

Tanner, Norman P., ed. *Decrees of the Ecumenical Councils 1: Nicaea I to Lateran V.* Washington, D.C.: Georgetown University Press, 1990.

Teresa of Avila. *The Life of Teresa of Jesus.* Ed. and trans. E. Allison Peers. New York: Image, 1960.

Theodore of Mopsuestia. *Opera Omnia.* PG 66:10–1020.

———. "Commentary on Obadiah." PG 66:303–18.

———. "Commentary on Haggai." PG 66:474–94.

———. "Commentary on Genesis." PG 66:633–46.

———. "Commentary on the Epistle to the Romans." PG 66:787–876.

———. "Commentary on the Incarnation." PG 66:971–94.

———. "Fragment of a Work against Apollinaris." PG 66:1001–1004.

———. "Epistle to Domnus." PG 66:1011–14.

———. *Commentaire sur les Psaumes I–LXXX.* Ed. Robert Devreese. Studi e Testi 93. Vatican City: Biblioteca Vaticana, 1939.

———. *Fragments syriaque du Commentaire des Psalmes* (Psalm 118 and Psalms 138–148). Ed. and trans. Lucas van Rompay. Corpus Scriptorum Christianorum Orientalium 189–90. Louvain: Peeters, 1982.

———. *Commentary on the Twelve Prophets.* Trans. Robert Hill. Fathers of the Church 108. Washington, D.C.: The Catholic University of America Press, 2003.

———. *Commentary of Theodore of Mopsuestia on the Nicene Creed* and *Commentary of*

Theodore of Mopsuestia on the Lord's Prayer and on the Sacraments of Baptism and the Eucharist. Ed. and trans. A. Mingana. Woodbrooke Studies 5 and 6. Cambridge: Heffer, 1932–33.

———. *Les Homélies Catéchétiques de Théodore de Mopsueste.* Trans. Raymond Tonneau, with Robert Devreese. Vatican City: Biblioteca Vaticana, 1949.

———. *Theodor von Mopsuestia Katechetische Homilien.* 2 vols. Trans. Peter Bruns. Fontes Christiani 17/1. Freiburg: Herder, 1994.

———. *Theodor von Mopsuestia und das Nicänum: Studien zu den katechetischen Homilien.* Trans. Simon Gerber. Leiden: Brill, 2000.

———. "Théodore de Mopsueste, Interprétation (du Livre) de la Genèse (Syr. 120, fols. 1–5)." Raymond Tonneau. *Le Muséon* 66 (1953).

———. *Theodori Mopsuesteni Fragmenta Syriaca.* Ed. and trans. Edward Sachau. Leipzig: G. Engelmann, 1869.

———. *Theodori Episcopi Mopsuesteni in Epistolas B. Pauli Commentarii.* Ed. H. B. Swete. 2 vols. Cambridge: Cambridge University Press, 1880, 1882.

———. *Theodori Mopsuesteni Commentarius in Evangelium Joannis Apostoli.* Ed. and trans. J.-M. Vosté. Corpus Scriptorum Christianorum Orientalium. 115–16/Syr. 62–63. Louvain: Officina Orientali, 1940.

———."L'homme créé 'à l'image de Dieu': quelques fragments grec unédits de Théodore de Mopsueste." Ed. and trans. Francoise Petit. *Le Muséon* 100 (1987): 269–77.

———. *Pauluskommentare aus der Griechischen Kirche,* 2d ed., 113–212. Ed. Karl Staab. Münster: Aschendorff, 1984.

———. *Teodoro di Mopsuestia: Replica a Guiliano Imperatore.* Trans. Augusto Guida. Firenze: Nardini, 1994.

———. "Ein unbekanntes Zitat aus *Contra Eunomium* des Theodorvon Mopsuestia." Ed. Luise Abramowski. *Le Muséon* 71 (1958): 97–104.

———. "Newly Discovered Fragments of the Gospel Commentaries of Theodore of Mopsuestia." Ed. William Macomber. *Le Muséon* 81 (1968): 441–47.

Theodoret of Cyrrhus. *Théodoret de Cyr Correspondance.* Ed. and trans. Yvan Azéma, 58–59. Sources chrétiennes 98. Paris: Cerf, 1964.

Secondary Sources

Abramowski, Luise. "Zur Theologia Theodors von Mopsuestia." *Zeitschrift für Kirchengeschichte* 72 (1961): 263–93.

———. *Drei christologische Untersuchungen.* Beiheft zur Zeitschrift für die neutestamentliche Wissenschaft und die Kunde der älteren Kirche 45. Berlin: de Gruyter, 1981.

Amann, Émile. "Théodore de Mopsueste." In *Dictionnaire de Théologie Catholique,* vol. 15, part 1. Paris: Letouzey, 1946.

Anastos, M. V. "Nestorius was Orthodox." *Dumbarton Oaks Papers* 16 (1962): 119–40.

Arnou, Robert. "Nestorianisme et Neoplatonisme: L'unité du Christ et l'union des'Intelligibles.'" *Gregorianum* 17 (1936): 16–31.

Baur, Chrysostomus. *John Chrysostom and His Time.* 2 vols. Trans. M. Gonzaga. Westminster, Md.: Newman, 1959–60.

Baus, Karl. "The Development of the Church within the Framework of the Imperial Religious Policy." In *The Early Church: An Abridgement of the History of the Church,* vols. 1–3. Ed. Hubert Jedin, trans. John Dolan, and abr. D. Larrimore Holland. New York: Crossroad, 1993.

Benoit, Pierre. "Corps. Tête et Plérôme dans les Épîtres de la Captivité." *Revue Biblique* 63 (1956): 5–44.

Brown, Raymond E. *Jesus: God and Man; Modern Biblical Reflections.* New York: Macmillan, 1967.

Bultmann, Rudolf. *Die Exegese des Theodor von Mopsuestia.* Ed. H. Field and K. Schelke. Stuttgart: W. Kohlhammer, 1984.

Chadwick, Henry. "Eucharist and Christology in the Nestorian Controversy." *Journal of Theological Studies,* n.s. 2 (1951): 145–64.

Chestnut, R. C. "The Two Prosopa in Nestorius' Bazaar of Heracleides." *Journal of Theological Studies* 29 (1978): 392–409.

Daniélou, Jean. *Sacramentum Futuri: Études sur les Origines de la Typologie Biblique.* Vol. 16 of *Études de Théologie Historique.* Paris: Beauchesne, 1950.

Devreese, Robert. *Essai sur Théodore de Mopsueste.* Studi e Testi 141. Vatican City: Biblioteca Vaticana, 1948.

———. "La méthode exégétique de Théodore de Mopsueste." *Revue Biblique* (April 1946): 207–41.

De Vries, Wilhelm. "Der 'Nestorianismus' Theodors von Mopsuestia in seiner Sakramentenlehre." *Orientalia Christiana Periodica* 7 (1941): 91–148.

Dewart, Joanne McWilliam. *The Theology of Grace of Theodore of Mopsuestia.* Catholic University of America Studies in Christian Antiquity 16. Washington, D.C.: The Catholic University of America Press, 1971.

———. "The Notion of 'Person' Underlying the Christology of Theodore of Mopsuestia." *Studia Patristica* 12 (1975): 199–207.

Doming, Daryl P. "Evolution, Evil and Original Sin." *America* (Nov. 12, 2001): 14–21.

Dorner, August. *The History of the Development of the Doctrine of the Person of Christ.* 5 vols. Edinburgh: Clark, 1863–66.

Downey, Glanville. *A History of Antioch in Syria from Seleucus to the Arab Conquest.* Princeton: Princeton University Press, 1961.

El-Khoury, Nabil. "Der Mensch als Gleichnis Gottes: Eine Untersuchung zur Anthropologie des Theodor von Mopsuestia." *Oriens Christianus* 74 (1990): 62–71.

Frei, Hans. *The Eclipse of the Biblical Narrative.* New Haven: Yale University Press, 1974.

Froelich, Karlfried, trans. and ed. *Biblical Interpretation in the Early Church.* Vol. 8 of *Sources of Early Christian Thought.* Philadelphia: Fortress, 1984.

Galtier, Paul. "Théodore de Mopsueste: Sa vraie pensée sur l'incarnation." *Recherches de science religieuse* 45 (1957): 161–86 and 338–60.

Gerber, Simon. *Theodor von Mopsuestia und das Nicänum.* Supplements to Vigiliae Christianae 51. Leiden: Brill, 2000.

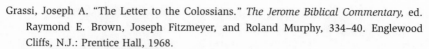

Grassi, Joseph A. "The Letter to the Colossians." *The Jerome Biblical Commentary,* ed. Raymond E. Brown, Joseph Fitzmeyer, and Roland Murphy, 334–40. Englewood Cliffs, N.J.: Prentice Hall, 1968.

Greer, Rowan A. *Theodore of Mopsuestia: Exegete and Theologian.* Westminster: Faith, 1961.

———. "Antiochene Christology of Diodore of Tarsus." *Journal of Theological Studies* 17 (1966): 327–41.

———. "Image of God and the Prosôpic Union in Nestorius' *Bazaar of Heracleides.*" In *Lux in Lumine: Essays for W. N. Pittenger,* ed. Richard A. Norris Jr., 46–59. New York: Seabury, 1966.

———. *The Captain of Salvation: A Study in the Patristic Exegesis of Hebrews.* Tübingen: Mohr, 1973.

———. "The Analogy of Grace in Theodore of Mopsuestia's Christology." *Journal of Theological Studies,* n.s. 34 (1983): 82–98.

Grillmeier, Alois. *Christ in Christian Tradition from the Apostolic Age to Chalcedon (451).* 2 vols. 2d rev. ed. Trans. J. Cawte and P. Allen. Atlanta: John Knox, 1975.

Gross, Jules. *La divinisation du chrétien d'après les pères.* Paris: Gabalda, 1938.

Guida, Augusto. *Teodoro di Mopsuestia: Replica a Guiliano Imperatore.* Firenza: Nardini, 1994.

Guillet, J. "Les exégèses d'Alexandrie et d'Antioche. Conflit ou malentendue?" *Recherches de Science Religieuse* (April 1947): 257–303.

Harrent, A. *Les Écoles d'Antioche.* Paris: Thorin, 1878.

Jugie, M. "Le Liber ad baptizandos de Théodore de Mopsueste." *Echoes d'Orient* 34 (1935): 257–71.

Kannengiesser, Charles. "Apollinaris." In *Encyclopedia of the Early Church,* 2 vols., ed. Angelo Di Berardino, trans. A. Wolford, 1:58–59. New York: Oxford University Press, 1992.

———. "Review of *Theodor von Mopsuestia und das Nicänum,* by Simon Gerber." *Revue des Études Augustiniennes* 49 (2003): 194–96.

Kasper, Walter. *God of Jesus Christ.* Trans. Matthew J. O'Connell. New York: Crossroad, 1986.

Kelly, B. "Divine Quasi-Formal Causality: Divinization by Grace: Inhabitation of the Trinity." *Irish Theological Quarterly* 28 (1961): 16–28.

Kelly, J.N.D. *Early Christian Doctrines.* Rev. ed. San Francisco: Harper, 1978.

Kepple, Robert J. "Analysis of Antiochene Exegesis of Galatians 4:24–26." *Westminster Theological Journal* 39 (1977): 239–49.

Kihn, Heinrich. "Über 'Theôria' und 'Allegoria' nach den verloren hermeneutischen Schriftender Antiochener." *Theologische Quartalscrift* 20 (1880): 531–82.

Kittel, Gerhard, and Gerhard Friedrich, eds. *Theological Dictionary of the New Testament.* Abr. Geoffrey W. Bromiley. Grand Rapids: Eerdmans, 1985.

Koch, Günter. *Die Heilsverwirklichung bei Theodor von Mopsuestia.* Münchener Theologische Studien. II. Systematische Abteilung 31. Munich: Hueber, 1965.

Köster, Helmut. *Theological Dictionary of the New Testament,* ed. Gerhard Friedrich, trans. Geoffrey W. Bromiley. Grand Rapids: Eerdmans, 1968.

Kugelman, Richard. "The First Letter to the Corinthians," in *The Jerome Biblical Commentary,* ed. Raymond E. Brown, Joseph Fitzmeyer, and Roland Murphy, 254–75. Englewood Cliffs, N.J.: Prentice-Hall, 1968.

Lampe, G.W.H., ed. *A Patristic Greek Lexicon.* Oxford: Clarendon Press, 1961.

Lane, Dermot A. *The Reality of Jesus: An Essay in Christology.* New York: Paulist Press, 1975.

Lera, José Maria. "Théodore de Mopsueste." In *Dictionnaire de Spiritualité Ascétique et Mystique: Doctrine et Histoire,* ed. M. Viller et al., 15:385–400. Paris: Beauchsne, 1991.

Malina, Bruce J., and Jerome H. Neyrey. *Portraits of Paul: An Archeology of Ancient Personality.* Louisville: John Knox, 1996.

Martin, Josef. *Antike Rhetorik: Technik und Methode.* Munich: Beck, 1974.

Matera, Frank J. *New Testament Christology.* Louisville: Westminster, 1999.

McKenzie, John L. *Dictionary of the Bible.* London: Geoffrey Chapman, 1965.

——. "A New Study of Theodore of Mopsuestia." *Theological Studies* (Sept. 1949): 394–408.

——. "The Commentary of Theodore of Mopsuestia on John 1:46–51." *Theological Studies* (March 1953): 73–84.

McLeod, Frederick G. *The Soteriology of Narsai.* Rome: Pontificium Institutum Orientalium Studiorum, 1973.

——. "Man as the Image of God: Its Meaning and Theological Significance in Narsai." *Theological Studies* 42 (Sept. 1981): 458–68.

——. "The Antiochene Tradition Regarding the Role of the Body within the Image of God." In *Broken and Whole: Essays on Religion and the Body,* ed. Maureen A. Tilley and Susan A. Ross, 23–53. The Annual Publication of the College Theology Society, 1993. Lanham, Md.: University Press of America, 1995.

——. "Judaism's Influence upon the Early Syriac Christians." In *Religions of the Book,* ed. Gerald S. Sloyan, 193–208. Lanham, Md.: University Press of America, 1996.

——. *The Image of God in the Antiochene Tradition.* Washington, D.C.: The Catholic University of America Press, 1999.

——. "The Theological Ramifications of Theodore of Mopsuestia's Understanding of Baptism and the Eucharist." *Journal of Early Christian Studies* 10 (spring 2002): 37–75.

McNamara, Kevin. "Theodore of Mopsuestia and the Nestorian Heresy." *Irish Theological Quarterly* (July 1952): 254–78, and (April 1953): 172–91.

McVey, Kathleen. "The Use of Stoic Cosmogony in Theophilus of Antioch's *Hexaemeron.*" In *Biblical Hermeneutics in Historical Perspective: Studies in Honor of Karlfried Froelich on His Sixtieth Birthday,* ed. M. S. Burrows and P. Rorem, 32–58. Grand Rapids: Eerdmans, 1991.

Meeks, Wayne A., and Robert L. Wilken. *Jews and Christians in the First Four Centuries of the Common Era.* Missoula: Scholars, 1978.

Mersch, Emile. *The Theology of the Mystical Body.* Trans. C. Vollert. St. Louis: Herder, 1951.

Nassif, Bradley. "'Spiritual Exegesis' in the School of Antioch." In *New Perspectives on Historical Theology: Essays in Memory of John Meyendorff,* ed. Bradley Nassif, 343–77. Grand Rapids: Eerdmans, 1996.

Norris, Richard A., Jr. *Manhood and Christ.* Oxford: Clarendon Press, 1963.

——. "Toward a Contemporary Interpretation of the Chalcedonian Definition." In *Lux in Lumine: Essays for W. N. Pittenger,* ed. Richard A. Norris Jr., 62–79. New York: Seabury, 1966.

——. "Antiochene Interpretation." In *A Dictionary of Biblical Interpretation,* ed. R. J. Coggins and J. L. Houlden. Philadelphia: Trinity, 1990.

——, ed. and trans. *The Christological Controversy.* Vol. 8 of *Sources of Early Christian Thought.* Philadelphia: Fortress, 1980.

O'Grady, John F. *Models of Jesus Revisited.* New York: Paulist Press, 1994.

O'Keefe, John J. "'A Letter that Killeth': Toward a Reassessment of Antiochene Exegesis, or Diodore, Theodore, and Theodoret on the Psalms." *Journal of Early Christian Studies* 8, no. 1 (2000): 83–104.

Oñatibia, I. "La vida christiana, tipo de las realidad celestes. Un concepto basico de la teologia de Teodoro de Mopsuestia." *Scriptorum Victoriense* 1 (1954): 100–133.

Patterson, Leonard. *Theodore of Mopsuestia and Modern Thought.* London: Society for Promoting Christian Knowledge, 1926.

Rahner, Karl. "Current Problems in Christology." In *Theological Investigations,* 1:149–200. Trans. Cornelius Ernst. Baltimore: Helicon, 1961.

Richard, Marcel. "La tradition des fragments du Traité Περι ἐνανθρωπήσεως de Théodore de Mopsueste." *Le Muséon* 46 (1943): 55–75.

Robinson, John A. T. *The Human Face of God.* Philadelphia: Westminster, 1973.

Romanides, John. "Highlight in the Debate over Theodore of Mopsuestia's Christology and Some Suggestions for a Fresh Approach." *Greek Orthodox Theological Review* 5 (winter 1959–60): 140–85.

Schäublin, Christoph. *Untersuchungen zu Methode und Herkunft der Antiochenischen Exegese.* Theophaneia 23. Cologne: Hanstein, 1974.

Simonetti, Manlio. "Diodore of Tarsus," "Exegesis, Patristic," "Theodore of Mopsuestia," and "Three Chapters." In *Encyclopedia of the Early Church.* 2 vols. Ed. Angelo Di Berardino, trans. A. Wolford. New York: Oxford University Press, 1992.

Sullivan, Francis A. *The Christology of Theodore of Mopsuestia.* Analecta Gregoriana 82. Rome: University Gregorianae, 1956.

[Swete, H. B.] "Theodorus." In *Dictionary of Christian Biography, Literature, Sects and Doctrines,* ed. W. Smith and H. Wace, 934–48. London: J. Murray, 1877.

Tillich, Paul. *The Dynamics of Faith.* New York: Harper, 1957.

Viciano, Albert. "Das Formale Verfahren der Antiochenischen Schriftauslegung: Ein Forschungüberblick." In *Stimuli,* ed. Georg Schöllgen and Clemens Scholten, 370–405. Munich: Aschendorff, 1996. 370–405.

Vööbus, Arthur. "Regarding the Theological Anthropology of Theodore of Mopsuestia." *Church History* (June 1964): 115–24.

Vosté, J.-M. "La chronologie de l'activité de Théodore de Mopsueste au II Councile de Constantinople." *Revue Biblique* 34 (Jan. 1925): 54–81.

——. "L'oeuvre exégétique de Théodore de Mopsueste au II Councile de Constantinople." *Revue Biblique* 38 (July 1929): 382–95, (Oct. 1929): 542–54.

Warne, Graham J. *Hebrew Perspectives on the Human Person in the Hellanistic Era: Philo and Paul.* Lewiston, N.Y.: Mellen, 1995.

Wickert, Ulrich. *Studien zu den Pauluskommentaren Theodors von Mopsuestia: Als Beitrag zum Verständnis der Antiochenischen Theologie.* Berlin: Töpelmann, 1962.

Wilken, Robert L. *John Chrysostom and the Jews: Rhetoric and Reality in the Late Fourth Century.* Berkeley and Los Angeles: University of California Press, 1983.

Woolcombe, K. J. "Le sens de 'type' chez les Pères." *Supplément de la Vie Spirituelle* 4 (1951): 84–100.

Young, Frances M. "The Rhetorical Schools and Their Influence on Patristic Exegesis." In *The Making of Orthodoxy: Essays in Honor of Henry Chadwick,* ed. R. Williams. Cambridge: Cambridge University Press, 1989.

——. *Biblical Exegesis and the Formation of Christian Culture.* Cambridge: Cambridge University Press, 1997.

Zaharopoulos, Dimitri Z. *Theodore of Mopsuestia on the Bible: A Study of His Old Testament Exegesis.* New York: Paulist Press, 1989.

INDEX

276

Christological terms. *See* Nature *(physis)*; Person *(hypostasis/qenôma)*; Person *(prosôpon)*; Substance *(ousia)*

Christology: divisive, 159; functional, 15, 93–99, 117, 119n.23, 161–63, 173–75, 193–94, 236, 253; "low" vs "high," 19, 202, 261; organic, 159–60

Colossians, letter to, 14, 17, 95, 102, 108–9, 114, 117–18, 121, 132, 138, 142, 182–83, 203, 235–37, 253, 265

Communicatio Idiomatum: Cyril's understanding, 253, 265; Theodore's understanding, 238–41, 256–57

Constantine the Great, 70

Constantinople I, Council of (381), 30n.27, 148

Constantinople II, Council of (553), 71, 205–14, 246, 257–60

Constantinople III, Council of (680–681), 233, 238, 246, 258–59

Cyril of Alexandria, 2, 18, 162–63, 171, 197n.44, 207n.4, 208; meaning of *hypostasis*, 157, 179, 194, 196, 211, 220–21, 232–33; understanding of eucharist, 73–74, 82

Cyril of Jerusalem, 47n.71, 70

Devreese, Robert, 7–8, 38, 130–31

De Vries, Wilhelm, 8, 12, 59, 67, 71–74

Diodore of Tarsus, 2, 8, 11, 14, 21, 28–32, 42, 47, 53, 57, 118, 125–26, 138–39, 159, 197, 208–11

Divinization, 10, 61n.24, 66–68, 72–74, 87, 126, 238, 261–63

Ephesus, Council of (431), 2, 19, 208, 246, 257–59

Eucharist: as a type, 82–86; its effects, 86–90, 208, 246, 257–59; real presence, 82–83; Spirit's role, 83–86

Eusebius of Emesa, 28, 31, 223

Eustathius of Antioch, 28, 31, 223

Eve, 51, 78, 104, 138–40

Exegesis. *See* Antioch, exegetical exegesis; Theodore of Mopsuestia, exegetical method

Facundus of Hermiane, 43, 171, 206, 222–24

Fall. *See* Adam, effects of his sin

Flavian, Patriarch, 223, 259

Galtier, Paul, 8, 18–19, 166–67, 221–22; his suggested standard for judging, 258

Gerber, Simon, 8, 69n.26, 131

Greer, Rowan A., xiii, 8, 27n.14, 38, 40, 54, 60n.3, 137, 157, 167–68, 208n.6, 258n.2

Gregory of Nyssa, 70, 265

Grillmeier, Aloys, 3n.5, 3n.8, 147n.6, 159n.34, 192n.31, 218n.26

Historia, 31–32, 49n.76

Homo assumptus. *See* Union of Christ's natures, *assumens/assumptus*

Homoousios, 3

Human Nature. *See* Nature *(physis)*

Hypostasis. *See* Person *(hypostasis/qenôma)*

Ibas of Edessa, 2–5, 171, 212, 223–24, 258

Image of God: Adam and Eve, 127–29; as the bond of the universe, 125, 128–29; as a type, 125, 132; Christ's humanity, 129, 133–37; cultic role, 137–38; general meaning, 125–26; in an imitative sense, 130–32; referring to the whole human being, 126, 129; revealing the Trinity, 127; role in salvation, 137–38; signifying authority, 126, 138–39; sin's distortion, 132–33; women as God's image, 138–42

Indwelling of Good Pleasure, 16–17, 235–37; analogous to union of soul and body, 173–74, 192–94, 200–202; "as in God's Son," 181–85; drawn from Colossians 2:9, 182, 233; divine initiative, 66, 195–96; general meaning, 179–80; not in a substantive or an operational sense, 177–79; role of the Spirit, 186–88, 253–54

Inspiration. *See* Theodore of Mopsuestia, views on inspiration

Išo´dad of Merv, 140

Jesuit and Dominican Controversy, 260

Job, Book of, 43–44, 209

John Chrysostom, 9, 14, 25, 30, 40–41, 43, 49n.76, 57, 70, 125–25, 138–39, 223, 265

John of Antioch, Patriarch, 2, 196, 231, 238, 259

Jugie, Martin, 8

Julian of Halicarnum, 54

Justinian, Emperor, 4–6, 211, 218, 223–24, 232, 258

Kannengiesser, Charles, 9, 30n.27

Kelly, J. N. D., 8, 29, 120n.25, 155n.21, 196n.41, 238

Kihn, Heinrich, 38

Köster, Helmut, 146–47

Leo, Pope, Tome, 162, 221, 259

Leontius of Byzantium, 207, 208n.11

Lera, José Maria, 8, 20

Libanius, 25, 28

Lucian of Antioch, 28

Malchion, 159

Malina, Bruce, 164–65

Mary as the Mother of God, 9, 194, 196–97, 213, 221, 229, 266

278

The Roles of Christ's Humanity in Salvation: Insights from Theodore of Mopsuestia was designed and
composed in Slimbach with Trajan display by Kachergis Book Design, Pittsboro, North Carolina; and
printed on sixty-pound Natures Natural and bound by Thomson-Shore, Inc. of Dexter, Michigan.

Scripture Index

Scripture Index

Isaiah (*continued*)

7:11	40
7:13	67f., 75
7:14	40, 65ff., 70f., 73, 75, 77, 147, 215
7:15	77
7:15–17	68
7:16	67f.
7:17	66, 75
7:20	66
7:23–25	88, 97, 147
8:1–4	69
8:1–18	66
8:2	89
8:4	66, 68
8:5–8	69
8:6	87
8:8	147
8:9–10	37
8:10	147
8:11–15	69
8:12	87
8:14	68
8:16	89, 94
8:16f.	209
8:18	69
8:19–22	69
8:23	69, 86, 242
8:23–9:6	65, 242
9:2–7 (Heb. 1–6)	56ff., 69ff.
9:3	71
9:4 (Heb. 3)	176f.
9:5	66, 71, 75
9:5–6	54
9:6	69, 71
9:8–21	98
9:18	88
10:5	176
10:5–15	40, 73, 99, 183f.
10:6	87
10:15	176
10:16–19	73
10:17	88, 97, 147
10:17–19	183
10:20–22	88, 183, 186
10:20–23	41, 147, 177, 184f.
10:22	183
10:23	183, 185ff.
10:24	176
10:24–25	184
10:24–27	176
10:27b–34	37
10:33–34	73, 183
11:1–5	54, 57, 76, 228
11:6–9	58, 77
11:10	90
11:11	88, 147

11:12	90
11:12–16	96
11:16	58, 88, 147
13—14	95
13—23	95
13:1–14:23	95
13:1–14:32	46
13:6–8	102
13:17–22	102
14:4–21	40
14:24–27	99
14:25	73, 184, 186
14:26–27	184
14:28–32	37
14:32	46f.
17:4–6	46
18:7	96
19:23	96
24—27	10, 81, 97, 145, 201
27:2–5	97
27:2–6	205
27:4	88, 97, 147
27:12–13	96
28:9–10	186
28:14	87
28:14–21	185
28:15	185
28:22	177, 183, 185ff.
29:5–8	37
29:5–9	186, 257
29:13	87
29:18	85f.
30:9	87
31:5	37, 73
32:1–8	100
32:3	100
32:13	97
34—35	81
35	80, 100
35:5	85f., 100
35:5–6	49
36—39	73f., 96f.
36:1–37:8	37
36:1–37:38	8
36:1–39:8	35
36:4–9	36
36:13–20	36
37:2–35	36
37:14–20	36
37:22–29	40, 43f.
37:22–35	35ff., 40
37:30–32	40, 6f.
37:32	48
37:33–35	41f.
37:35	101
37:36	36, 41
38:1–32	35
38:6	38
38:7–8	40
38:9–20	96
39	80, 95, 101

39:1–8	35
39:6–7	38
40	96, 98, 102
40—55	2, 13, 16, 48, 78ff., 82ff., 94, 96ff., 103, 123, 132, 246f.
40—66	13, 16, 96f., 217
40:1	86
40:1–2	102
40:9	48
41:8–9	86
41:21	80
41:27	48
42	85f.
42:1–4	87
42:4	89
42:9	99
42:16	83
42:18–19	84
42:18–20	100
42:21	89
42:21–25	84
43	85f.
43:6–7	86
43:8	84, 89, 100
43:9f.	89
43:10	88
43:10–13	89
43:12	88
43:20–21	87
44:1–2	87
44:5	87
44:8	88
44:9–20	84
44:18	84
44:21–22	87
44:26	89
45:4	87
45:9–10	87
45:14	97
46:13	48
48:3	99
49:22–23	90
51:4	87
51:11	48
51:16	48, 87
52:5	87
52:7f.	48
55:4	88
55:11–17	103
56—66	78, 81, 94, 97f., 103, 145, 201
62:6–12	103

Jeremiah

1—25	107ff., 114, 118ff., 148, 222
1—52	122
1:1–3	107

276